ESCHER

ESCHER

MEETS ISLAMIC ART

THOTH PUBLISHERS BUSSUM

The *Escher Meets Islamic Art* exhibition and this publication have been partly financed by the Prins Bernhard Cultuurfonds and the Mondriaan Fund.

This publication accompanies the *Escher Meets Islamic Art* exhibitions in the Tropenmuseum, Amsterdam, and Escher in Het Paleis, The Hague. Both exhibitions can be seen from 11 July – 3 November 2013.

It is a joint publication of the Tropenmuseum, Amsterdam and the Gemeentemuseum Den Haag | Escher in Het Paleis, The Hague.

Nieuwe 's-Gravelandseweg 3, 1405 HH Bussum,
The Netherlands
WWW.THOTH.NL

Illustration front cover: M.C. Escher, *Sky and Water I* (detail), 1938, woodcut, 43.5 x 43.9 cm, © the M.C. Escher Company B.V. – www.mcescher.com

Exhibition concept
Tropenmuseum, Amsterdam
(Hans van de Bunte, Mirjam Shatanawi and Titia Zoeter)
Escher in Het Paleis, The Hague
(Micky Piller and Benno Tempel)

Translation
Jean Vaughan Engelse TaalService, Amsterdam
Biographical chronology: Annette Mills, Heemstede

Design
Femke Tomberg, Haarlem

Printing
drukkerij Mart.Spruijt bv, Amsterdam

Binding
Epping Boekbinders bv, Woerden

Illustration credits
Eric Broug: pp. 20 (both), 21 (below), 22 (all), 23 (top left and top right), 25, 27
Escher Archive, Gemeentemuseum Den Haag: pp. 8 (all), 9 (all, except top left), 10 (all), 11, 12, 13 (all, except left centre)
Gemeentemuseum Den Haag: pp. 6 (top), 9 (top left), 14 (all), 15 (all), 16 (above and below), 18, 19 (below)
G.K. Lieten: pp. 13 (below), 17 (top left and top right)
Dr Stephen R. Turner, p. 24

Photography
The image material is from the photo collections of various museums, as stated in the captions. In addition the following must be mentioned:
Gemeentemuseum Den Haag: J&M Zweerts Fotografie p. 16 (below), 43, 90, 98
Museum Boijmans Van Beuningen: Tom Haartsen
Tropenmuseum: Irene de Groot
Wereldmuseum: Aad Hoogendoorn

ISBN 978 90 6868 631 9

CONTENTS

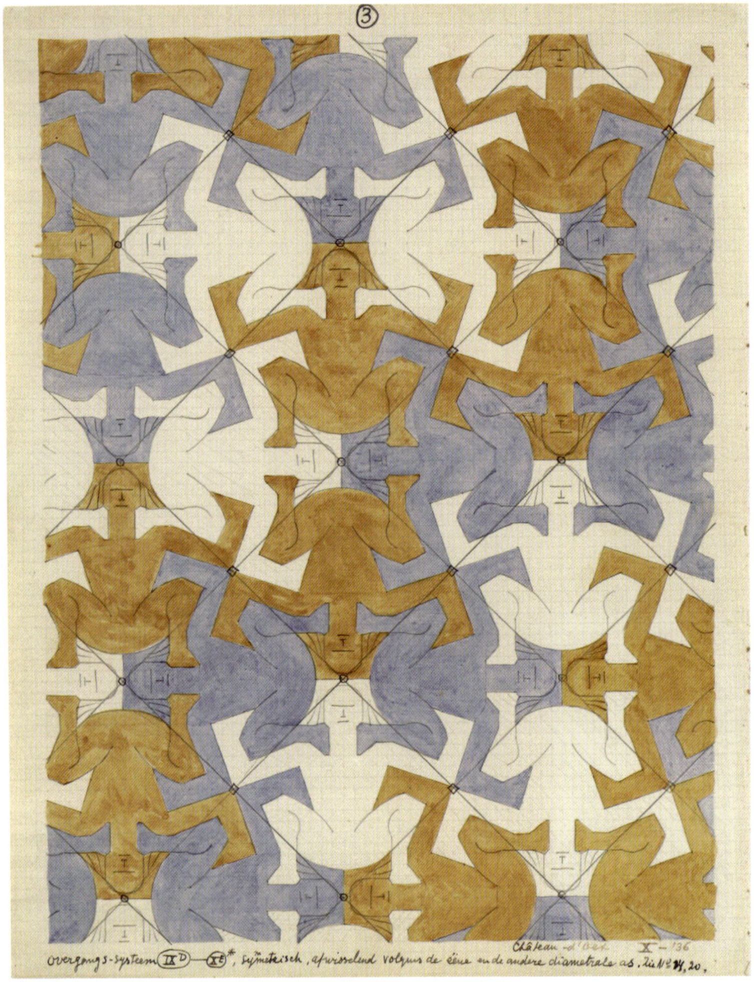

This study from October 1936 is Escher's variation of a tile pattern he copied in the Alhambra (see illustration below). First he analysed the mathematical structure of the pattern. He kept this in his own drawing but replaced the abstract shapes with human figures.

Regular Division of the Plane with human figures no. 3, 1936
M.C. Escher
Pencil, ink
Collection Gemeentemuseum Den Haag

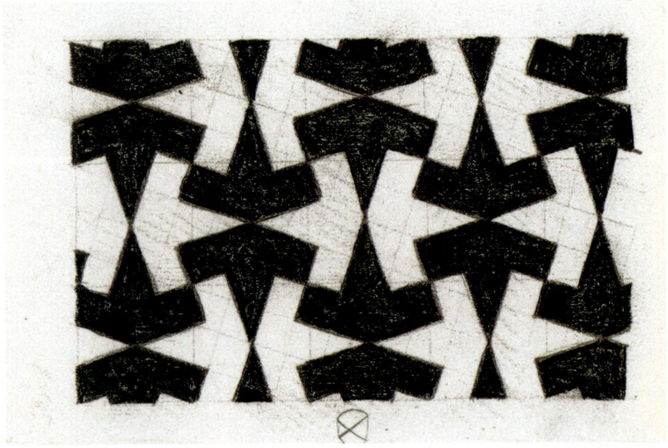

Sketch of tile work in the Alhambra (detail), 1936
M.C. Escher
Pencil
Collection Dr Stephen R. Turner

FOREWORD

The work of Maurits Cornelis Escher (1898–1972) is famous worldwide. For almost twenty years Escher lived and worked abroad, including thirteen years in Italy. He visited Andalusia in Southern Spain twice in those twenty years. During his first visit to the Alhambra in Granada in 1922 he made copies of tessellations. The Alhambra is a fourteenth-century palace complex that is considered to be one of the highlights of Islamic architecture in Europe. When he visited a second time in 1936, Escher and his wife Jetta spent several days copying tessellations in both the Alhambra and the Mezquita mosque in Córdoba. His brother Berend, a geologist and crystallographer, introduced him to the mathematical analysis of tessellations. Escher hence discovered the basis of how a tessellation fits together. During years of research, with the help of this analysis he developed his own special tessellations in which figures can change shape or undergo unexpected visual transformations. Many of these analyses and sketches and all of his prints are in the collection of the Gemeentemuseum Den Haag.

The similarities between the tessellations in Islamic art and Escher's work lie in these mathematical patterns. Although Escher never saw the Islamic artworks exhibited here, they are remarkably similar in form, mathematical approach and sometimes theme. It is both fascinating and astonishing to see the similarities between these two great but different manifestations of art – the prints and studies of M.C. Escher and the magnificent Islamic works of art from Southern Spain to India.

In the two exhibitions a unique artistic encounter has been realized: never before has Escher's work been presented side by side with Islamic works of art. The Amsterdam Tropenmuseum, the largest ethnographical museum in the Netherlands, and the Gemeentemuseum Den Haag, the owner of an important collection of Islamic art and the biggest collection in the world of M.C. Escher's work, have joined forces to achieve this.

Without the help of many people the exhibitions and this book would not have been possible. Many thanks to Hüseyin Sen, who approached the Tropenmuseum with the original idea for the exhibition. Mirjam Shatanawi, Titia Zoeter and Liza Swaving curated the exhibition at the Tropenmuseum. Micky Piller and Benno Tempel organized and designed the exhibition at Escher in Het Paleis. For the accompanying publication *Escher & Schatten uit de islam / Escher Meets Islamic Art,* our thanks to Hans van de Bunte, Anna Brolsma, Micky Piller and Eric Broug for their valuable contributions. We are grateful to the M.C. Escher Foundation and to those who have lent their artwork for their kind cooperation. The beautiful design of this book is by Femke Tomberg, and it has been produced with care and affection by Marja Jager and Kees van den Hoek of THOTH Publishers.

Peter Verdaasdonk
Director Tropenmuseum

Benno Tempel
Director Gemeentemuseum Den Haag
Director Escher in Het Paleis

BIOGRAPHICAL CHRONOLOGY

1898
Maurits Cornelis Escher is born on 17 June in Leeuwarden, in the Dutch province of Friesland. His father was a civil servant at the Dutch Ministry of Water Management. He rented the Princessehof. Mauk is the youngest of five sons.

1903
The family moves to Arnhem.

1916
First graphic work.

1917
The family moves to Oosterbeek.

1919-1922
Escher attends the School for Architecture and Decorative Arts in Haarlem; lessons from S. Jessurun de Mesquita.

1921
Spring holiday trip with his parents along the French Riviera and through Italy. In November the booklet *Flor de Pascua*, with text by his friend A.P. van Stolk, woodcuts by Escher, is published.

1922
Spring journey through northern Italy. In September Escher travels by cargo ship to Tarragona; trip through Spain by train and walking. His first visit to the Alhambra where he copied mosaics. On another cargo ship to Italy, where he stays in Siena from mid-November onwards.

1923
From March to June Escher stays in Ravello, where he meets Jetta Umiker. Back in Siena end of June. 13-26 August: first one-man exhibition in Siena. Moves to Rome in November.

1924
In February first exhibition in Holland. Escher and Jetta are married on 12 June in Viaréggio, Italy in company of their parents.

1925-1935
Yearly spring trips through inhospitable areas of Italy.

1925
They live in their apartment in Rome from October onwards.

1926
2-16 May: exhibition in Rome. Son George is born on 23 July.

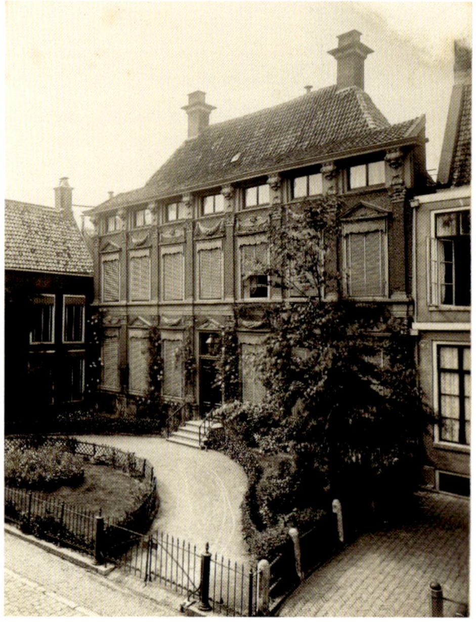

Princessehof in Leeuwarden, capital of the Dutch province of Friesland. In the eighteenth century members of the House of Oranje lived here.

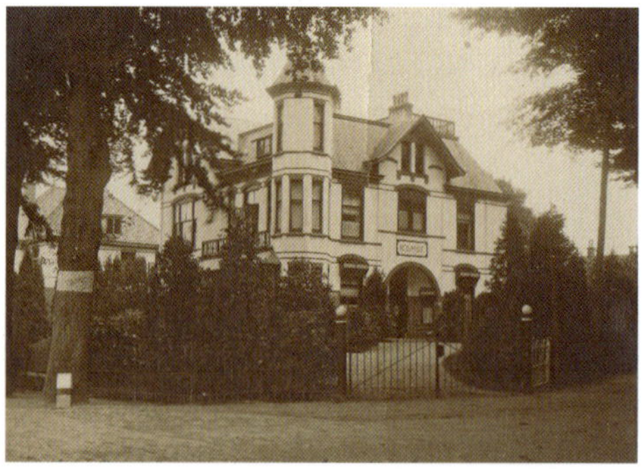

In 1917 Eschers parents moved from Arnhem to Villa Rosande in Oosterbeek

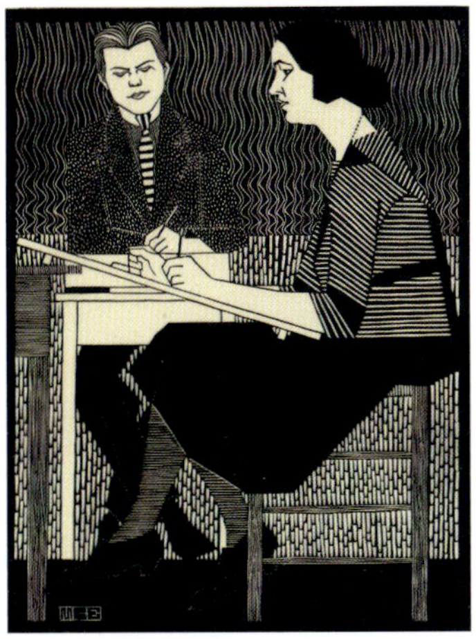

In the classroom of Mesquita, woodcut, 1920–21

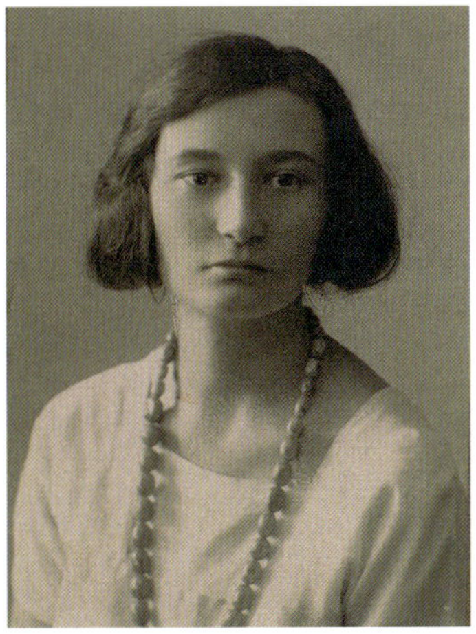

Jetta in 1923 in Zürich, Switzerland

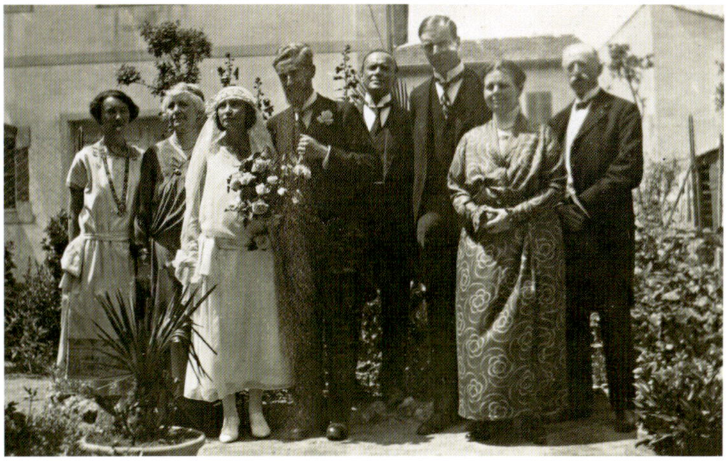

Wedding photo June 16, 1924

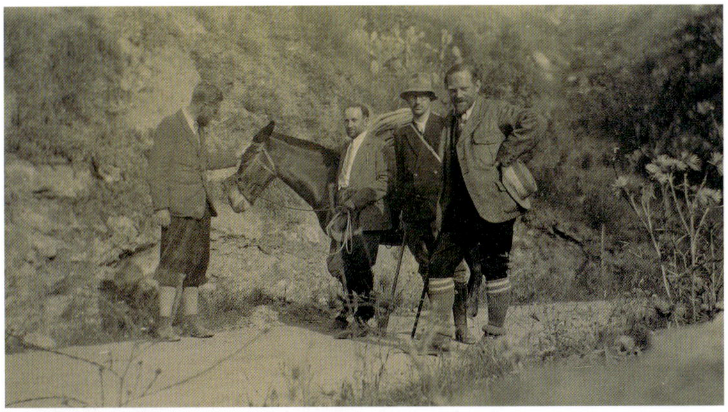

During the annual springtime hike in the Italian mountains together with his friend Guiseppe Haas-Triverio on the far right, two companians and a mule. Escher is on the left

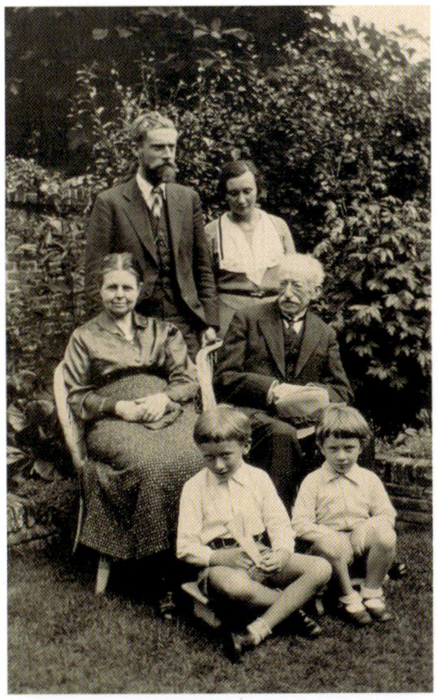

July 17 1933, with their sons George and Arthur at the 90th birthday of Eschers father in The Hague

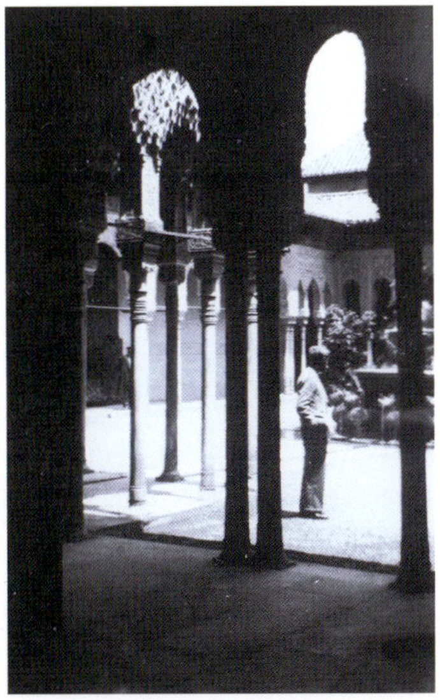

In the Alhambra, 1936

1928
Son Arthur is born on 8 December.

1932
In the summer the book *XXIV Emblemata dat zijn zinne-beelden*, with woodcuts by Escher, is published.

1933
In the autumn *De vreeselijke avonturen van Scholastica* (*The Terrible Adventures of Scholastica*) is published, also with woodcuts by Escher.

1934
Escher's litograph *Nonza* is awarded a third prize at an exhibition in Chicago. 12–22 December: exhibition at the Dutch Historical Institute in Rome.

1935
Both sons George (1926) and Arthur (1928) catch tuberculosis. In July the Escher family moves to Switzerland.

1936
April–May: sea trip along the coasts of Italy and France to Spain, where Escher visits the Alhambra for the second time, as well as the mosque in Córdoba. They copy together Arab-Andalusian mosaics. Escher makes a large drawing in the former Mezquita mosque in Córdoba.

1937
In August the Eschers move to Ukkel, very near to Brussels, Belgium.

1938
Son Jan is born on 6 March.

1939
Escher's father dies on 14 June.

1941
February 20 the Eschers move to Baarn in Holland.

1951
Articles on Escher are published in *The Studio* and *Time* and *Life* magazines.

1954-61
Each year Escher makes a sea voyage to and/or from Italy.

1954
In September, large one-man exhibition at the Stedelijk Museum in Amsterdam on the occasion of the International Mathematical Conference. In October and November, exhibition in the Whyte Gallery, Washington, D.C.

1955
In February the Eschers move to a new house in Baarn. On 30 April Escher is knighted.

1958
Early in the year Escher's book *Regelmatige vlakverdeling* (*The Regular Division of the Plane*) is published.

1960
In August exhibition and lecture in Cambridge during an international conference of crystallographers. August-October: sea voyage to Canada. Lecture at MIT in Cambridge, Massachusetts, end of October.

1961
Article on Escher by E.H. Gombrich in the *Saturday Evening Post* of 29 July.

1962
In April Escher is admitted to hospital for an emergency operation; he takes a long time to recover.

1965
In March Escher is awarded the cultural prize of the city of Hilversum. In August *Symmetry Aspects of M.C. Escher's Periodic Drawings* by Caroline H. MacGillavry is published. An article on Escher appears in the October issue of *Jardin des Arts*.

1966
Scientific American publishes a long article on Escher in its April issue.

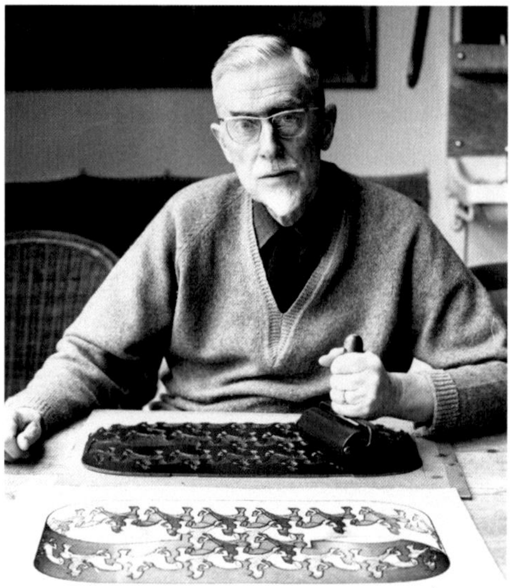
Escher at work

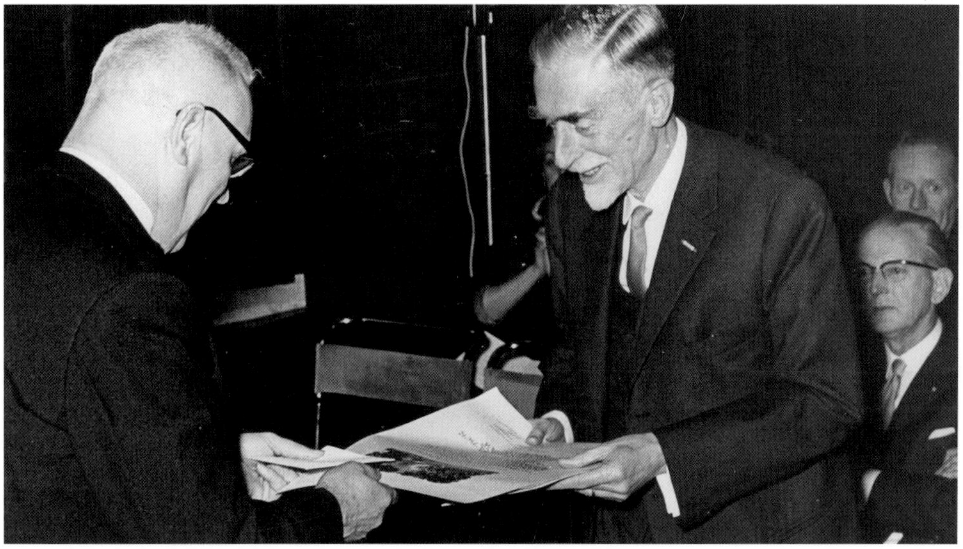

The presentation of the cultural prize of the city of Hilversum, 1965

1967
Second decoration.

1968
Exhibitions in Washington, D.C. (Mickelson Gallery) and The Hague (Gemeentemuseum).

1969
February 20 the painted *Metamorphosis III* of 42 metres is showed to the public in de General Post Office in The Hague. Nowadays it hangs in Schiphol Airport Lounge 4. In July Escher finishes his last print: *Snakes.*

1970
In the spring Escher is re-admitted to hospital for another major operation. In August he moves to the Rosa Spier House in Laren.

1972
Escher dies on 27 March in the hospital in Hilversum, the Netherlands.

2002
November 15 opening of Escher in Het Paleis in The Hague dedicated to the work of M.C. Escher.

ESCHER VISITS ANDALUSIA

MICKY PILLER

'My profession is artist, draughtsman and woodcutter,' M.C. Escher wrote to the Italian shipping company Compagnia di Navigazione ADRIA on 1 February 1936. The Escher family had been living in the Swiss Château-d'Oex for a few months. Maurits Cornelis Escher, his wife Jetta and both their sons left Rome in 1935, after living there for some years, because the children proved to be suffering from tuberculosis. While they played in the snow and Jetta skied, Escher became deeply unhappy in the 'misery of this snow'. His solution was to go on a voyage with Jetta. He thought of a scheme to finance it. In the letter to the Italian shipping company he asked if it was possible to sail on one of their ships for nothing. In return he would 'pay' with prints of harbours. He had sailed on their ships in the past, knew the advertising brochures and thought that his work would be suitable.
The Compagnia was agreeable. On 27 April 1936 Escher arrived at the head office in Fiume, a port now called Rijeka and located in Croatia. Here he chose the Mediterranean route and was introduced to the captain. Jetta joined him later. Although these ships were really cargo ships, they did take passengers. They travelled in comparative luxury, given the photos from the advertising leaflet. Escher and Jetta were served wine with their meals every day. In Andalusia they went on a tour, which included visits to both Granada and Córdoba.
During the journey Escher did drawings of harbours, such as Marseille, but also of the ship itself. A photo from his album from 1936 shows him in plus fours sitting drawing on deck. He has a drawing board on his lap, probably the one that he made especially for this journey. It cost him 62,80 Swiss francs, which he calculated precisely in his diary. In that diary he kept a record, as always, of his itinerary. The boat mainly sailed at night, so that the cargo could be unloaded during the day. Then the passengers went on excursions. During the night of 21-22 May 1936 the ship sailed to the port of Almería in Southern Spain. The next

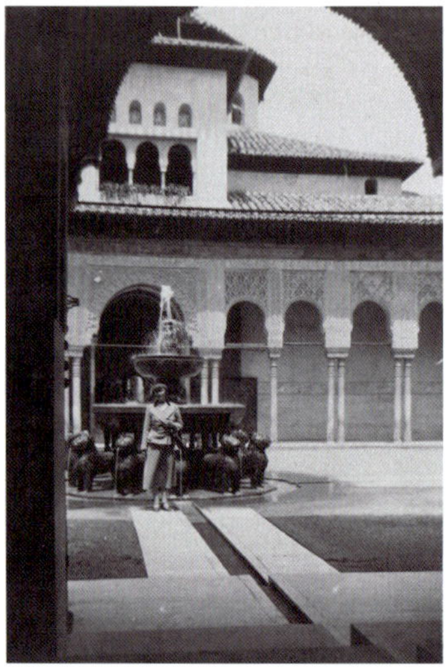
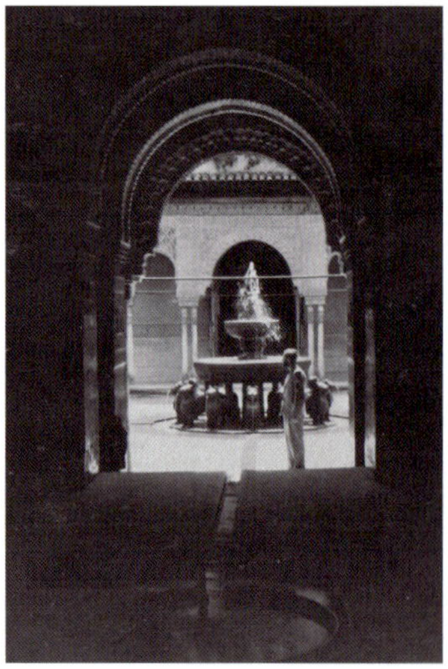

Jetta (left photo) and Mauk Escher (right photo) at the Lion Fountain in the Alhambra, May 1936. The photos are from the album the Eschers made about their sea voyage in 1936 visiting the harbours along the Italian, French and Spanish coasts and trips like those to Andalusian cities.

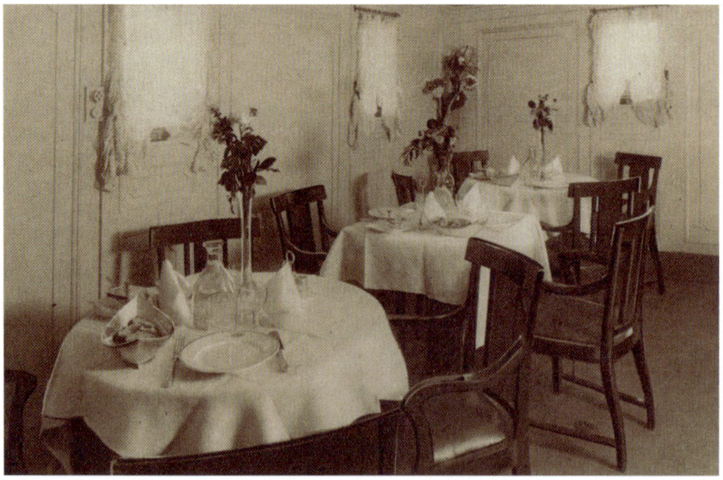

From the advertising leaflet of the Italian shipping company, Compagnia di Navigazione ADRIA

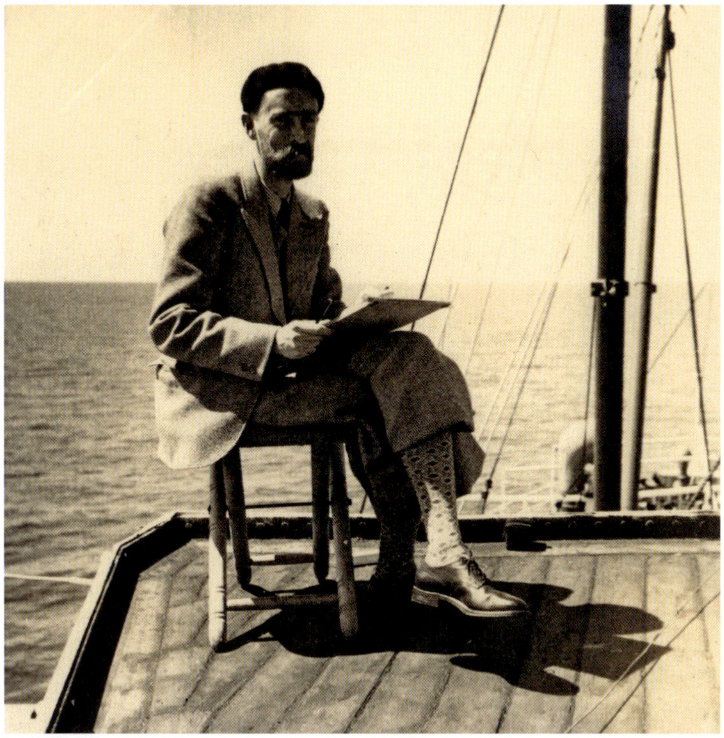

During the voyage in 1936

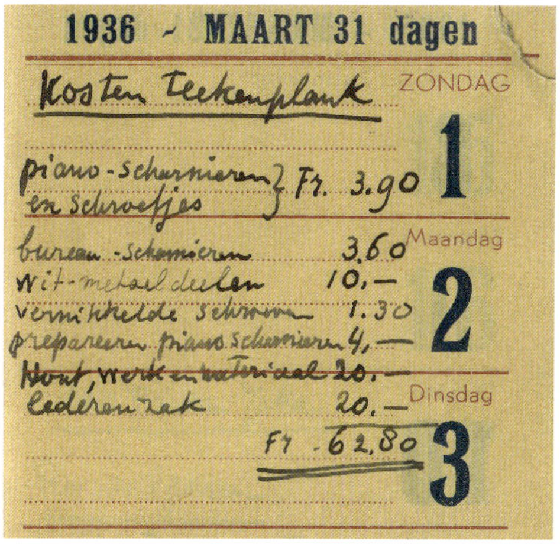

The calculation of the cost of the drawing board

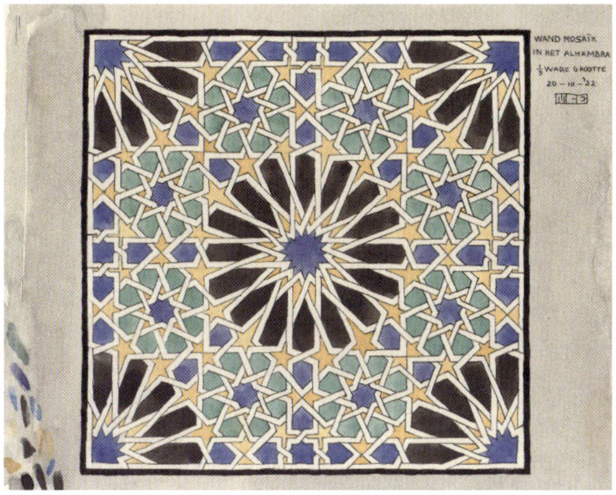

M.C. Escher, drawing of wall mosaic in the Alhambra, 1922

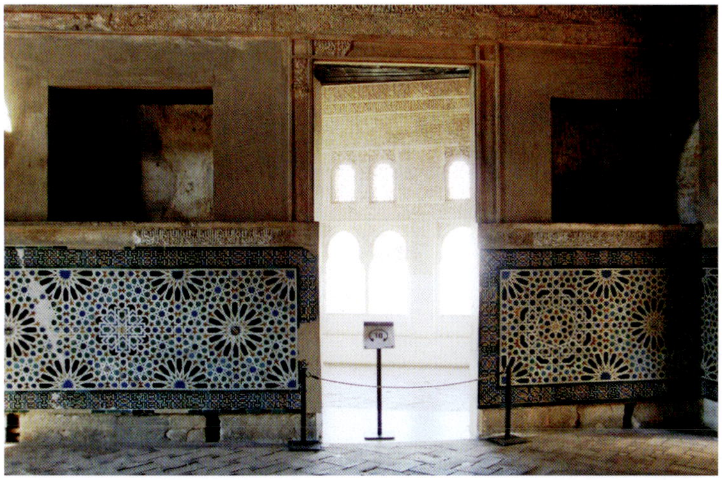

The wall, left section, with the tile motif Escher copied here in 1922. Alhambra, situation 2011

day the Eschers took the train to Granada where they stayed for three days. This was Escher's second visit. He visited the Alhambra, an Arab-Andalusian palace complex for the first time in 1922, also after a sea voyage. The Alhambra was built between the thirteenth and four-teenth centuries by the Nasrid dynasty and is one of the most important monuments that have been preserved from the time when Muslims ruled Southern Spain. Escher carefully copied a tile motif from a wall there.

At the time of his first visit to the Alhambra in October 1922, Escher had just finished his training as a graphic artist at the School of Architecture and Decorative Arts in Haarlem. His parents sent him to this school because his father hoped that his youngest son would still study architecture. Escher had failed his final exams at second-ary school in Arnhem. After the mediation of his father, who himself had studied in Delft, Escher followed a sort of preparatory year for the Higher Technical School in Delft, but that was also unsuccessful. Father Escher thought this course in Haarlem would, albeit in a roundabout way, put him on the right path to architecture.
Mauk Escher, as family and friends called the youngest of his five sons, thought otherwise. He had known for a long time that he wanted to become a graphic artist and he had already taken his work to Richard Roland Holst, a professor at the State Academy in Amsterdam. Holst confirmed his choice. During his first week at the school in Haarlem he walked from the Department of Architecture to the Depart-ment of Graphic Art to show his work to the well-known graphic artist and teacher Samuel Jesserun de Mesquita. He recognized the young Escher's talent and thought that he should join his class, so suggested a meeting with his parents. After this meeting Mauk's parents were convinced and he could start the course.

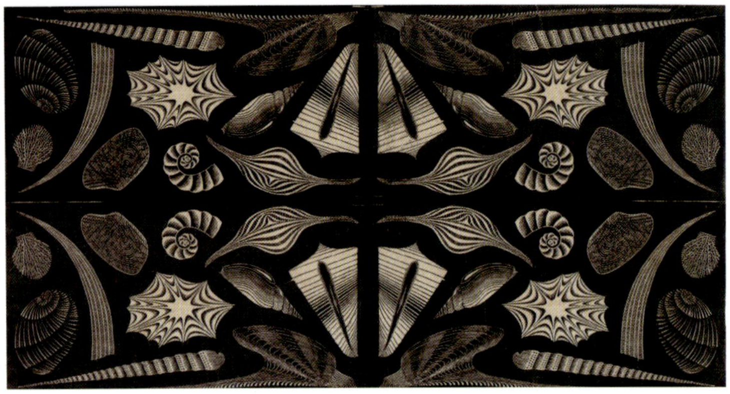

Shells, woodcut, 1920 or 1921

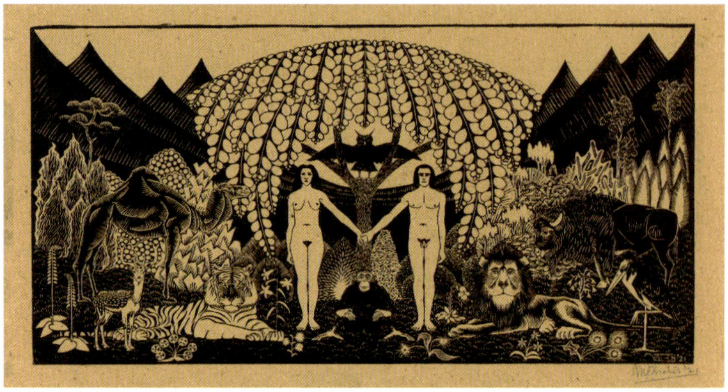

Paradise, woodcut, 1921

During his training in Haarlem, Escher's work already showed evidence of a strong symmetry, as is seen in *Shells*. Sometimes there is evidence of set symmetry even when the subject, as in *Paradise*, does not require it. During his time at school he also made a woodcut and a lithograph in which he produced a rudimentary tessellation by repeating the motif (see p. 15). In these two prints he repeated a motif set in a geometric pattern, a diamond. It is comparable to a series of stamps. A tessellation is a motif in which the outer lines seamlessly join on all sides. The motifs are placed against each other, like paving stones, and can then be endlessly repeated: upwards, downwards, to the left and to the right.
A year later, in the spring of 1922, Escher made his first real tessellation, *Eight Heads*. Although there is a profusion of heads in this print, the basic block or motif has eight heads, as seen to the right. Escher then used parts of this motif, as can be seen in the illustration on the next page. A, A1 and A2 are taken completely or partly from the horizontal bottom row of heads in the central motif; B1 comprises the four heads from the vertical right half of the central motif; B2 comprises the four heads from the vertical left half; C, C1 and C2 are taken completely, or partly from the horizontal top row of four heads in the central motif. Seen from the middle downwards, the horizontal bottom row of men's heads comes first (row A); all eight heads are in the middle (row B); at the bottom (row C) are the four women's heads from the horizontal top row of the central motif. In the corner A1, the right men seamlessly join the left man's head; all four men are in A; in the corner A2, the two left men seamlessly join the right man's head.

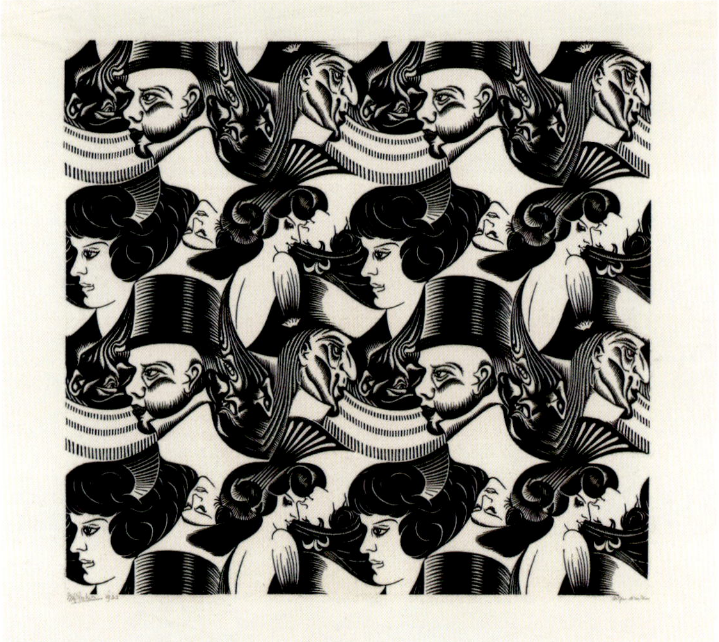

Eight Heads, 1922, woodcut from one block printed once in its entirety and eight times in sections

Escher visited Granada for the first time on 20 October 1922. The same year he had already been to Italy with friends in the spring and in the autumn he travelled around Spain. In the Alhambra he saw walls, niches and galleries full of colourful abstract decorations, including tessella-

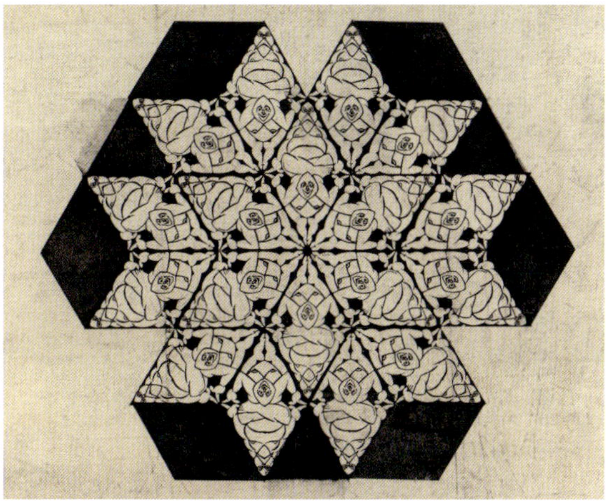

Plane-filling motif of men and women, woodcut, 1920–1921

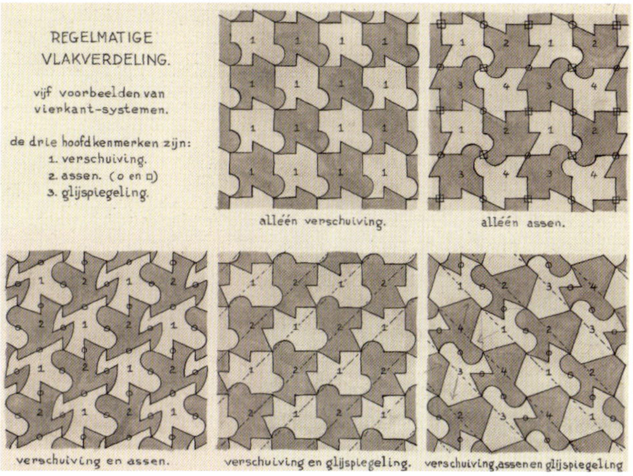

Example used during lectures, around 1960, ink on paper

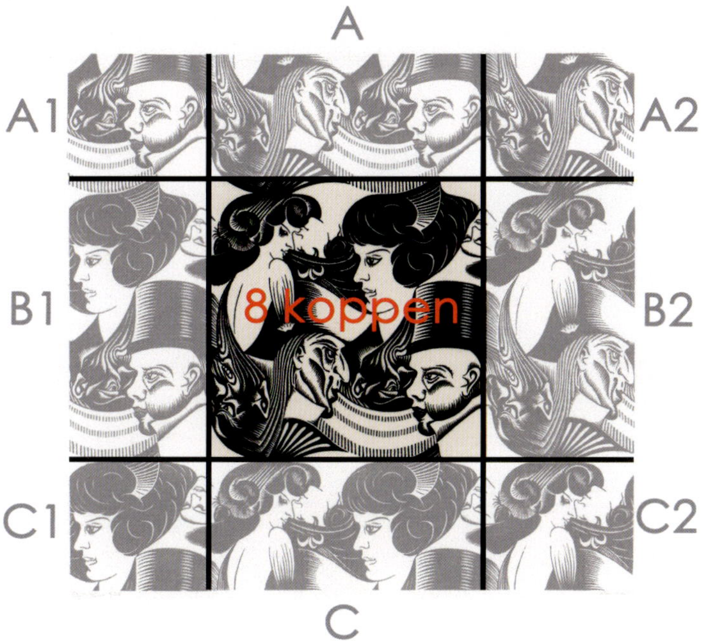

Diagrammatic division of the *Eight Heads* around the central motif

tions made up of lines. Five months earlier he had made *Eight Heads*; so it isn't surprising that he copied the motifs here. Contrary to what is mostly thought, this first visit left no mark on Escher's work. For the next thirteen years he lived in Italy and explored the possibilities of the landscape and the perspective. He was not working with tessellation. During his second visit in May 1936 Escher and his wife Jetta copied motifs in the Alhambra, like they had done earlier in Catholic churches in Italy. They stayed three days in Granada, then travelled via Ronda to Córdoba and ultimately ended up in Seville. The importance of this journey through Andalusia was to become clear later in his career.

In her book *Visions of Symmetry*[1] Doris Schattschneider has worked out the origin of Escher's tessellations and how he used them. Thanks to Schattschneider it is possible to ascertain which drawings he did during his second visit to Andalusia. From this we know which tessellations Escher chose in the Alhambra and what captivated him in the upper parts of the archways of the famous Mezquita mosque in Córdoba.

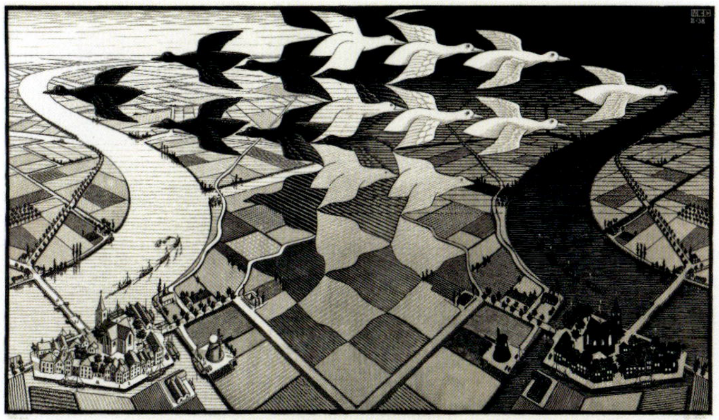

Day and Night, grey black woodcut, February 1938

A year after the visit to Andalusia and after moving to Uccle in Belgium, between May 1937 and February 1938, Escher made three prints in which tessellation played the main role: *Metamorphosis I, Development I* and *Day and Night.* The first and the last of these have become world famous. During a visit to his parents in The Hague his oldest brother Berend (Beer) saw *Metamorphosis I.* Berend Escher was a geologist at the University of Leiden. At that time crystallography was part of that discipline. He sent Mauk a bibliography of scientific developments in his field. Two publications were to have an important influence on Escher. These were the article about the seventeen systems written by the Hungarian crystallographer George (*György*) Pólya in 1924[2] and a study by the German scientist Friedrich Haag[3] from 1923. Here Escher found congruent, more

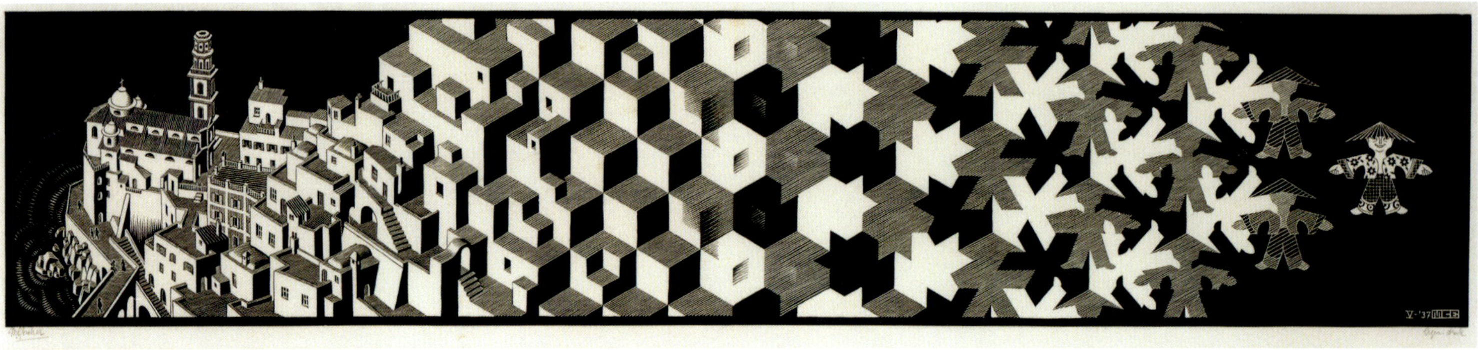

Metamorphosis I, woodcut, May 1937

complex shapes than the systems drawn by Pólya.
During World War II Escher examined and worked on the diagrams developed by these scientists in exercise books and note pads. He researched the structure and possibilities of tessellations in a classical way. These hundreds of variations on endlessly continuing motifs were a reservoir from which he would continue to draw. From the drawings in pencil next to the diagrams or below independent tessellations, it can be deduced which systems he used.
In 1947 Escher explained in the monthly journal *Phoenix* what a tessellation is: 'According to certain systems a plane can be divided into geometric figures, whose forms can be endlessly varied and can be extremely complicated but nevertheless comply with the rule: to fill the plane with congruent figures and in rhythmic repetition, leaving no empty space. When you seek to fit these figures together so that they arouse an association in the viewer with something familiar – an object, an animal, whatever – then it becomes a fascinating game, both because it offers endless possibilities and the huge restrictions imposed by the rules of play.'[4]
Two important elements come to the fore in this definition of tessellation. Firstly, it is a series of recognizable figures that fit seamlessly together, whereby Escher, secondly, plays a game with strict rules but offering infinite possibilities. These two conditions are the backbone of the hundreds of tessellations Escher drew, but even more so off all the prints in which he used tessellations.
Although Pólya dealt exclusively with crystals and how they divide, these systems also proved to correspond with the structures of centuries-old Islamic tessellations. Thus there is a huge visual parallel between the growth of crystals, as defined by Pólya and Haag, and decorative abstract motifs from Islamic art. There are hence similarities between the geometric patterns Escher used as the basis for his tessellations and those applied by the makers of Islamic art centuries ago.

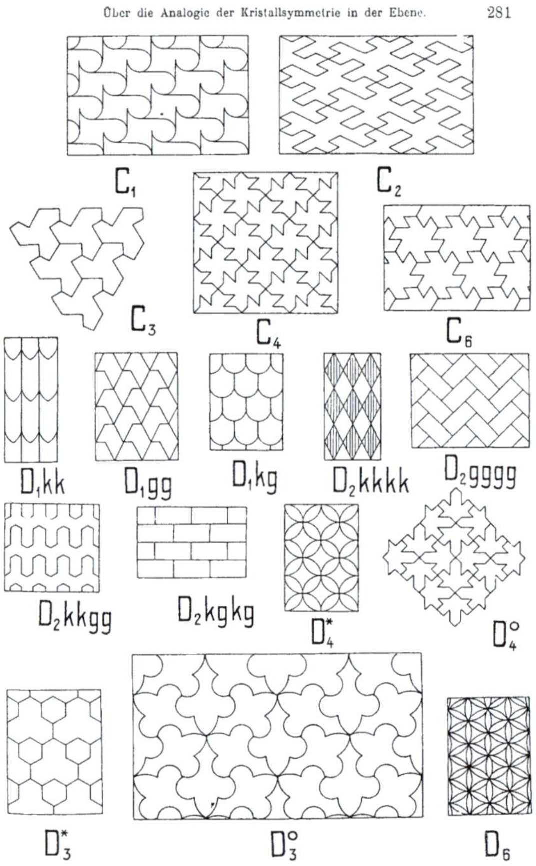

Pólya's 17 systems

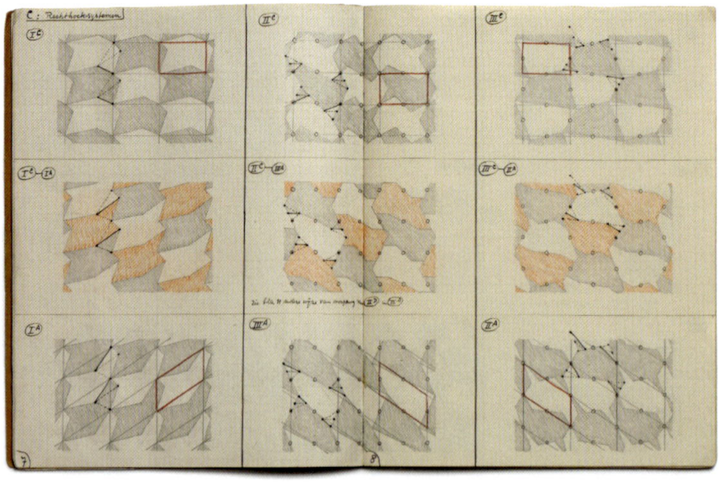

Double page from one of the exercise books

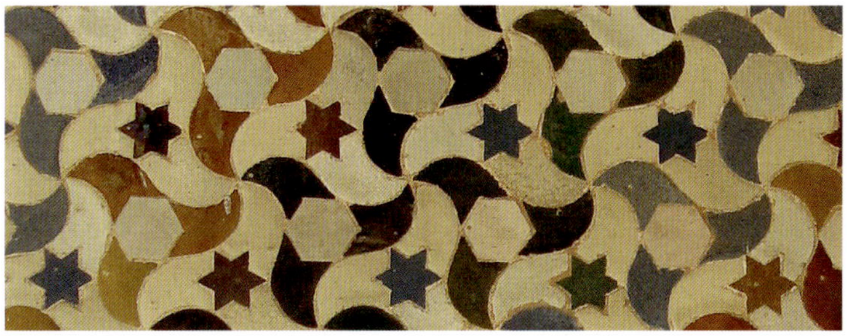

Detail of motif, Alhambra wall

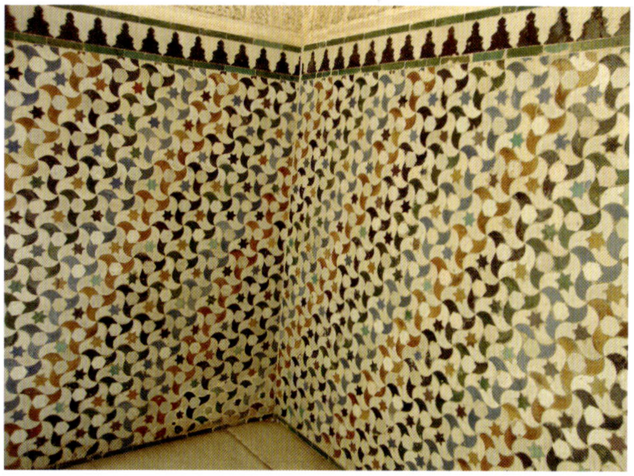

Alhambra, wall with the motif Escher copied, situation 2011

In Granada Escher saw wall mosaics that appeared to have movement and dynamics by linking a clear pattern with a set colour system. From a distance the large surface acquires a rhythmic division. Bigger lines originate from a small motif. On a photo of a wall in the Alhambra you can see that the series of coloured triangles run over the wall in diagonal bands: light blue, ochre, black and dark green. The lighter colours create rhythm and structure between the darker colours.
If you look at the details on such a large wall, you don't immediately see any rhythm; it is a simple system of undulating triangles with a hexagon at the centre. In the top row, the points of the undulating triangle are coloured and the centre is white. In the row below, the triangle is white and is placed at the heart of a diagonally positioned star with six points. White is dominant in this mosaic. It forms both the background to coloured triangles, as well as an independent motif with a star in the centre. This creates the feeling that the foreground and background run into each other. The layered structure only becomes visible if you continue to look carefully.

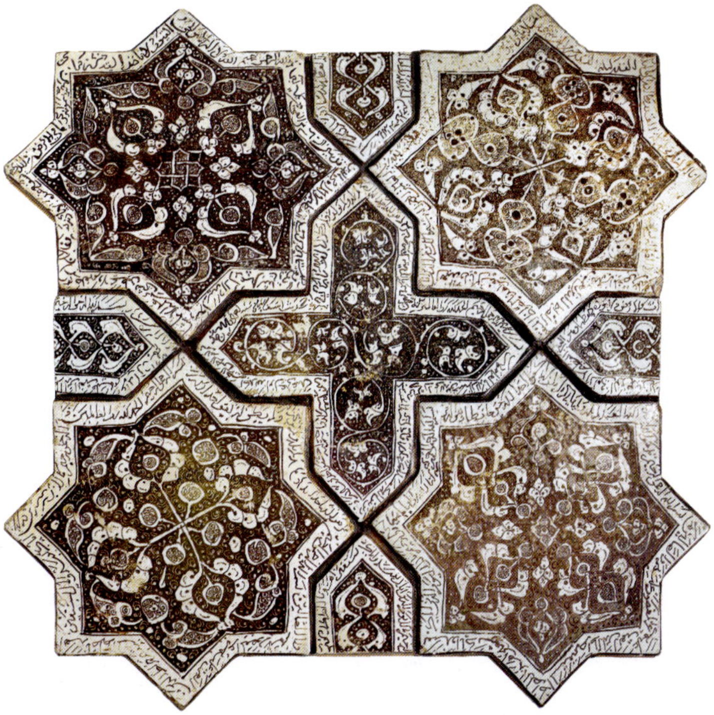

Tile panel from Iran, 1220-1300, fritware, glaze

How are the dynamics and the problem of the foreground and background of this wall related to M.C. Escher's work? Escher copied this mosaic in Granada. So he carefully drew the structure and its details. He also used movement in his prints but that was the result of changing shapes, which literally create movement, dynamics. Although Escher and the makers of Islamic art used the same geometric patterns, Escher 'distorts' them into recognizable figures: birds, fish, human males, horses and so on. Living beings seldom occur in Islamic tessellations. But figuration does occur in Islamic art in general – think of Ottoman, Persian and Indian miniature paintings. Furthermore, abstract patterns and motifs based on plants and flowers are frequently used in Islamic art, such as the large wall mosaics.

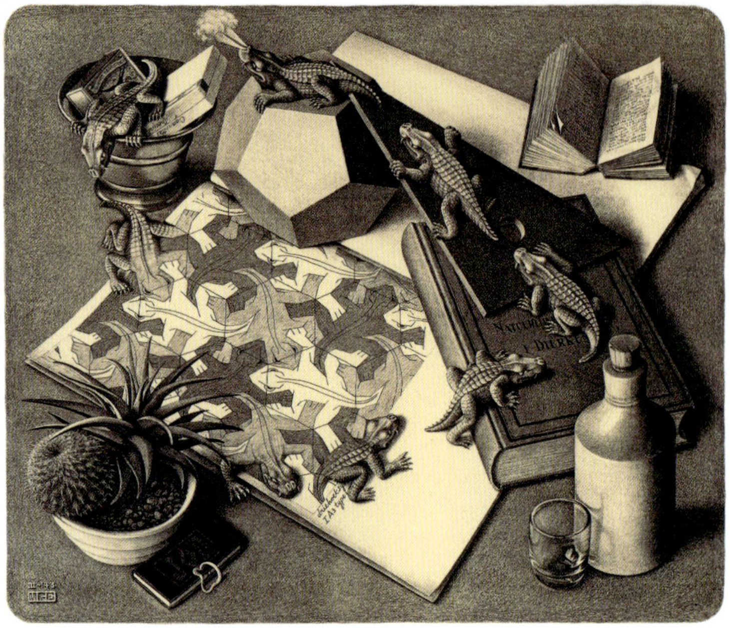

Reptiles, lithograph, 1943

The change in form is crucial. In Escher's most famous prints, fish become birds, houses become blocks and reptiles crawl out of a drawing. Regarding the latter, think of the famous lithograph *Reptiles.* The tessellation with the same name, a colour drawing, is the subject of this lithograph.

This brings us back to his own definition from 1947: Escher found working with tessellations 'a fascinating game, both because it offers endless possibilities and the huge restrictions imposed by the rules of play'. Endless variations that are astonishing, his work cannot be better typified.
In his game Escher combined tessellations with optical illusions, as in *Reptiles*, in which salamanders climb out of a drawing and then seem to disappear into it again. Here he ingeniously made use of the confusion in our perception of the conflict between foreground and background, which he had also seen in the Alhambra.
In the middle part of the woodcut *Horseman*, Escher combined a tessellation of horsemen with a Möbius band – a figure eight (see top of next page). Here it is uncertain whether the grey horseman in the middle is in front of the red horseman, or the other way round. The grey horsemen are riding on a red background towards the left and the red horsemen are riding towards the right on a grey background. Apart from in the middle section where two red horsemen are riding in the red and two grey horsemen are riding in the grey. There the red and the grey horsemen swap places in the foreground and the background. A confusing, contradictory movement is created in our heads: are the grey horsemen in front of the red or is it the other way round?
In *Reptiles* and *Horseman* a cycle forms the core of the print: the beginning and end coincide in perpetuum mobile, the ever continuing movement. A principle that we also know from Islamic art. The perpetuum mobile is typical of Escher: he combines cycles with a change in

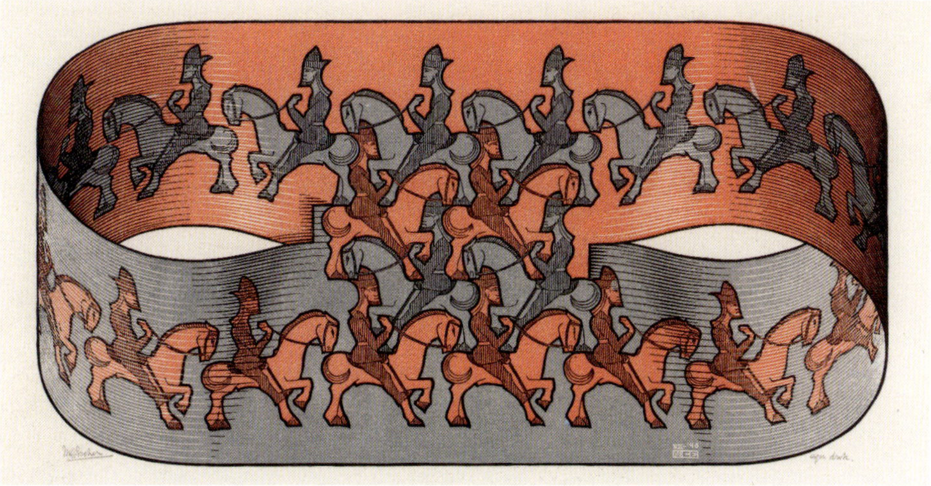

Horseman, woodcut, 1946

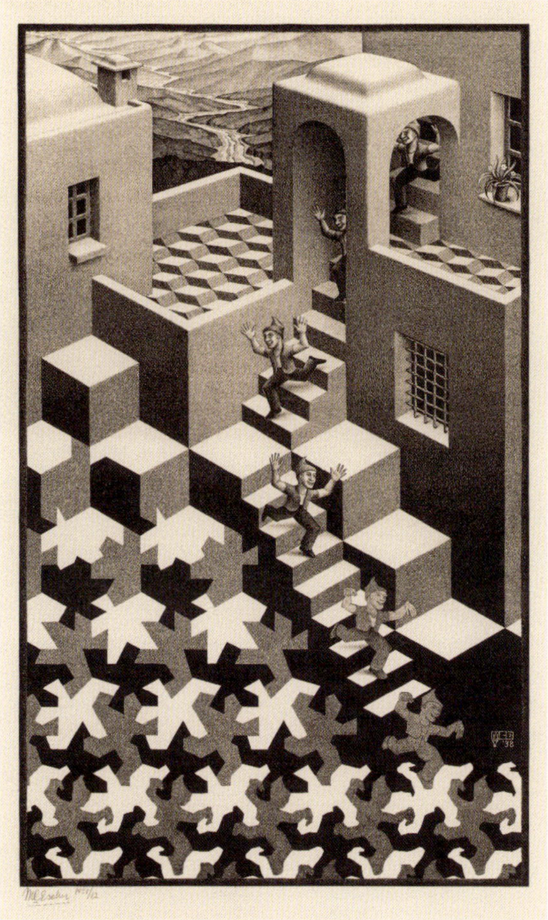

Cycle, lithograph, 1938

form, a metamorphosis. Both in *Metamorphosis I* from 1937 and *Metamorphosis II* from 1939–1940, as well as *Metamorphosis III* which he made in 1968, tessellation was the means to change the form and content.

The most beautiful way to exhibit the seven-metre long *Metamorphosis III* is in a large round frame. Then it becomes an architectonic object in space, as *Metamorphosis III* was originally intended, in the form of a painted enlargement, 42 metres long, for the post office in The Hague.

Whoever has walked through the galleries of the Alhambra and gazed at the tessellations there, sees the influence on Escher. You see how he put movement into his tessellations. In the spring of 1922 he made his first tessellation *Eight Heads.* Then he discovered the systems of Pólya and Haag, but his inspiration also came from the Islamic art of Andalusia.

1 Doris Schattschneider, *Visions of Symmetry: Notebooks, Periodic Drawings and Related Work of M.C. Escher*, first edition 1990 (reprint 2005), Abrams, New York.

2 G. Pólya, 'Über die Analogie der Kristallsymmetrie in der Ebene', *Zeitschrift für Kristallographie*, 1924.

3 F. Haag, 'Die regelmässigen Planteilungen und Punktsysteme', *Zeitschrift fur Kristallographie* 58 (1923) pp. 478–488.

4 *Phoenix, Maandblad voor beeldende kunst*, volume two, 1947, no. 4 June, in the section 'Nederlandse Grafici vertellen van hun werk'.

ESCHER AND ISLAMIC GEOMETRIC DESIGN

ERIC BROUG

The craftsmen who created the great variety of Islamic geometric design in art and architecture were not mathematicians. They didn't calculate angles. Instead they used a few basic tools to make all their compositions, from the relatively simple to the very complex. Their most important tool was a pair of compasses with which they could draw circles and arcs. The other tool was a simple ruler with which they could draw straight lines. Every Islamic geometric design is created by lines, circles and arcs. Craftsmen would seek and create intersections using these three elements. Choosing which intersections to use (and which not to use) creates the immense variety of patterns that can be seen across the Islamic world.

They didn't draw an entire composition with these tools but instead drew a small pattern or part of a pattern that they could repeat to create a composition. This principle of drawing a small pattern in, for example, a hexagon or a square is at the root of almost all Islamic geometrical compositions.

What we can do with this one small pattern is repeat it to cover a larger area. In other words, it can be tessellated to make a composition. A simple eightpointed star can be designed in a square (see ill. 1). This square can be tessellated and a composition is created. When it is tessellated, the square in which the star appeared is no longer needed and is invisible and the cross shapes that now sit between the stars have appeared (see ill. 2). This principle can apply to small patterns in squares but also to

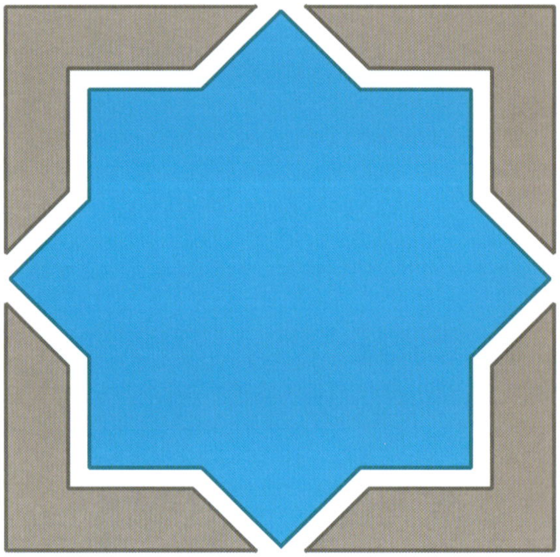

1. Eightpointed star set in a square

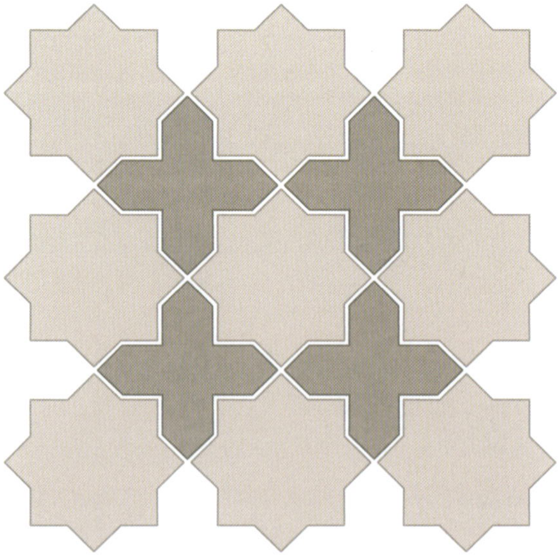

2. Eightpointed star tessellated

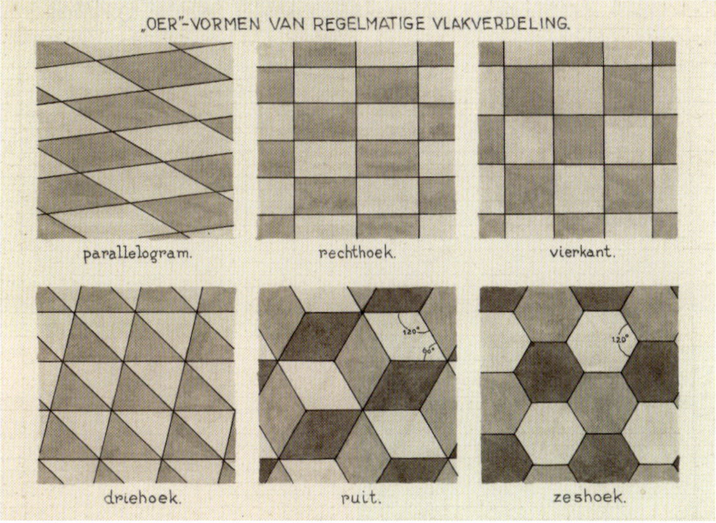

3. M.C. Escher, the top row of sketches shows three fourfold tessellations, the bottom row shows three sixfold tessellations

small patterns in hexagons, triangles, diamond shapes and many other polygons. One of M.C. Escher's sketches shows that this was also the way he structured many of his compositions (see ill. 3). In his sketch he has a top row of drawings showing tessellations where squares, diamonds and rectangles are arranged to cover a surface area. The bottom row shows drawings where triangles, hexagons and lozenge shapes are arranged to cover a surface area.
A pattern or part of a pattern in a square, hexagon or any other polygon can be called a 'repeat unit'. Repeat units can have many different shapes and can create many different grids. The sketch by Escher shows six such grids. The most simple grid is a grid of squares. Many patterns in Islamic geometric design can be made using a repeat unit that is tessellated in a grid of squares. Using a simple grid doesn't mean that the composition is therefore less complex. This depends entirely on the content of the repeat unit. A composition that can be found in the Alhambra Palace was created in a grid of squares. The craftsmen would draw a small pattern and then tessellate it (see ill. 4). The pattern was drawn using only a pair of compasses and a ruler.

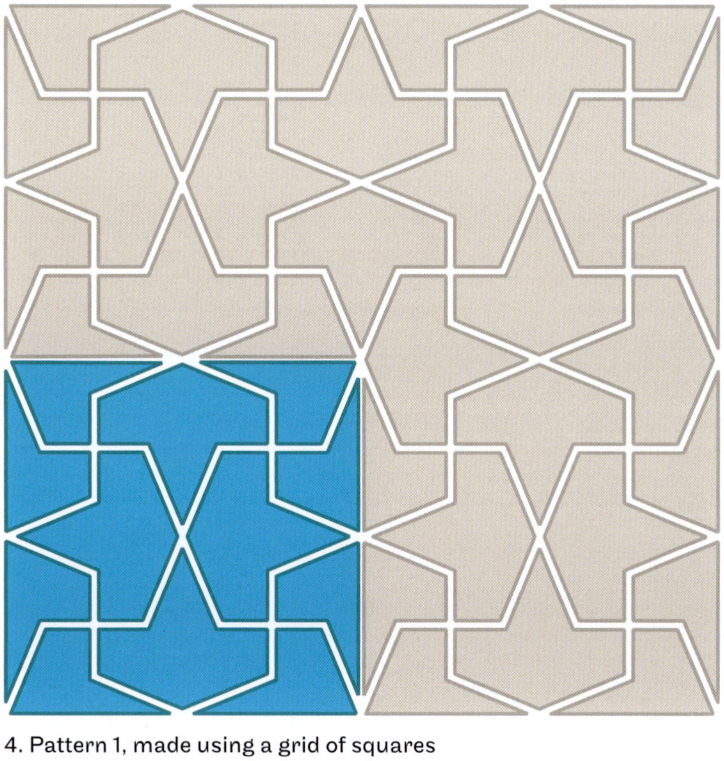

4. Pattern 1, made using a grid of squares

One of the main practical benefits of using a grid is that a craftsman can modify the size of the repeat unit to take into account the size of the composition. All the compositions in the Alhambra had to cover a specific surface area; the craftsman had to create his composition knowing that it had to be of a specific height and width. It had to fit. A grid makes this possible. It allows the craftsmen to determine the size of the repeat unit before he commits himself to making the composition. Another composition that can be found in the Alhambra Palace can be created in a grid of hexagons. This pattern can also be drawn using just a pair of compasses and a ruler.

The vast majority of patterns in the Alhambra can be created in either of these two grids; a grid of squares or a grid of hexagons. They are also the most common grids in Islamic geometric design in general. One of the observational skills that Escher demonstrated in his sketches from the Alhambra was that he was able to identify which grids were used for which compositions. There are different ways to do this. One of the easiest ways is to identify the type of star pattern that is used. This can be best done by counting the 'petals' that surround a central star (see ill. 6). The thousands of different geometric compositions that have been created by craftsmen over the centuries can generally be categorized according to what kind of star patterns feature. There are compositions with eightpointed stars, tenpointed stars, twelvepointed stars etc. These stars give clues to what kind of grid was used by a craftsmen to make a composition. A six-pointed star fits in a hexagon. Similarly, an eightpointed star fits in a square. In the case of compositions where there are no star

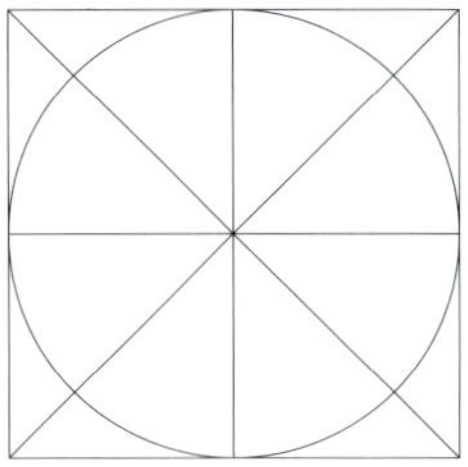

Step 1: The starting point for many Islamic geometric patterns: a circle in a square, divided into eight equal sections

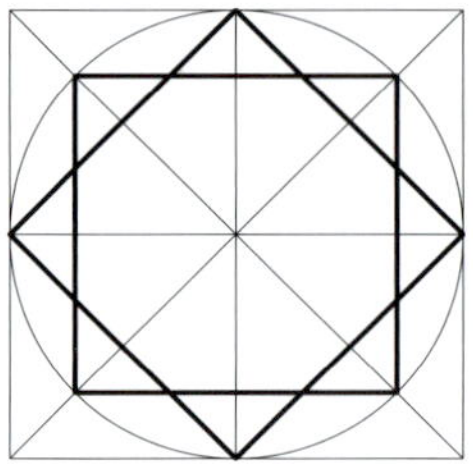

Step 2: Draw two squares inside the circle

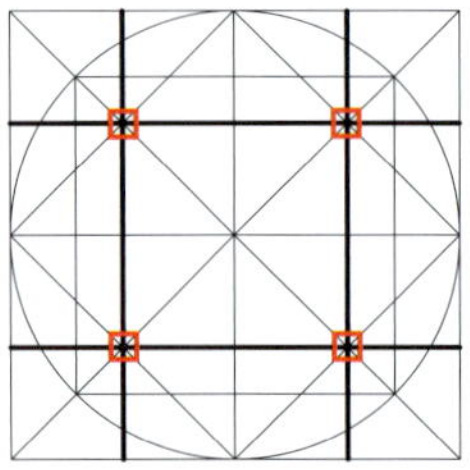

Step 3: Draw two pairs of parallel lines that pass through the intersections indicated with red squares

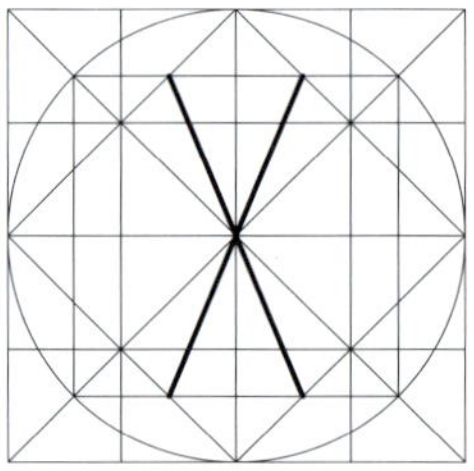

Step 4: Draw an X shape as indicated

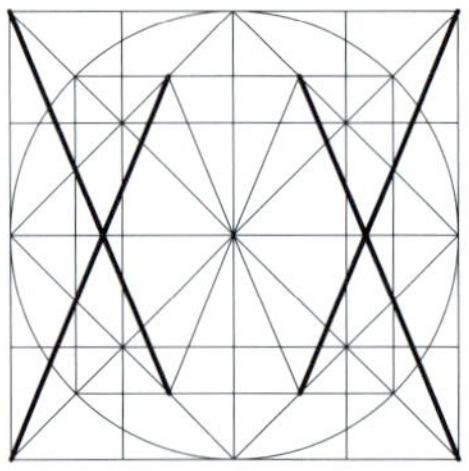

Step 5: Draw four lines that connect with corners of the square and the X shape from the previous step

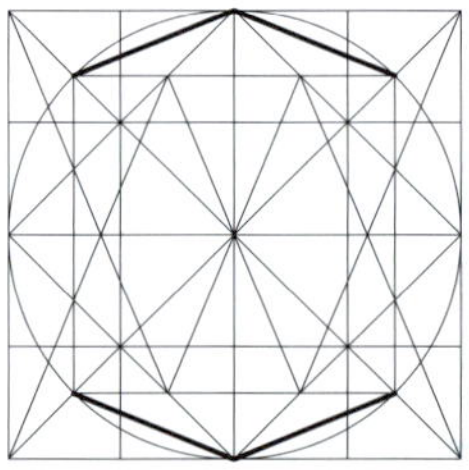

Step 6: Draw four lines as indicated

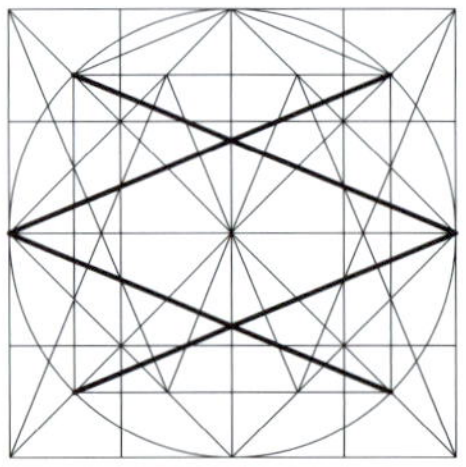

Step 7: Draw four lines. Consider them as two V-shapes on their side. Look carefully at the intersections they connect with

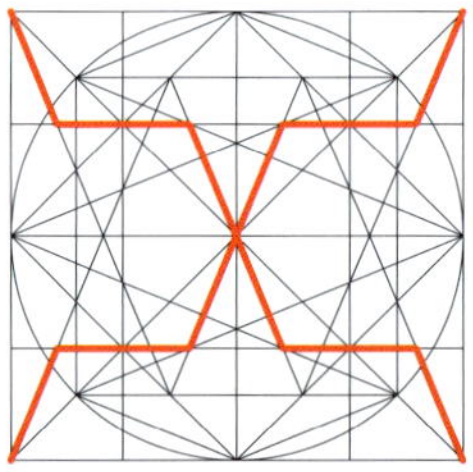

Step 8: All the construction lines have now been drawn. Take a different colour pen or pencil and trace the sections of lines as indicated

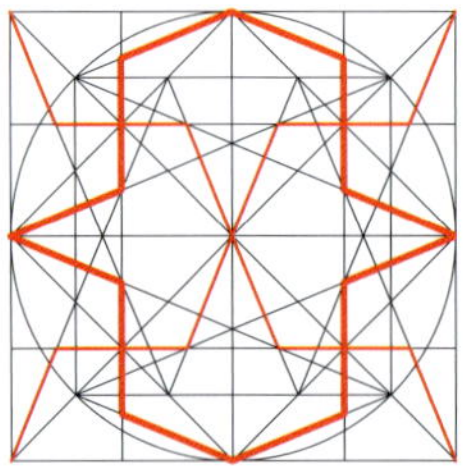

Step 9: Trace the sections of lines as indicated

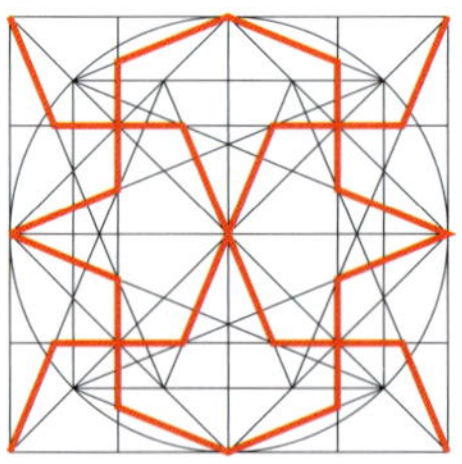

Step 10: All lines have now been drawn. The design is now complete and can be tessellated in a grid of squares to create pattern 1 on page 21

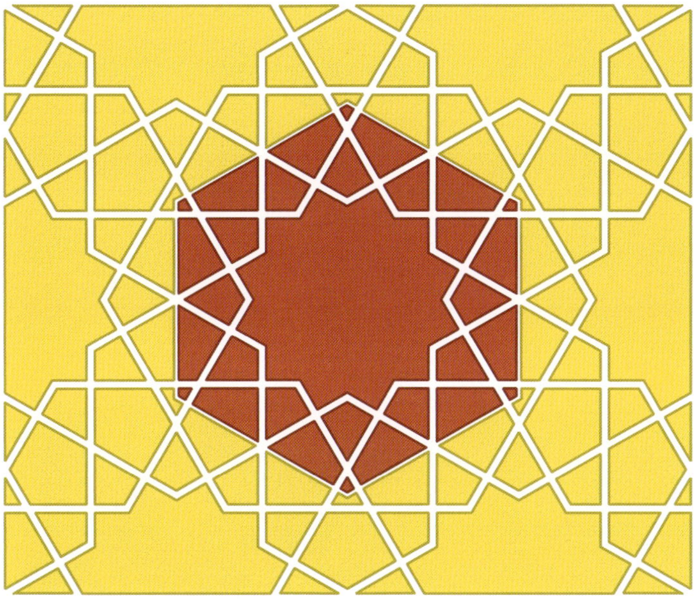

5. Pattern 2, made using a grid of hexagons

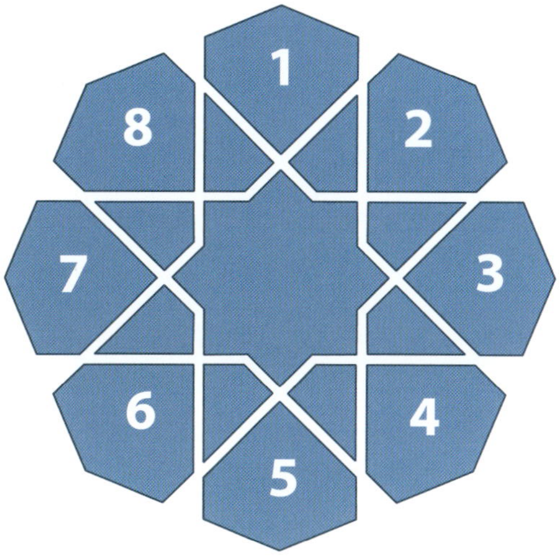

6. An eightpointed star surrounded by eight petal shapes

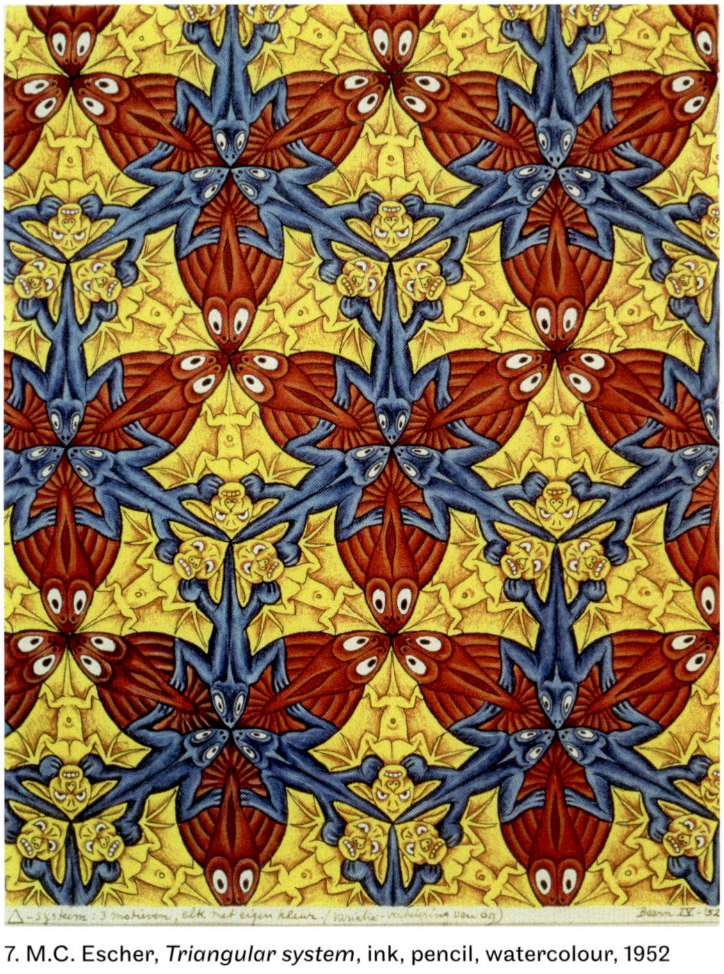

7. M.C. Escher, *Triangular system*, ink, pencil, watercolour, 1952

patterns with surrounding petals to count, a different approach needs to be used. Escher's compositions also do not feature star patterns. The best way to identify what grid was used to structure the composition is to look how recurring elements can be seen to be grouped together and spatially related to each other. There are many Escher compositions in which this method of identification can be tested. If we take his composition with red fish, yellow bats and blue lizards we can see that each creature can be seen to be grouped in threes (see ill. 7). Alternatively, we can focus only on the blue lizards and they can be seen to make a structure of hexagons. Alternatively again, the red fish and yellow bats can be seen to create a grid of alternating yellow and red triangles. The presence of triangles and hexagons are evidence that this composition was created in a grid of hexagons or triangles.

Escher's complex compositions typically offer different visual possibilities. Different elements will draw attention at different times and looking more closely and more frequently at his compositions will give the viewer different visual rewards over time. This is one of the more profound visual similarities between Escher's work and the geometric patterns that can be seen at the Alhambra. The style of geometric design at the Alhambra, where small glazed tiles with bold contrasting colours were used, meant that these compositions offered different visual rewards depending on the distance

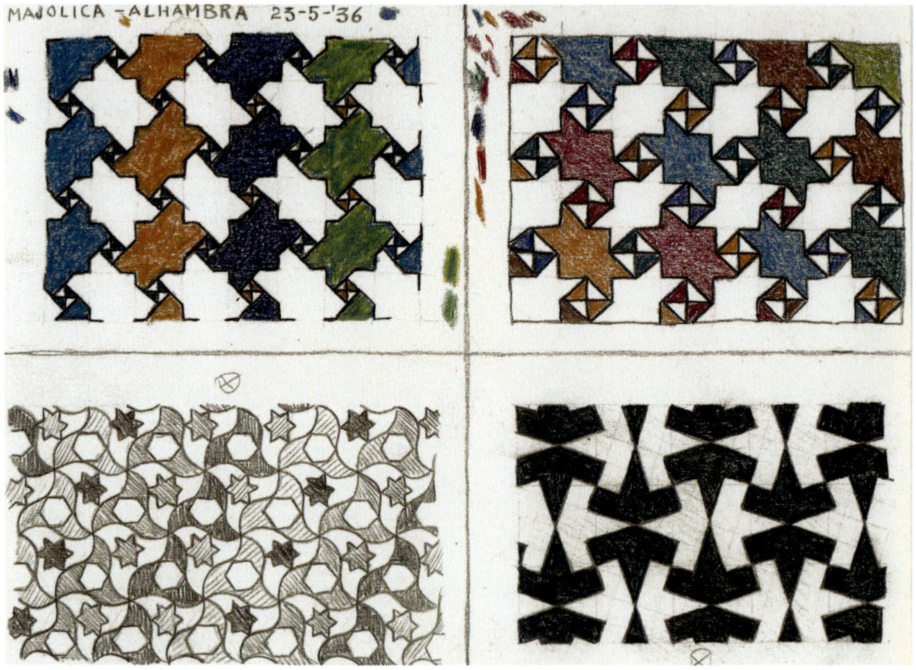

8. M.C. Escher, Sketch of tile work in the Alhambra, 1936, Collection Dr Stephen R. Turner

between the observer and the composition. The pattern that was drawn in the step-by-step sequence was also drawn by Escher on his trip to the Alhambra (see ill. 8). The lower right black and white drawing features the familiar arrows shapes that point left and right and up and down. What is clear from this drawing and the two colour drawings in the same illustration (ill. 8) was that Escher was especially interested in how shapes interact with each other. The arrow pattern shows this well: the black arrows need the white arrows to exist and vice versa. The two colour drawings show how Escher experimented with modifying the size of shapes in a composition. The original composition appears in the Alhambra. Both colour drawings show Escher altering the size of shapes without significantly altering their appearance. Nevertheless, when seen side by side, both drawings show compositions that are subtly different.

If all compositions in Islamic geometric design were created with grids with just one shape, the creative potential would soon be exhausted. If the only creative opportunity for the craftsman was to decide what pattern he created in his square or hexagons, there would not be the rich diversity of patterns and compositions that we can see in Islamic geometric design. This rich diversity was in part created by combining different polygonal shapes to create new grids. These new grids could form the basis for new patterns. For example, a simple grid of hexagons with a repeat unit can

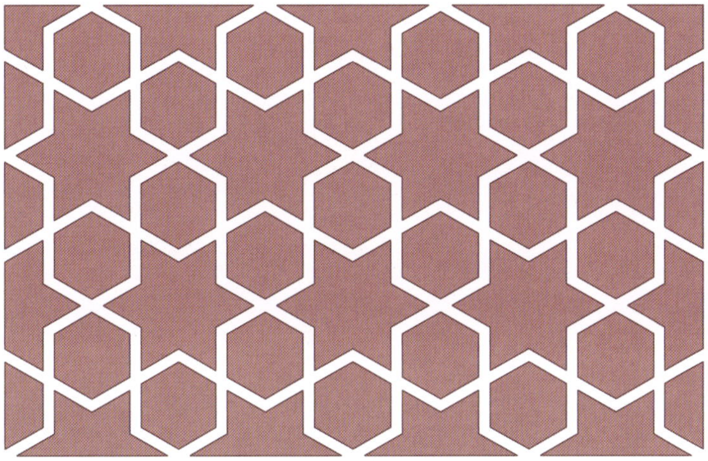

9. Pattern 3, without the hexagonal grid being visible

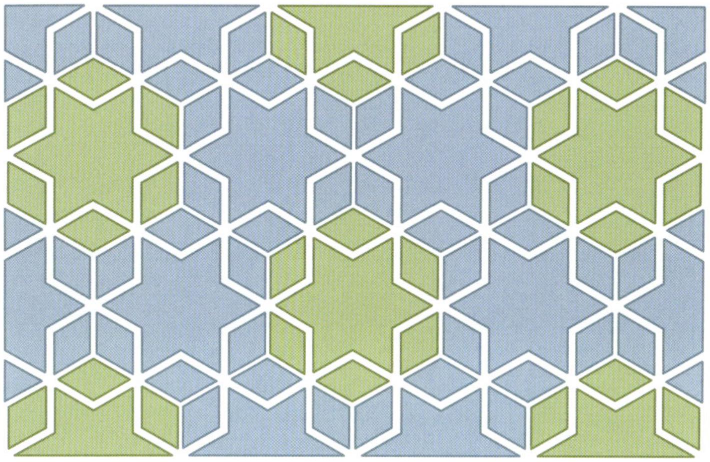

10. Pattern 3, made by tessellating a simple sixpointed star in a hexagonal grid

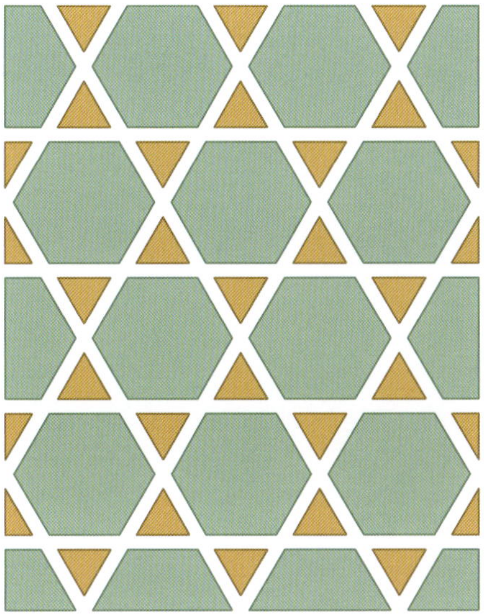

11. A grid of hexagons and triangles

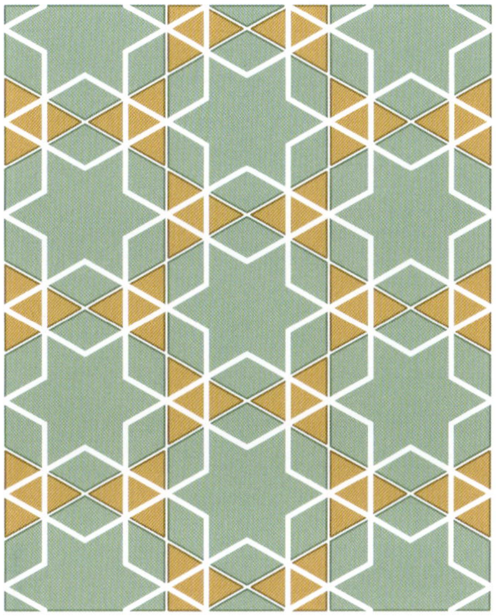

12. Pattern 4, made using a grid of hexagons and triangles. The hexagons have the same content as the hexagons in pattern 3

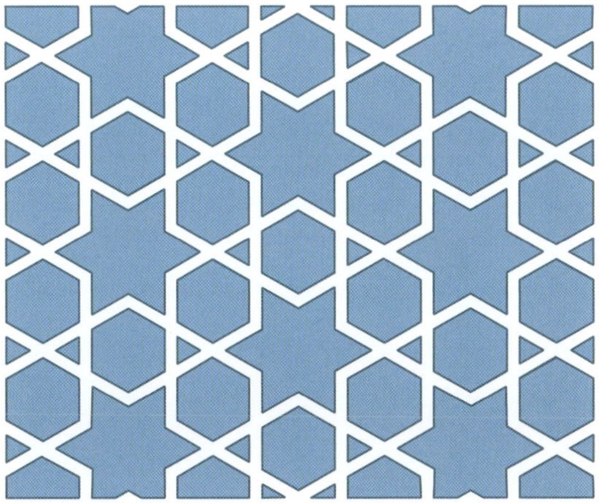

13. Pattern 4, without the grid of hexagons and triangles being visible

create a pattern. Illustration 10 shows the repeat units, illustration 9 shows the same composition but without the repeat units. When a triangular element is added to this grid, it becomes a grid of hexagons and triangles (see ill. 11). The triangular shapes can be treated as new repeat units that can contain part of a pattern and they can now contribute to the creation of a new pattern. Illustration 12 shows the composition with the repeat units visible, illustration 13 shows the compositions without the repeat units visible. What becomes clear is that the simple addition of a small triangular repeat unit significantly changes the pattern. There are hundreds of such modifications that can be done to grids and repeat units. This is the creative source of Islamic geometric design.

The Nasrid craftsmen at the Alhambra Palace worked exclusively with fourfold and sixfold compositions. They did not try their hand at fivefold compositions (based on the division of a circle into five or ten equal sections). Why this is the case is not clear. Some eras in Islamic history are especially renowned for the beauty and innovation of their Islamic geometric design. The work of the Nasrid craftsmen at the Alhambra should certainly be considered in this light. However, it seems that they found sufficient creative expression in fourfold and sixfold geometric design. This is untypical. If we consider the geometric design of the Mamluks of Cairo (1250–1517) or of the Seljuks of Anatolia (1077–1307), we can see that they also sought to find new creative

expression in Islamic geometric design. They found this frequently in fivefold (and tenfold geometric compositions). However, this was not the case for the Nasrid craftsmen. Interestingly, the Marinids who had their capital in Fes, Morocco and had friendly relations with the Nasrids in the Alhambra Palace, built many madrasas where the decorative theme is evidently indebted to the style of decoration used at the Alhambra. One such madrasa, the Bu Innaniya madrasa (1350–1355), has Islamic geometric decorations all around its central courtyard. It features several tenfold star patterns that have been tessellated as if they were fourfold patterns. The craftsman who made these compositions seemingly knew how to draw tenfold star patterns but not how to tessellate them in a way that is most suitable.
Tessellating a tenfold pattern is not as straightforward as tessellating a sixfold or fourfold patterns. That is why, for example, Mamluk and Seljuk craftsmen were so attracted to them: they posed unique design challenges (see ill. 15). Escher showed some interest in fivefold geometric design but not in the context of his compositions that feature tessellation. He certainly wouldn't have come across any examples of fivefold tessellation at the Alhambra Palace.
Escher's fivefold star pattern composition is a rare instance where he used this category of geometric design. Tessellating fivefold geometric design is more difficult because it doesn't work to the same rules as fourfold or sixfold design. Squares and

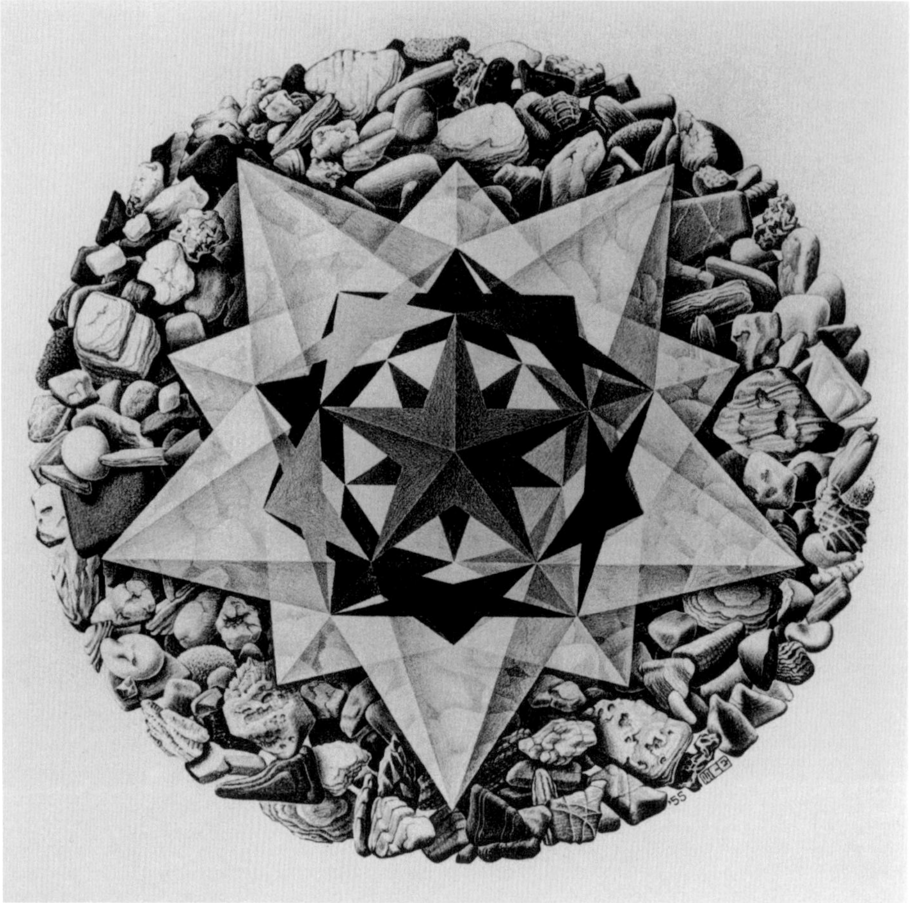

14. M.C. Escher, *Order and Chaos II*, Lithography, 1955

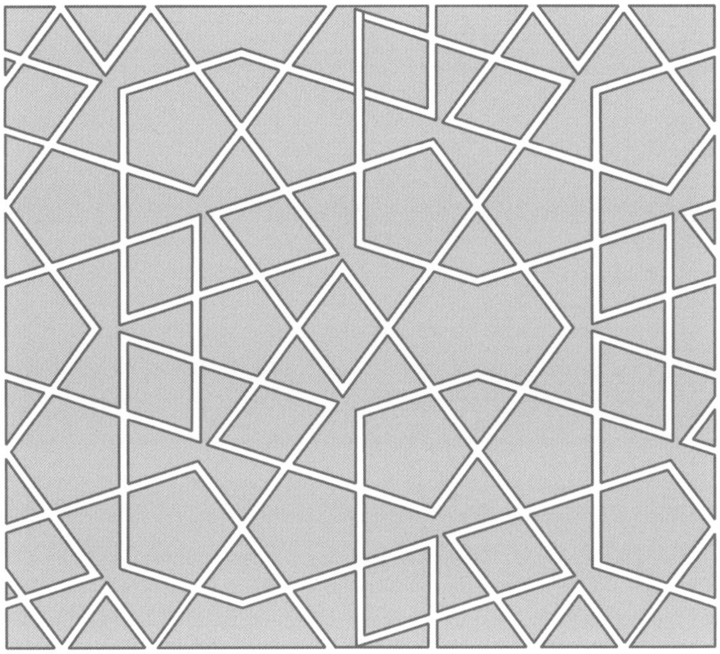

15. A fivefold composition

hexagons can be repeated ad infinitum. This is not the case with pentagons. They can not be tessellated to cover an area; they overlap or they leave gaps. Over the centuries, Islamic craftsmen have found creative solutions to still be able to make large fivefold compositions. They did this mostly by creating unusually shaped repeat units.

When Escher's work is placed next to Islamic geometric design, it is clear how he was inspired by it. The way shapes interact in a composition, the way grids are used behind the scenes to give structure and more creative freedom, the way different elements can give various visual rewards, they way in which colour and contrast feature in the Alhambra, these are all characteristics of Islamic geometric design that Escher subsequently used in his own work. It is interesting to wonder what would have happened if Escher had managed to make a trip to Cairo or Anatolia in Turkey. He would have seen a whole new geometric language expressed in the many fivefold and tenfold compositions that were made by Mamluk and Seljuk craftsmen, respectively. It would undoubtedly have had an impact on his work in the same way that his trip to the Alhambra had a formative impact on his work.

INSPIRATION

From 1936 Escher worked on tessellations, also known as plane fillings. In a tessellation, figures completely fill a plane without overlapping each other and with no space in between them – just like paving stones. He made his first tessellation in 1922, immediately after his studies at the School of Architecture and Decorative Arts in Haarlem.
The same year, at the age of 24, Escher visited the Alhambra for the first time. The Arab-Andalusian palace complex was popular with many artists. Like Escher they were fascinated by the geometric patterns on the buildings.
In the Alhambra Escher saw how different combinations of shapes and colours could work. When Escher returned there fourteen

ESCHER WORKED ON SO-CALLED TESSELLATIONS HIS ENTIRE CAREER. IN A TESSELLATION, FIGURES COMPLETELY FILL A PLANE WITHOUT OVERLAPPING EACH OTHER AND WITH NO SPACE IN BETWEEN THEM – JUST LIKE PAVING STONES

years later he decided to study the patterns in depth. With his wife Jetta, for days on end he made sketches of the tiled walls and plaster-work. He later described plane-filling patterns as 'the richest source of inspiration that he encountered in his life'.
On his return home he began making his own variations of the material he had collected. He applied the mathematical rules he had discovered in the Islamic tessellations to his own designs. Abstract shapes were replaced by recognizable animal and human figures. Over the years Escher's tessellations became increasingly complex and more and more imaginative, with for example transformation of the figures and the suggestion of spatiality.

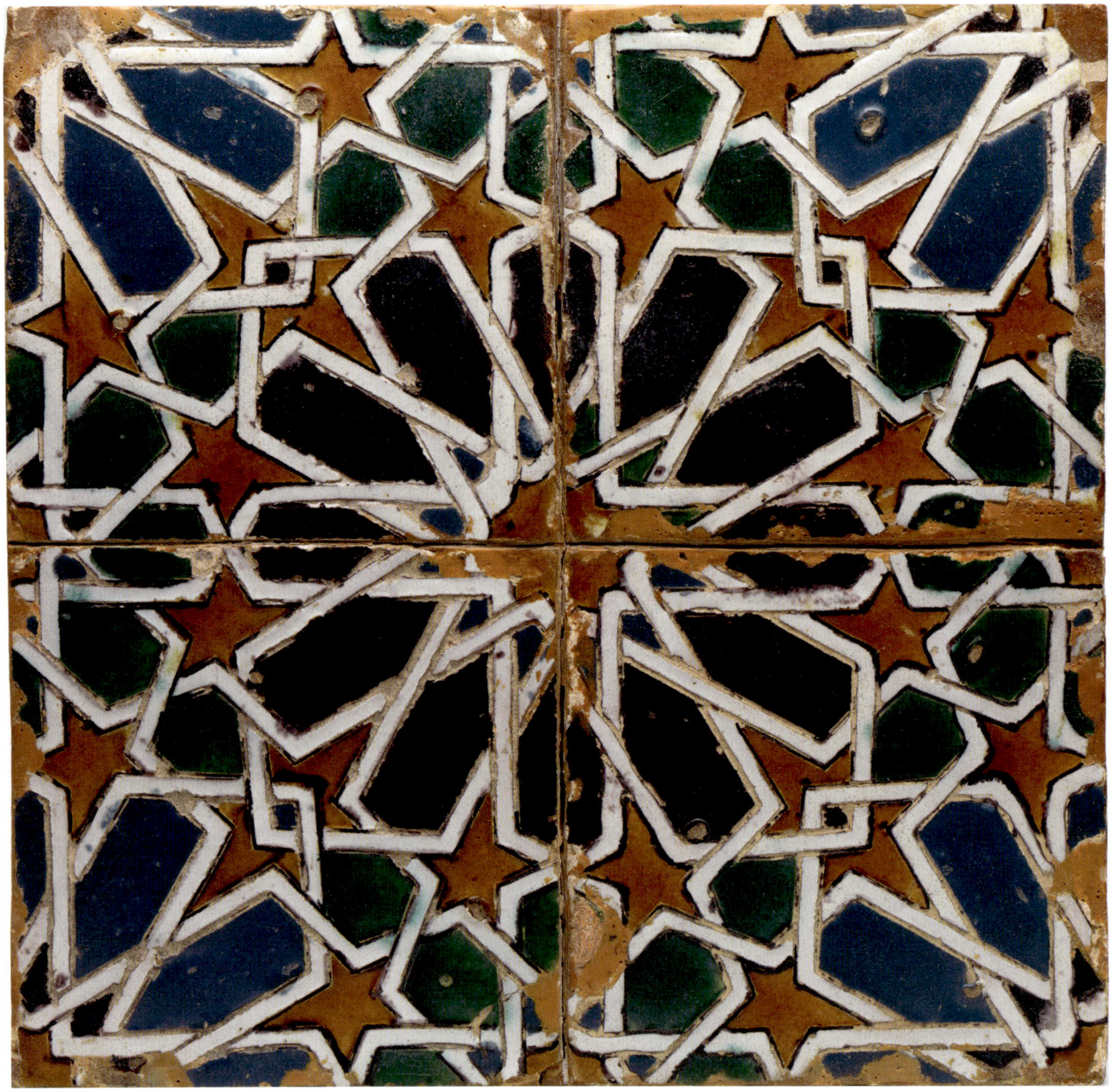

Alhambra tiles
This tile panel is in the same style as the tiles Escher drew in 1922 in the Alhambra (see Escher's drawing to the right). He made a note in his diary about the palace complex: 'It was wonderfully Eastern. What was strange to me was the immense richness of the decoration and the great dignity and its simple beauty as a whole.'

Tile panel, 16th century
Spain
Cuerda seca, majolica earthenware
Collection Museum Boijmans Van Beuningen, Rotterdam

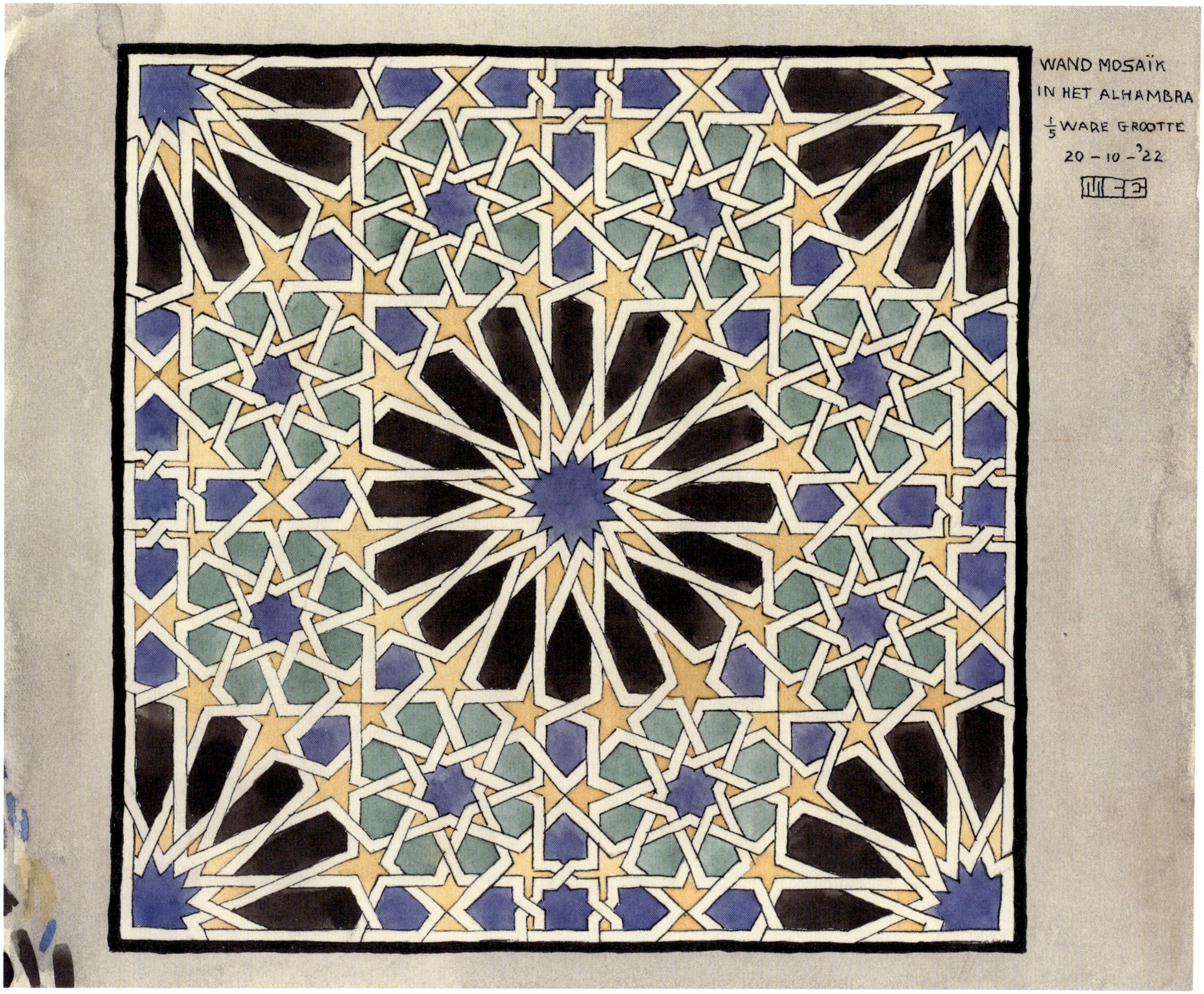

First sketch
During his first visit to Spain Escher spent a whole afternoon in the Alhambra copying tiles with geometric patterns. That evening and the following morning he worked on his sketches to produce this drawing.

Wall Mosaic in the Alhambra, 1922
M.C. Escher
Watercolour, ink
Collection Gemeentemuseum Den Haag

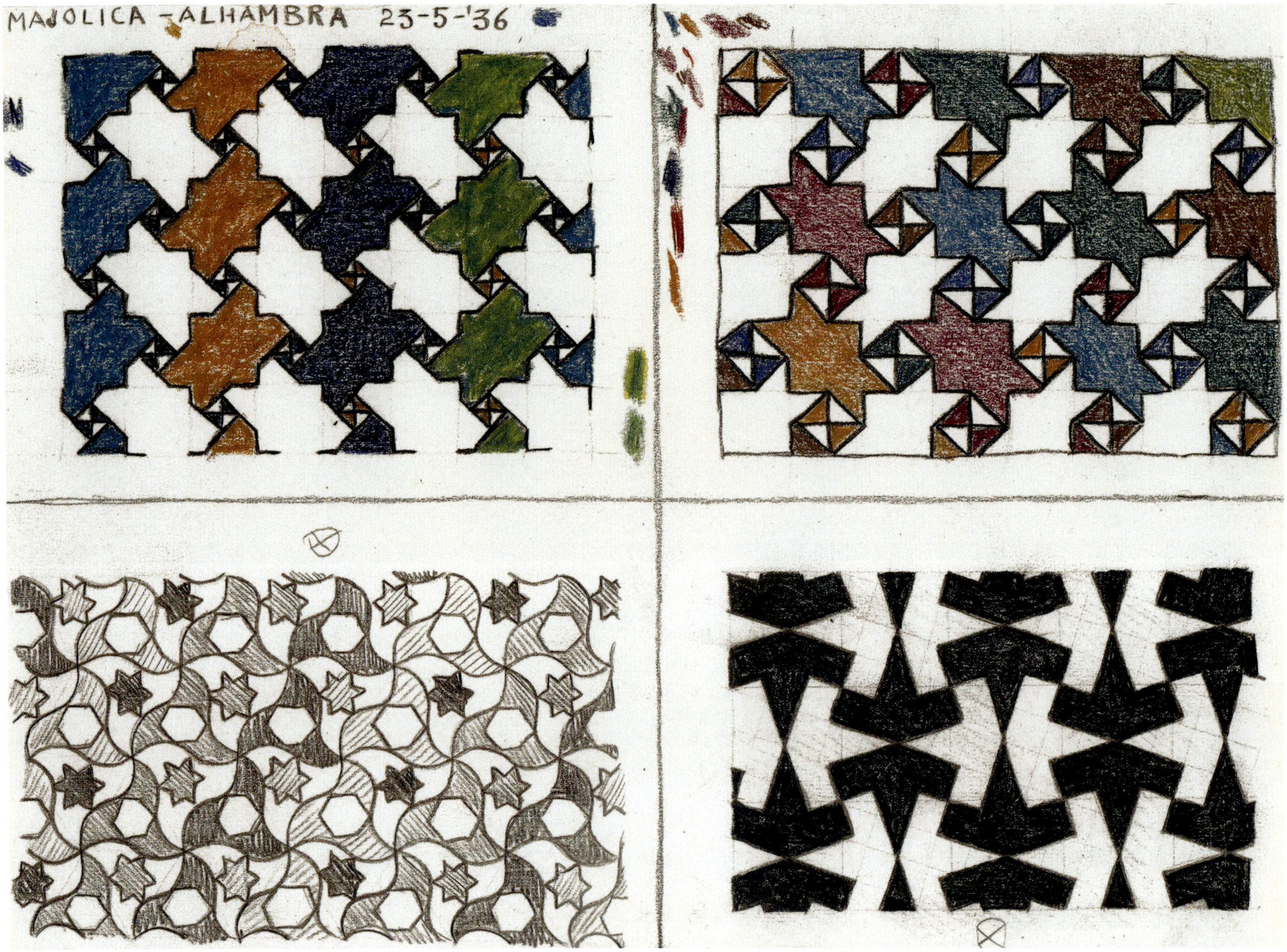

Tile patterns
During his second visit to the Alhambra, Escher also made a series of sketches of the tiled walls. He joyously recognized the geometric patterns and was later to write: 'Long before I discovered an affinity with the regular division of the plane in the Alhambra with the Moors, I'd already recognized it in myself.'

Sketch of tile work in the Alhambra, 1936
M.C. Escher
Pencil
Collection Dr Stephen R. Turner

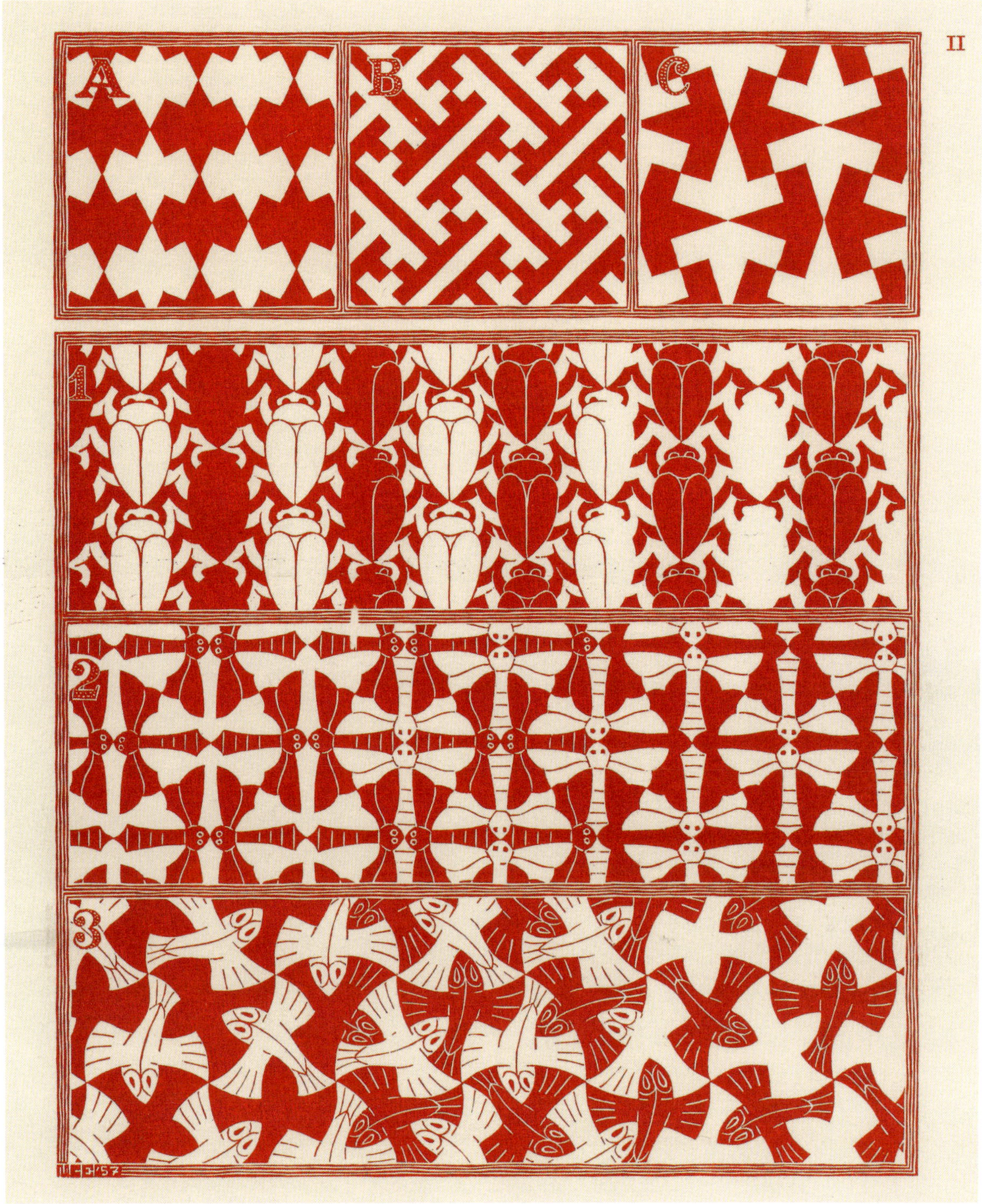

Variations
Escher thought it a shame that the tessellations in the Alhambra only depicted abstract shapes. Top left and top right on this print are patterns that he copied there. In the three rows below are Escher's later variations on these, now with animal figures.

Regular Division of the Plane II, 1957
M.C. Escher
Woodcut
Collection M.C. Escher Foundation

INFINITY

Figures that are repeated again and again evoke the illusion of infinity. There is seemingly no beginning or end and the pattern can continue in all directions. Despite the finite plane this gives a feeling of boundlessness. Continuous geometric patterns frequently occur in Islamic art. The meaning of this is a subject of discussion. Is the endless repetition simply beautiful to look at? Does this type of pattern have a meditative effect or does it have a deeper meaning, like the immensity of God? *The* answer doesn't exist because too little is known about the concepts behind Islamic art.

FIGURES THAT ARE REPEATED AGAIN AND AGAIN EVOKE THE ILLUSION OF INFINITY

Escher felt the need to express infinity in his tessellations. He wrote: 'If you want to depict an infinitely large number you have to resort to shrinking the figures gradually, until at least theoretically, you reach the limit of the infinitely small format.' As well as reduction in size he applied for example metamorphosis. Shapes that gradually move from the plane to the ostensibly spatial, from abstract to figurative – and back again – intensify the idea of never-ending movement.

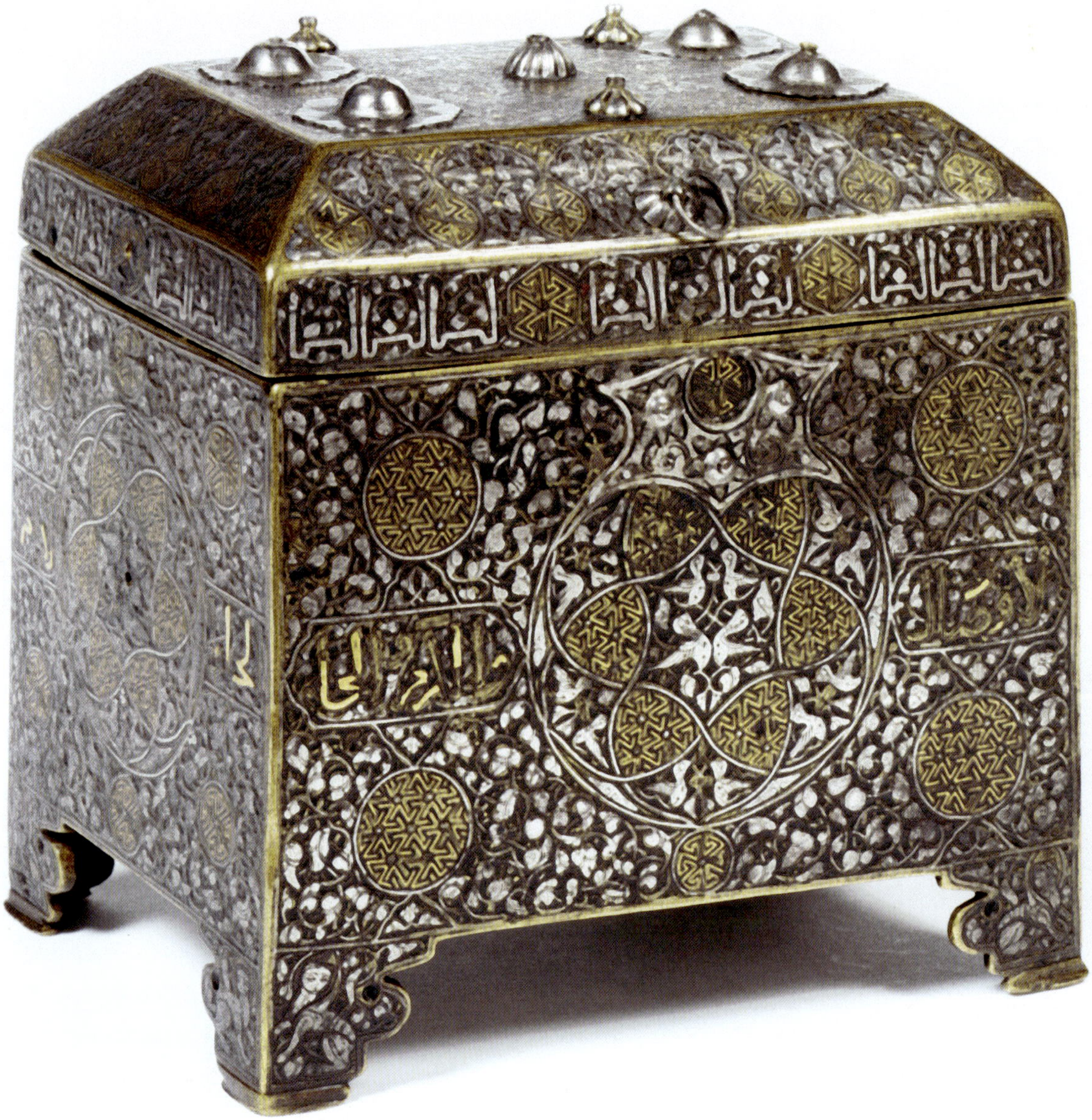

Islamic art
This casket is a textbook example of Islamic art. It is a luxury item made for someone from well-to-do circles. The four main decorative forms found in Islamic art – calligraphy, geometry, flower and plant motifs, and living beings – are all found on this casket.

The concept of Islamic art is a European invention from the nineteenth century. Nowadays the term is problematic owing to the preconceptions associated with it, namely that all cultural expressions in Muslim regions are derived from the faith.

Casket, early 14th century
Western Iran, Ilkhanid period
Brass, gold, silver
Collection Victoria and Albert Museum, London

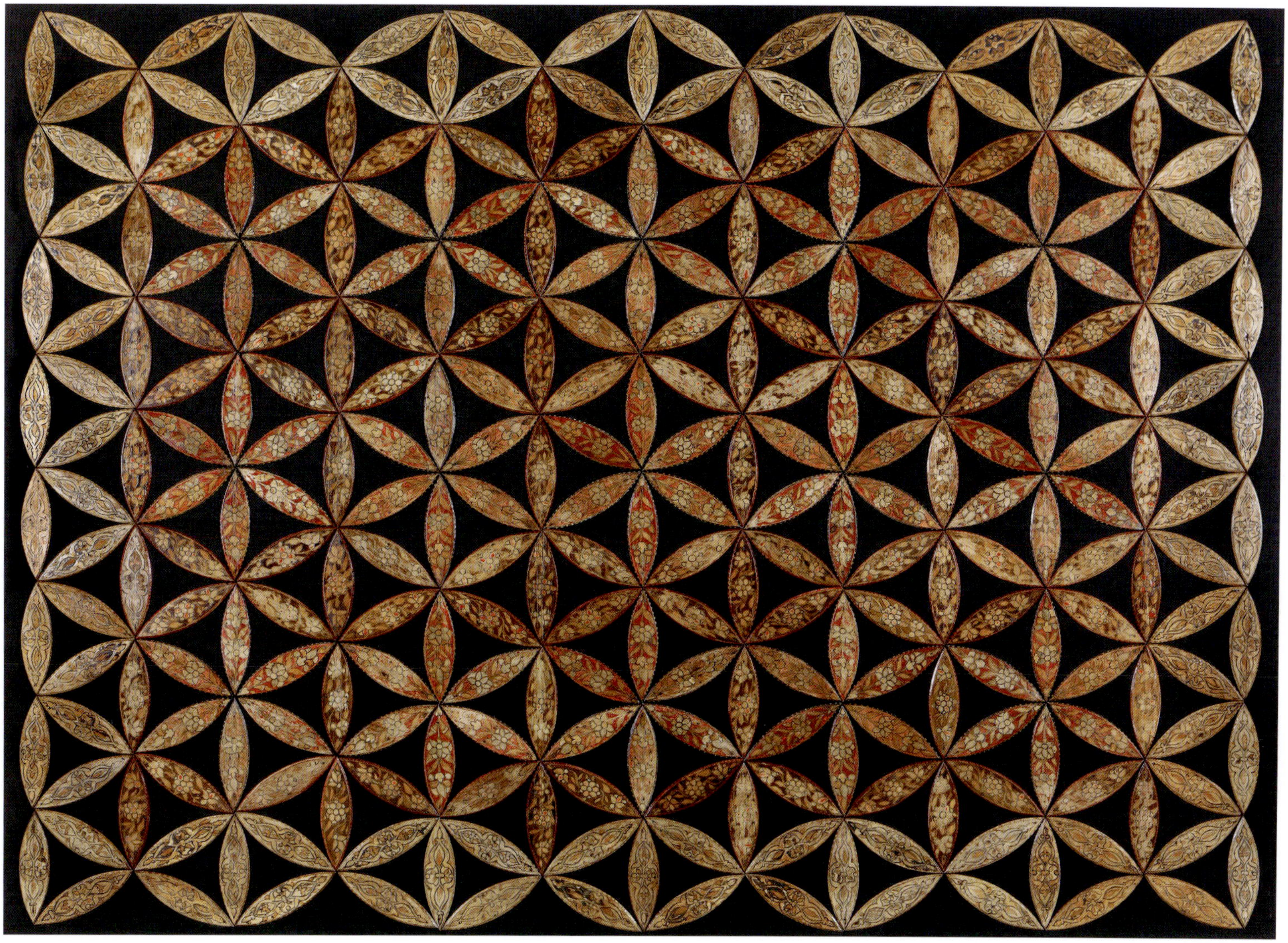

Continuous circles
This ceiling decoration is from the house of a wealthy family in the Turkish city of Bursa. The pattern of overlapping circles could continue in all directions. This evokes the suggestion of infinity.

Ceiling decoration, 18th century
Bursa, Turkey, Ottoman period
Wood, varnish
Collection Wereldmuseum, Rotterdam

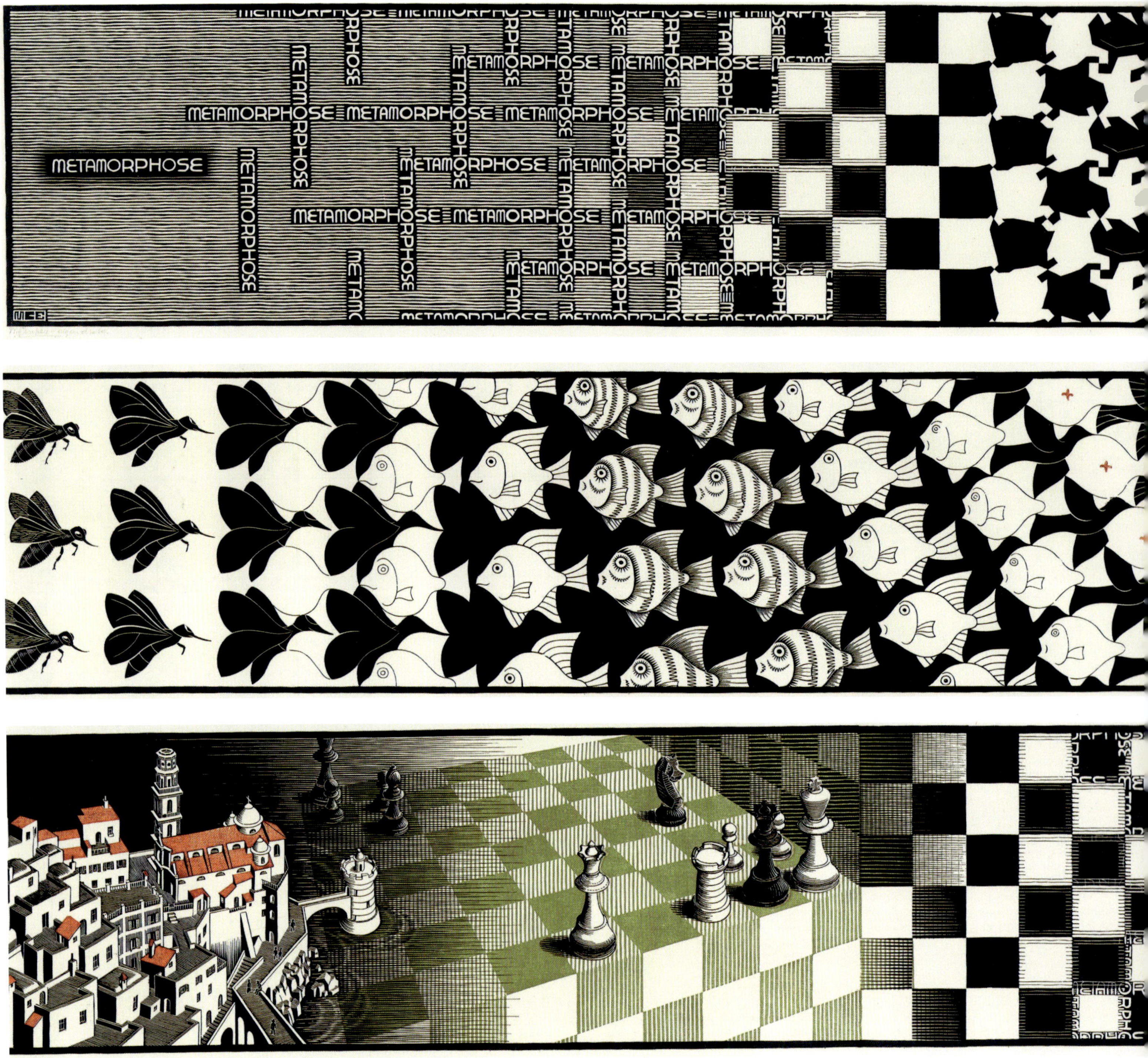
METAMORPHOSE

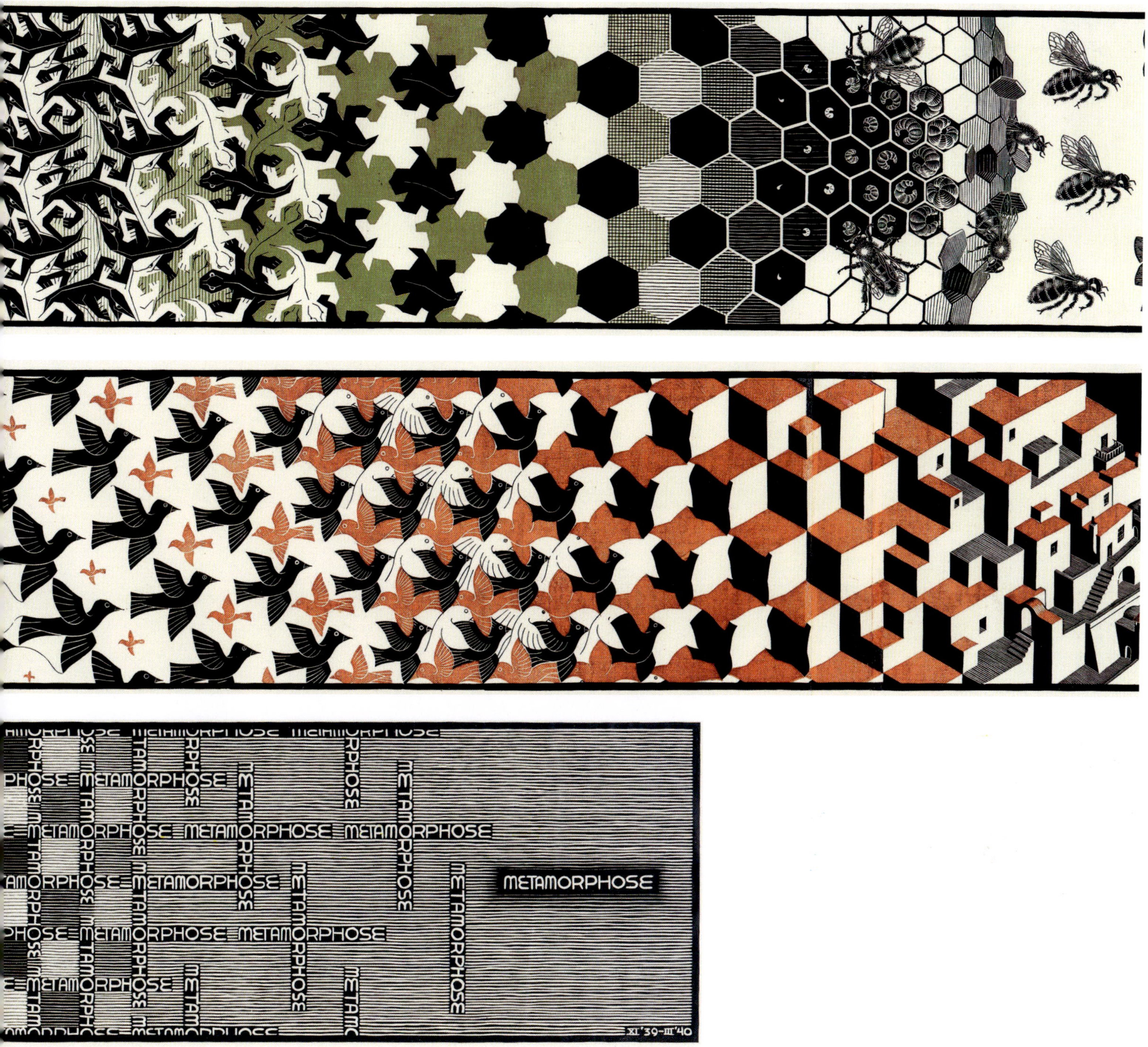

Metamorphosis
Escher tried to express the concept of infinity in this famous print. Letters change into geometric shapes, which in turn transform into animal figures and even a town on the coast. The series of possible transformations is in theory inexhaustible.

Metamorphosis II, 1939–1940
M.C. Escher
Woodcut
Collection Gemeentemuseum Den Haag

PATTERNS

The use of patterns is a clearly visible similarity between Escher's work and much Islamic art. Patterns occur when figures – for example lines, letters or depictions of plants or animals – are continually repeated.
Abstract patterns with an interplay of lines, which together form star motifs, often occur in Islamic art. Objects like books and candle-sticks are decorated with them and they are also found as decorative elements in buildings. In architecture these patterns are not only executed on flat surfaces but also three dimensionally.

THE USE OF PATTERNS IS A CLEARLY VISIBLE SIMILARITY BETWEEN ESCHER'S WORK AND MUCH ISLAMIC ART

Owing to these abstract forms Escher thought that no Islamic tessellations with people or animals existed. He was mistaken, as many figurative images are found on Islamic objects, particularly on non-religious artefacts. Escher himself preferred to include living beings in the patterns he drew. According to him, the ease of recognition of animal figures, like fish and birds, made them particularly suitable for a tessellation.

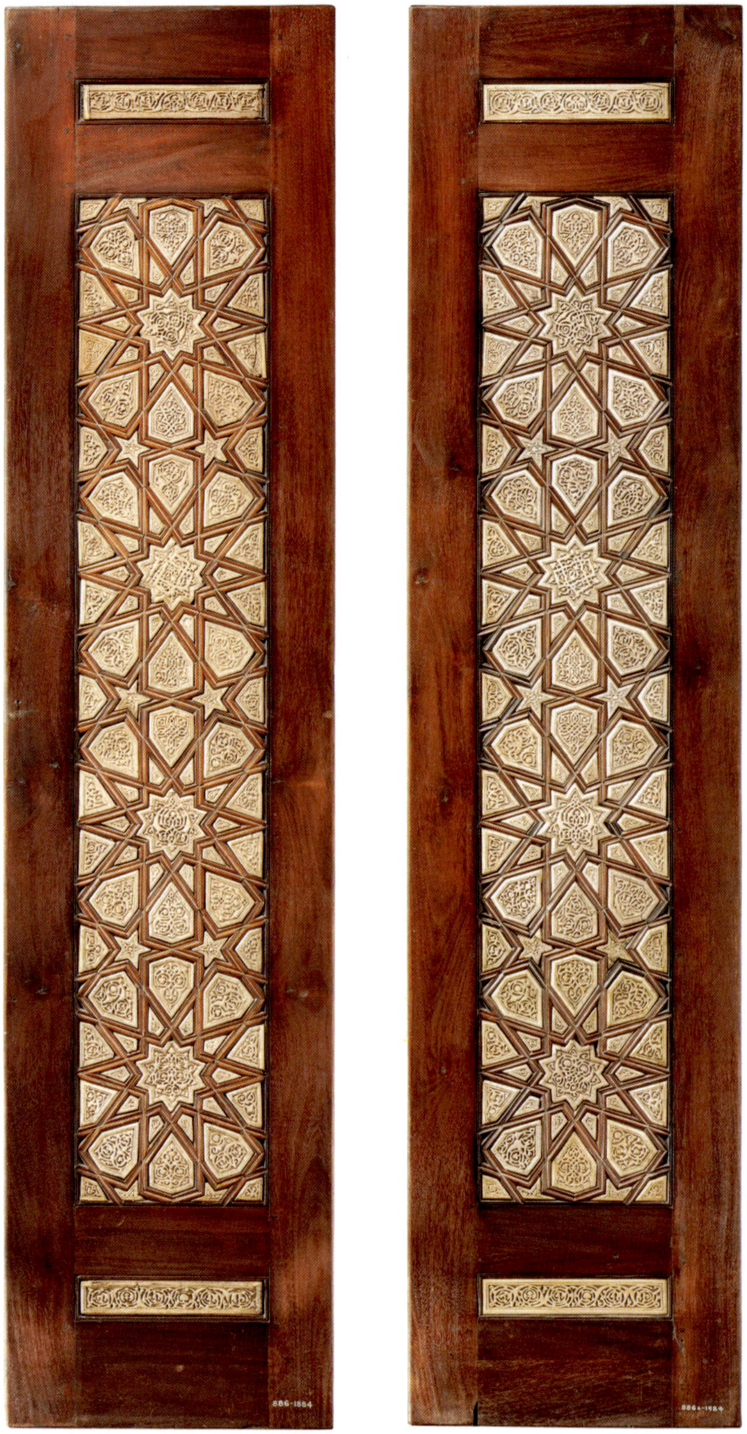

Tenpointed stars
The ivory inlaid work dates from the fourteenth century. Five centuries later it acquired a place in these doors. Abstract patterns with star figures are found in virtually all regions and periods of Islamic art and architecture.

Pair of doors, 1860–1883
Cairo, Egypt, Mamluk style
Wood, ivory
Collection Victoria and Albert Museum, London

Abstract
Inspired by the patterns in the Alhambra, Escher did eleven drawings with geometric shapes in a notebook. He also described his own mathematical theories in the notebook and sketched many variations of the drawings. They are some of the few abstract studies Escher did.

Drawing in *Regular division of the plane; abstract motifs; geometric problems* notebook, 1941
M.C. Escher
Watercolour
Collection Gemeentemuseum Den Haag

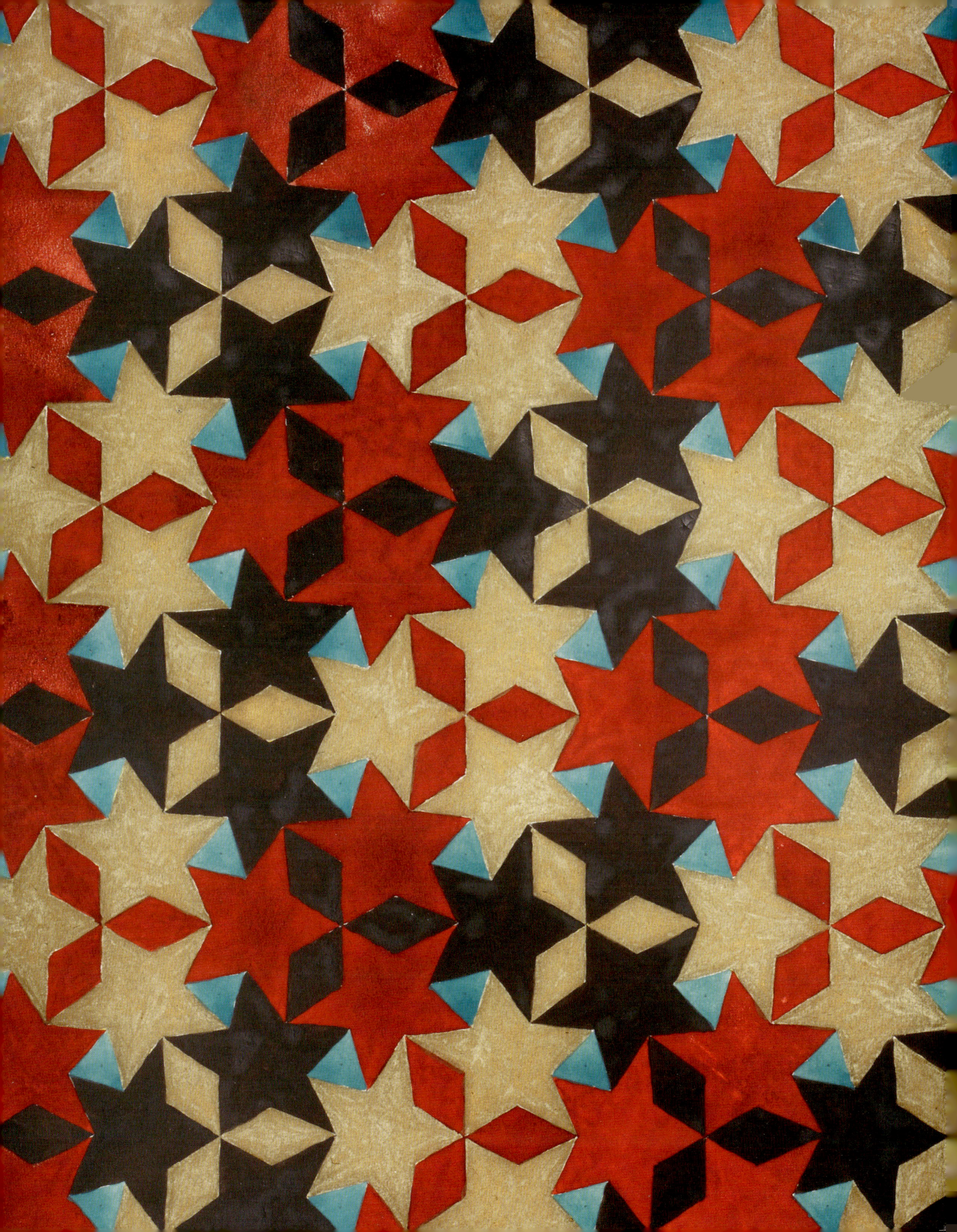

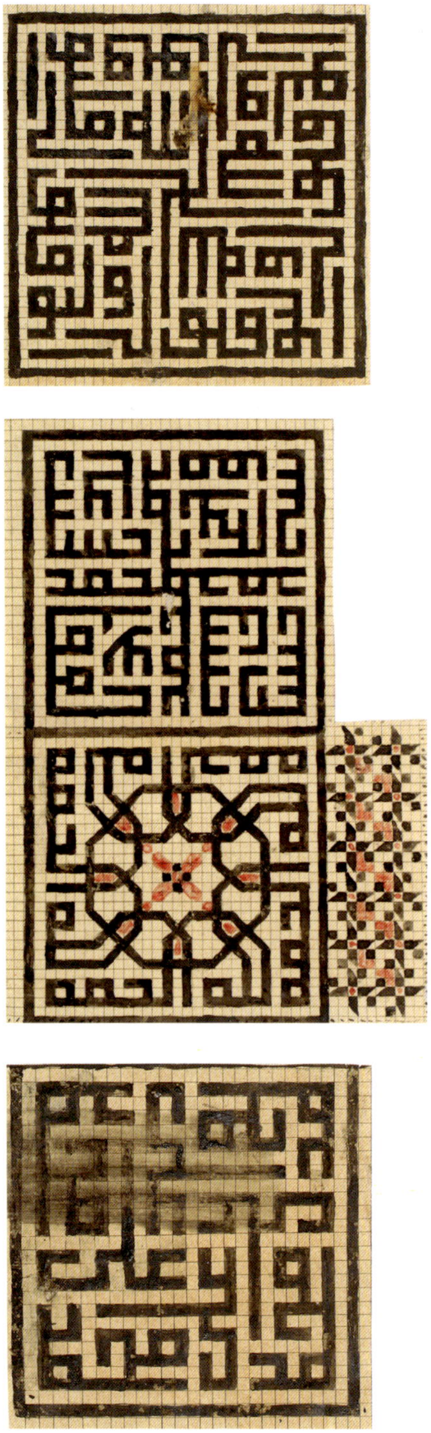

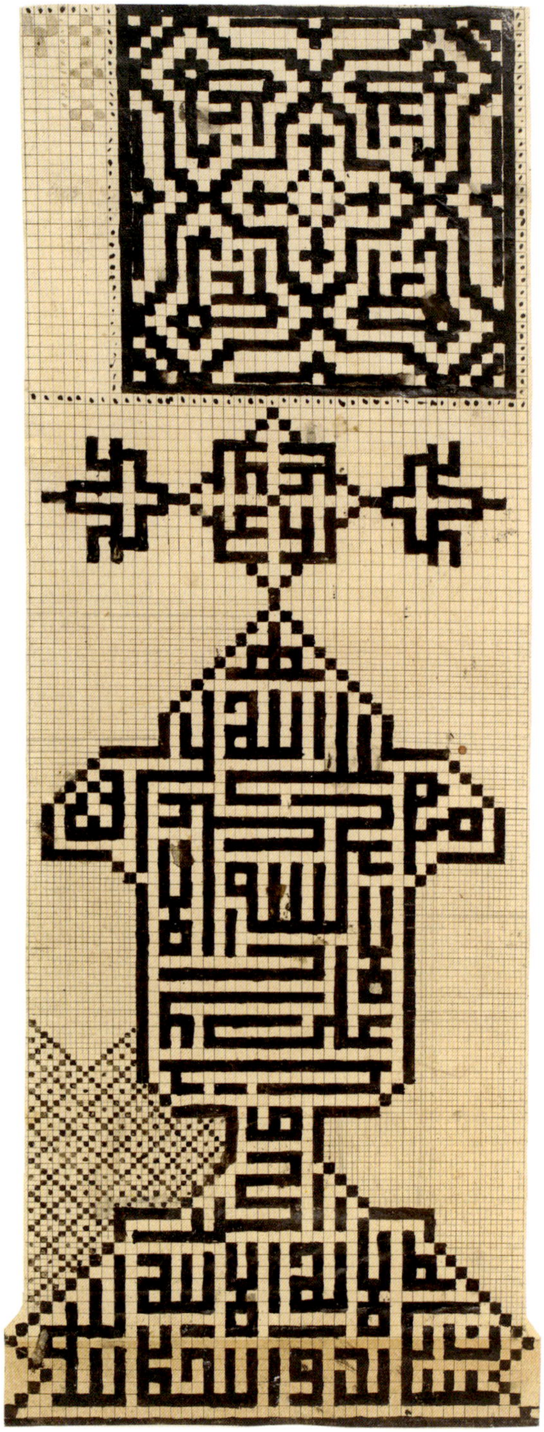

Letters
Geometric patterns comprising Arabic letters decorate the interior and exterior of many buildings in the Middle East and Central Asia. Owing to its angular form the Kufic typeface is particularly suitable for square or rectangular patterns like this.

Designs from a pattern scroll, 1840–1870
Mirza Akbar (architect)
Tehran, Iran, Qajar period
Graphite, ink
Collection Victoria and Albert Museum London

Design for wrapping paper for Jelmoli, 1933
M.C. Escher
Woodcut
Collection Gemeentemuseum Den Haag

ELMO

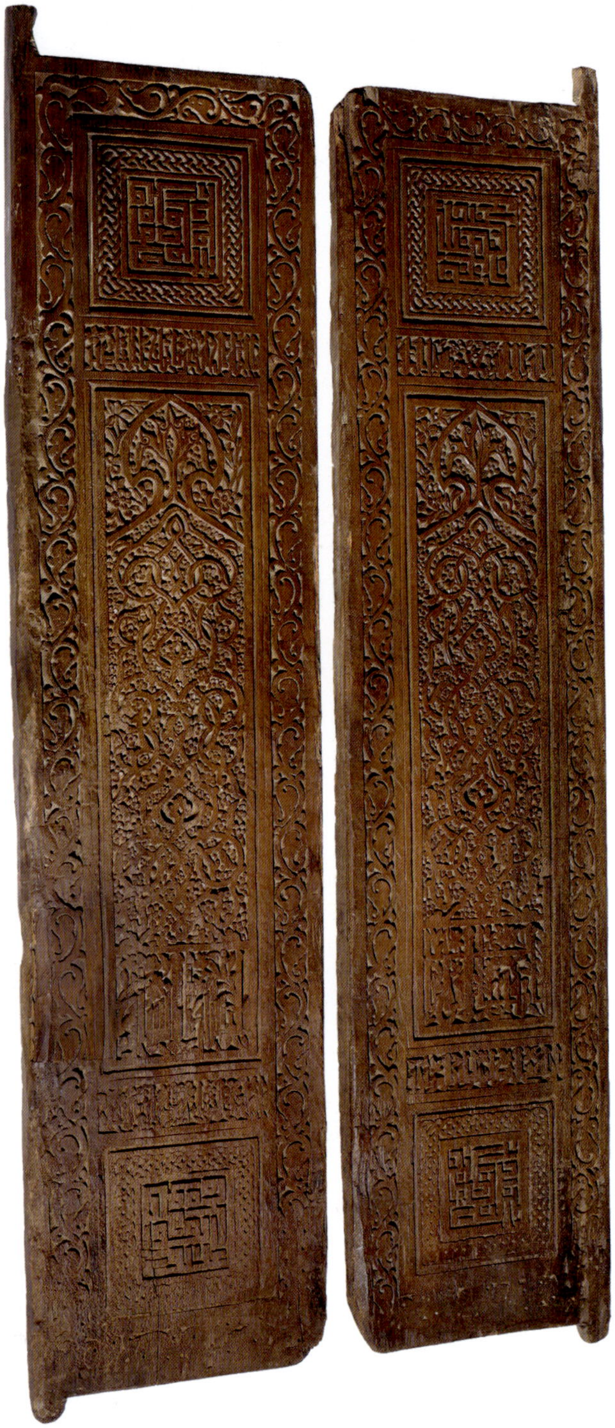

Letters
The four square planes above and below have different geometric patterns in Kufi script.
The Arabic texts are religious sayings and exhortations.

Pair of panelled doors, 15th century
Central Asia, Timurid period
Wood
Collection Gemeentemuseum Den Haag

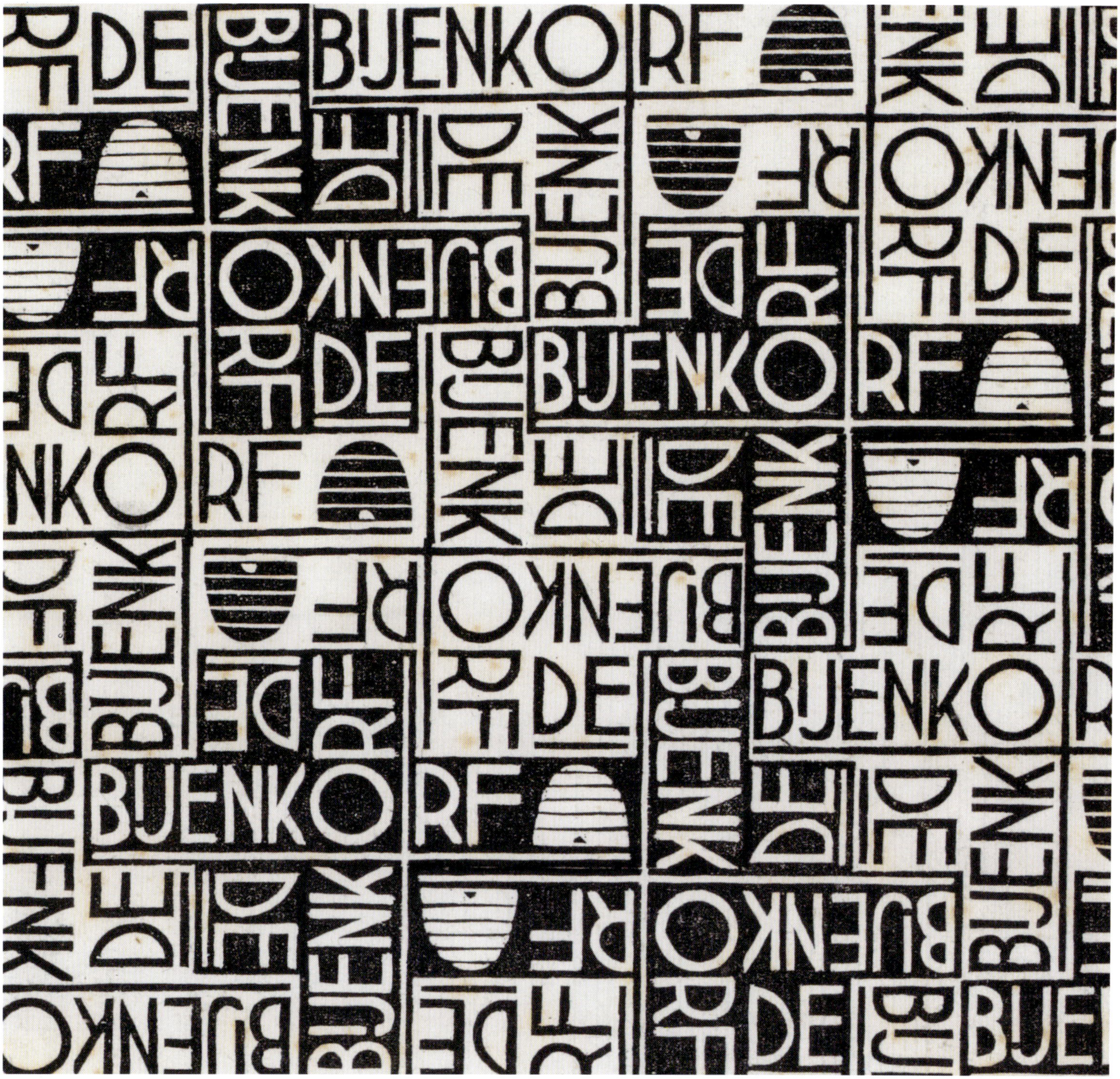

Wrapping paper
Escher designed wrapping paper for several department stores, including De Bijenkorf in Amsterdam and the Swiss Jelmoli. All these designs have a geometric pattern of bands with the name of the shop. Only the paper for de Bijenkorf was actually produced.

Design for wrapping paper for De Bijenkorf, 1933
M.C. Escher
Woodcut
Collection Gemeentemuseum Den Haag

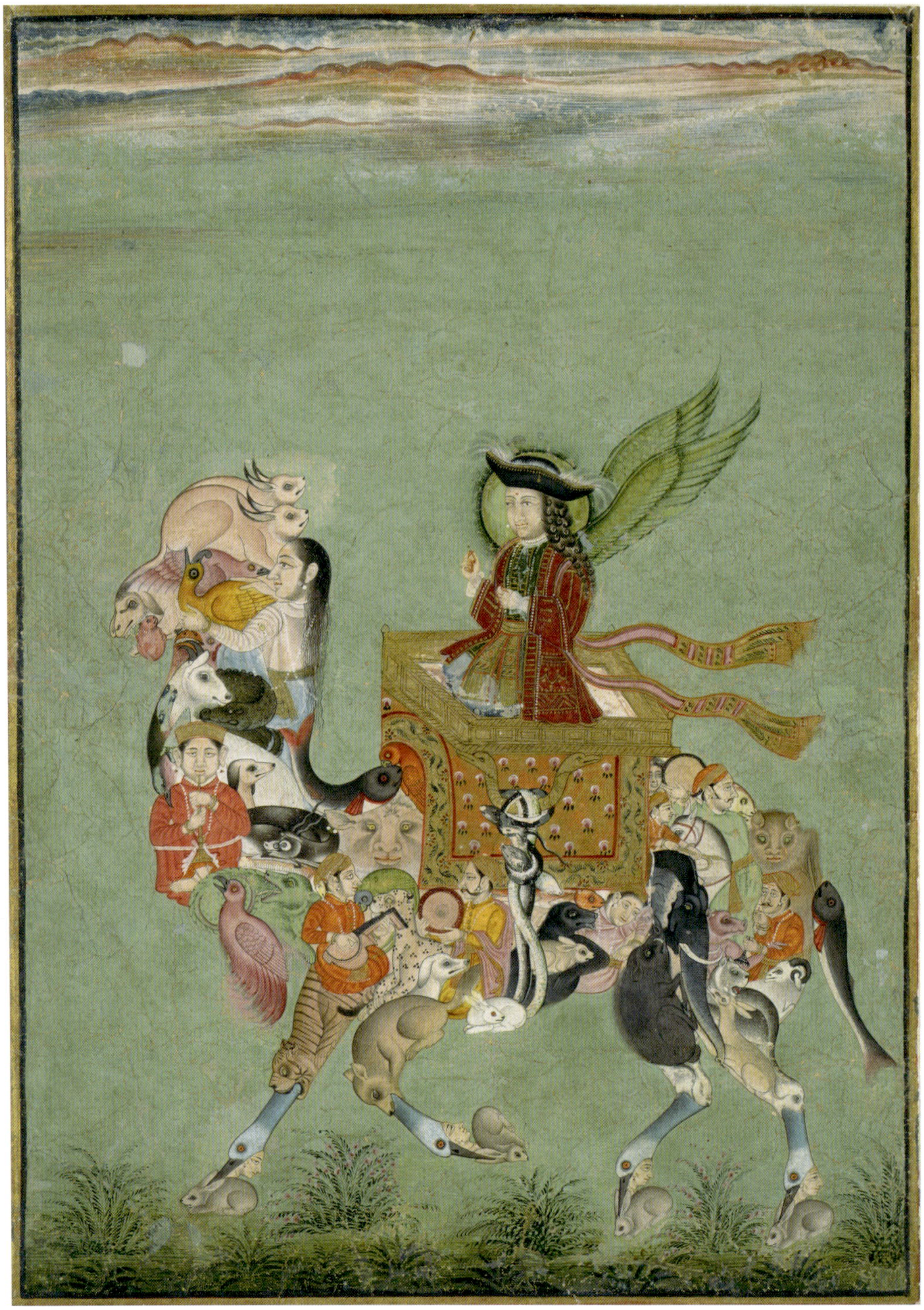

Irregular tesselation
The camel depicted is highly imaginatively composed of animals and humans. It forms an irregular tessellation. Almost every figure is unique; only the rabbits and the birds' heads in the camel's legs are repeated. This composition was popular in the art of the Mughal period. The figures possibly refer to a poetic description of the camel.

Miniature painting, c. 1725
Mewar, India, Mughal period
Watercolour
Collection Victoria and Albert Museum, London

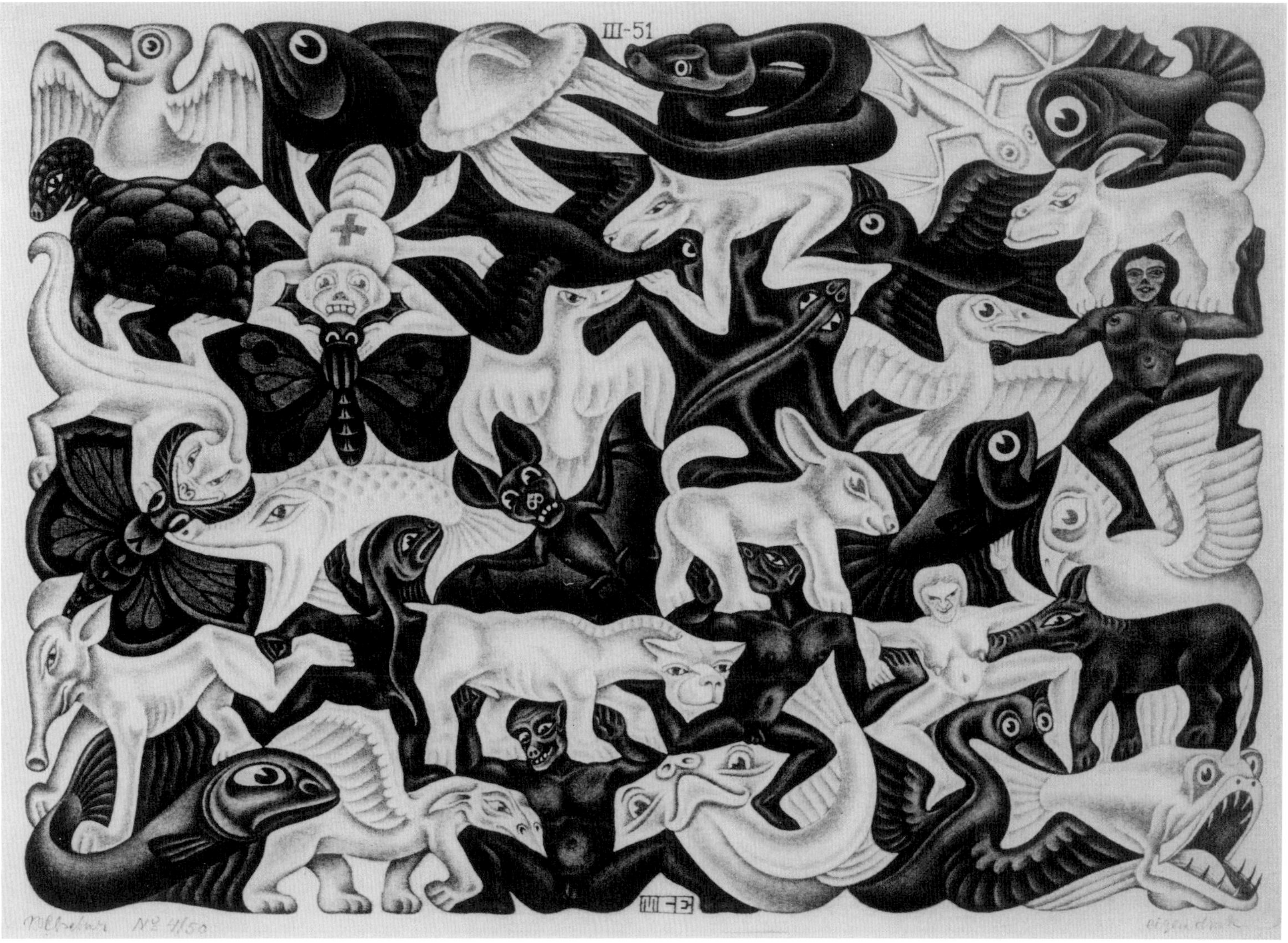

Animals and humans
The tessellation in this print is irregular: not a single animal or human is depicted twice. By consistently alternating black and white and using an even number of figures, Escher evokes the suggestion of regularity. He said himself that he could only make this print after years of practice in regular tessellation.

Plane filling I, 1951
M.C. Escher
Mezzotint
Collection M.C. Escher Foundation

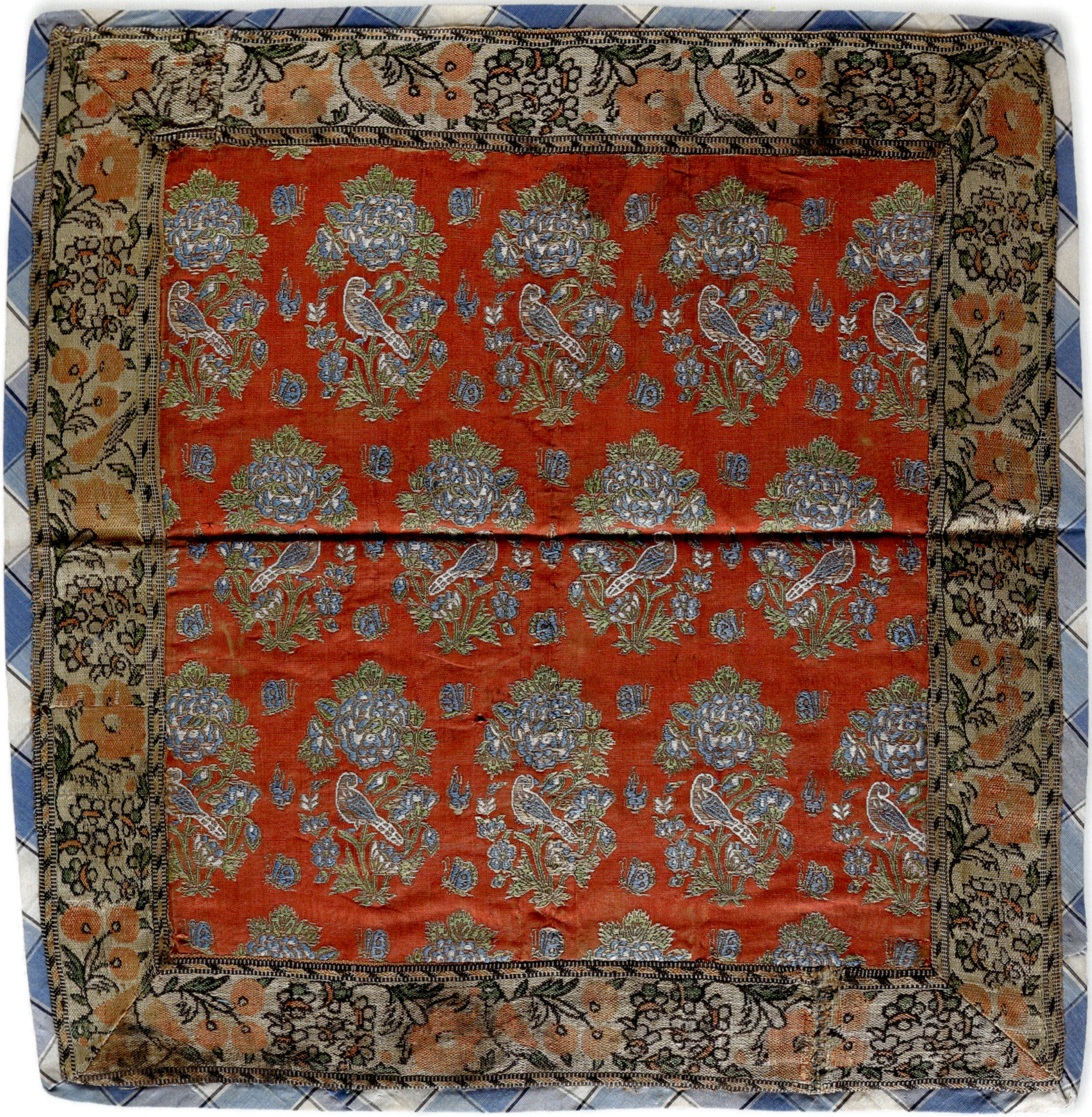

Birds

The motif of a bird on a branch is repeated absolutely regularly. The pattern isn't tessellation, as space remains between the figures. The cloth was possibly used to wrap a present.

Textile, 17th century
Iran, Safavid period
Silk, gold thread
Collection Wereldmuseum, Rotterdam

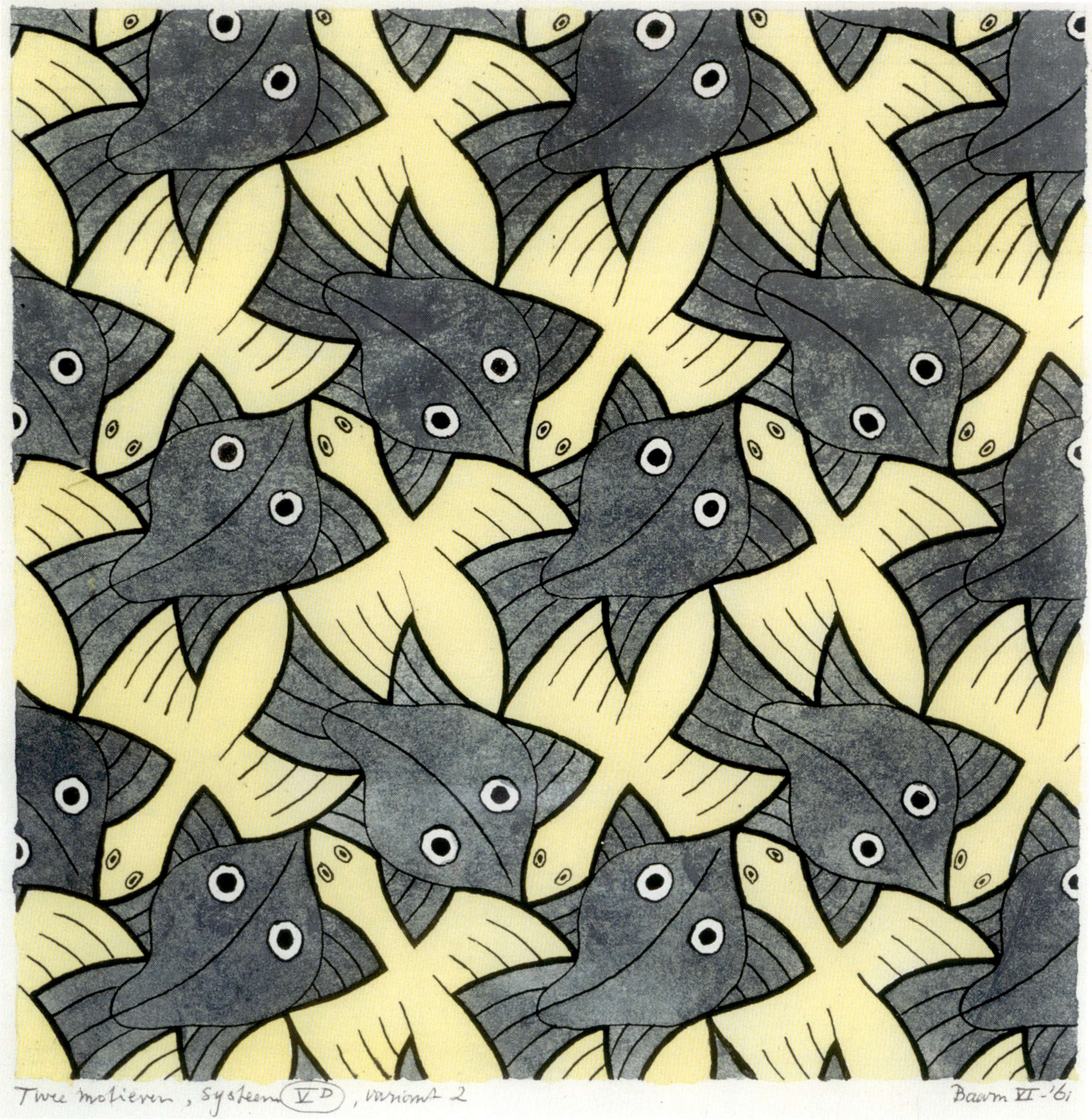

Regular tesselation
Escher did more than a hundred drawings with regular tessellations. He experimented with colours, shapes and mathematical principles, which he called systems. Each 'system' was given its own number. The drawings formed the basis of the more complex works he executed in various graphic techniques.

System Vd variant 2, 1961
M.C. Escher
Ink, watercolour
Collection M.C. Escher Foundation

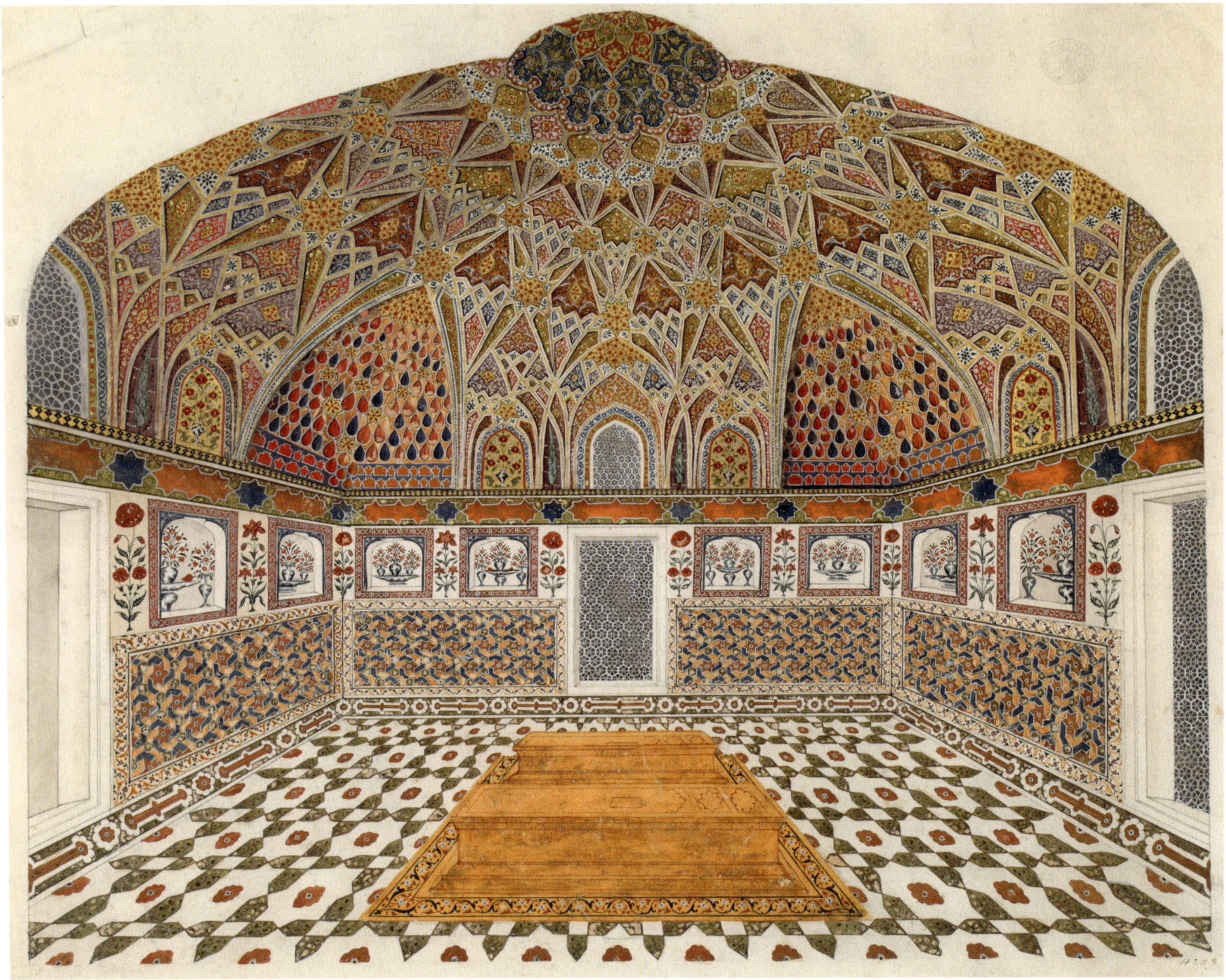

Three dimensional
The painting depicts the tomb of the high-ranking official Itimad ud-Daula (d. 1622) in the Indian city of Agra. His daughter, who was married to the emperor, had the mausoleum built for him. A three-dimensional geometric pattern based on star shapes can be identified in the vaulted ceiling of painted plasterwork.

Watercolour painting, c. 1820
India, Mughal period
Watercolour
Collection Victoria and Albert Museum, London

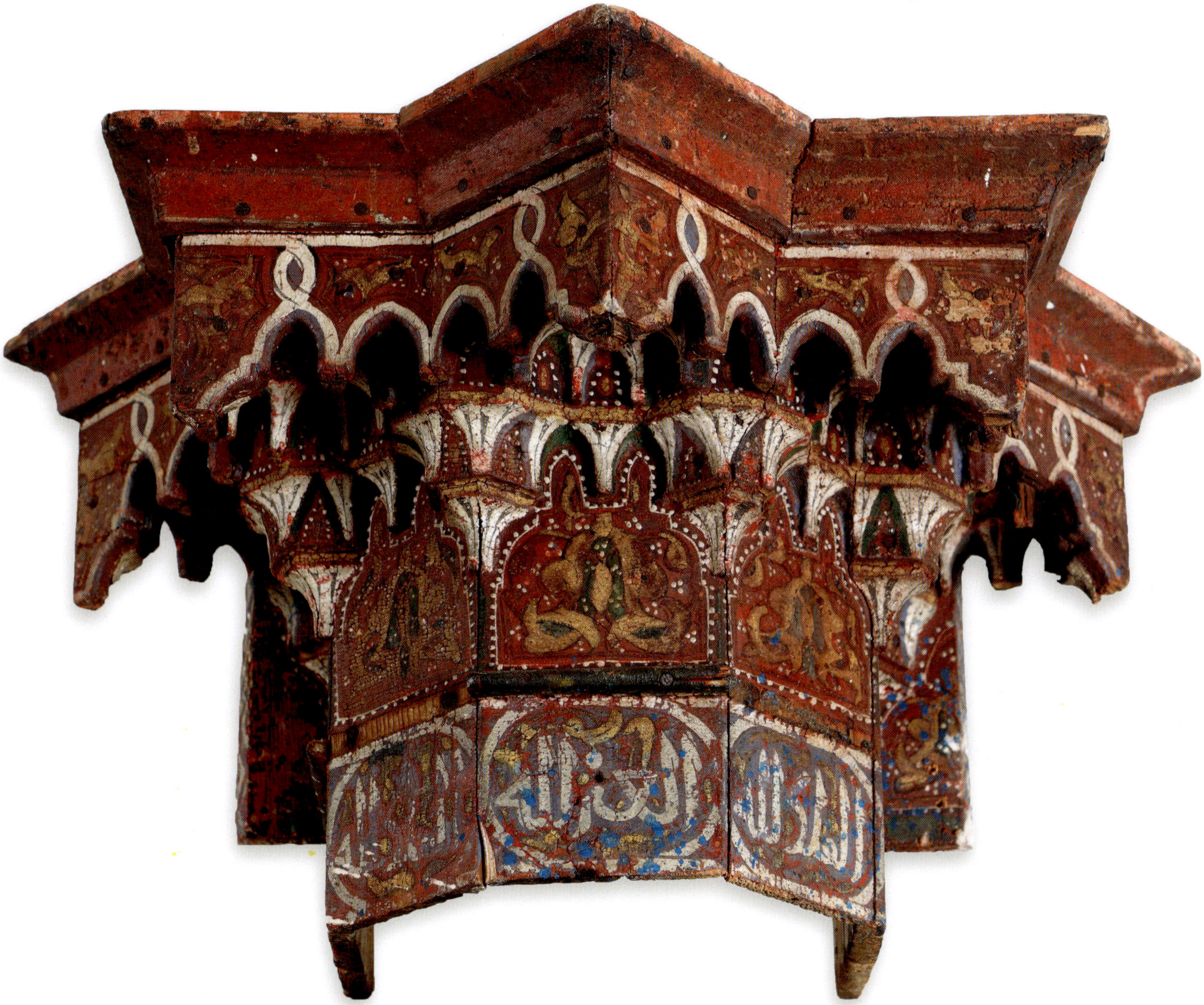

Muqarnas
This ornament was mounted at the top of a heavy door in a *riad*, a house with an inner courtyard. It's a spatial decoration with geometric shapes built up from layers of wood. An ornament with a pattern resembling a honeycomb like this is known as *muqarnas.*

Door ornament, early 20th century
Marrakech, Morocco
Wood
Collection Wereldmuseum, Rotterdam

MATHEMATICS

When designing his tessellations Escher used mathematical principles like grids and symmetry. These basic rules from mathematics make it possible for patterns to be repeated endlessly. They are also found in Islamic artefacts.
What a pattern looks like depends on how the figures are repeated, the symmetry.
A shape can shift (translation symmetry), rotate (rotation symmetry), be reflected (reflection symmetry), or various combinations of these. The grid forms the structure

WHEN DESIGNING HIS TESSELLATIONS ESCHER USED MATHEMATICAL PRINCIPLES LIKE GRIDS AND SYMMETRY

behind a pattern. This network of identical polygons, such as triangles and squares, results in the equal distribution of figures over the plane.

Escher was self-taught in the field of mathematics. By frequently experimenting with shapes, he discovered the mathematical rules that are the basis of tessellations. He also studied geometry and corresponded with scientists. Ultimately he understood the seventeen combinations that can occur in symmetry and can also be seen in Islamic art.

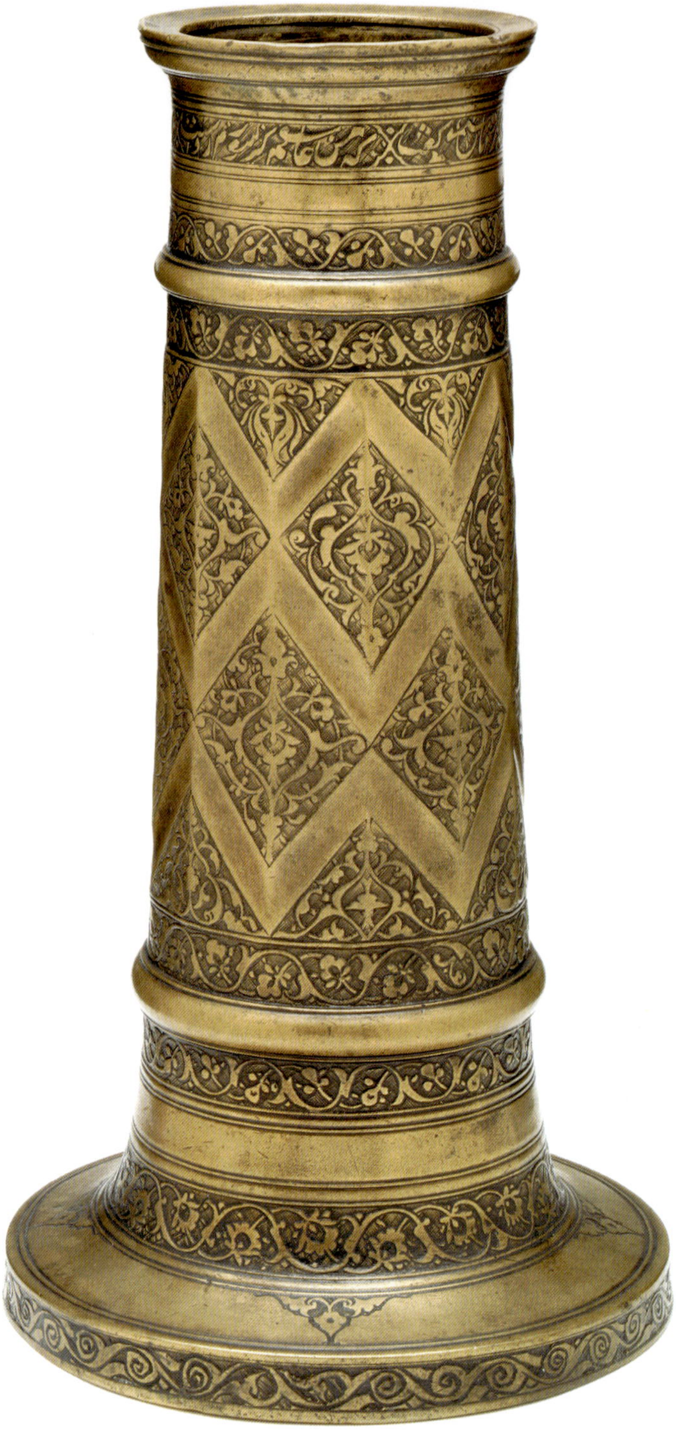

Translation symmetry
The zigzagging bands together represent the diamond grid. Each diamond, filled with plant motifs, constantly shifts horizontally. A cheerful poem by the famous Persian poet Sa'adi is engraved on the neck of the torch-stand.

Torch-stand, 17th century
Iran, Safavid period
Brass
Collection Victoria and Albert Museum, London

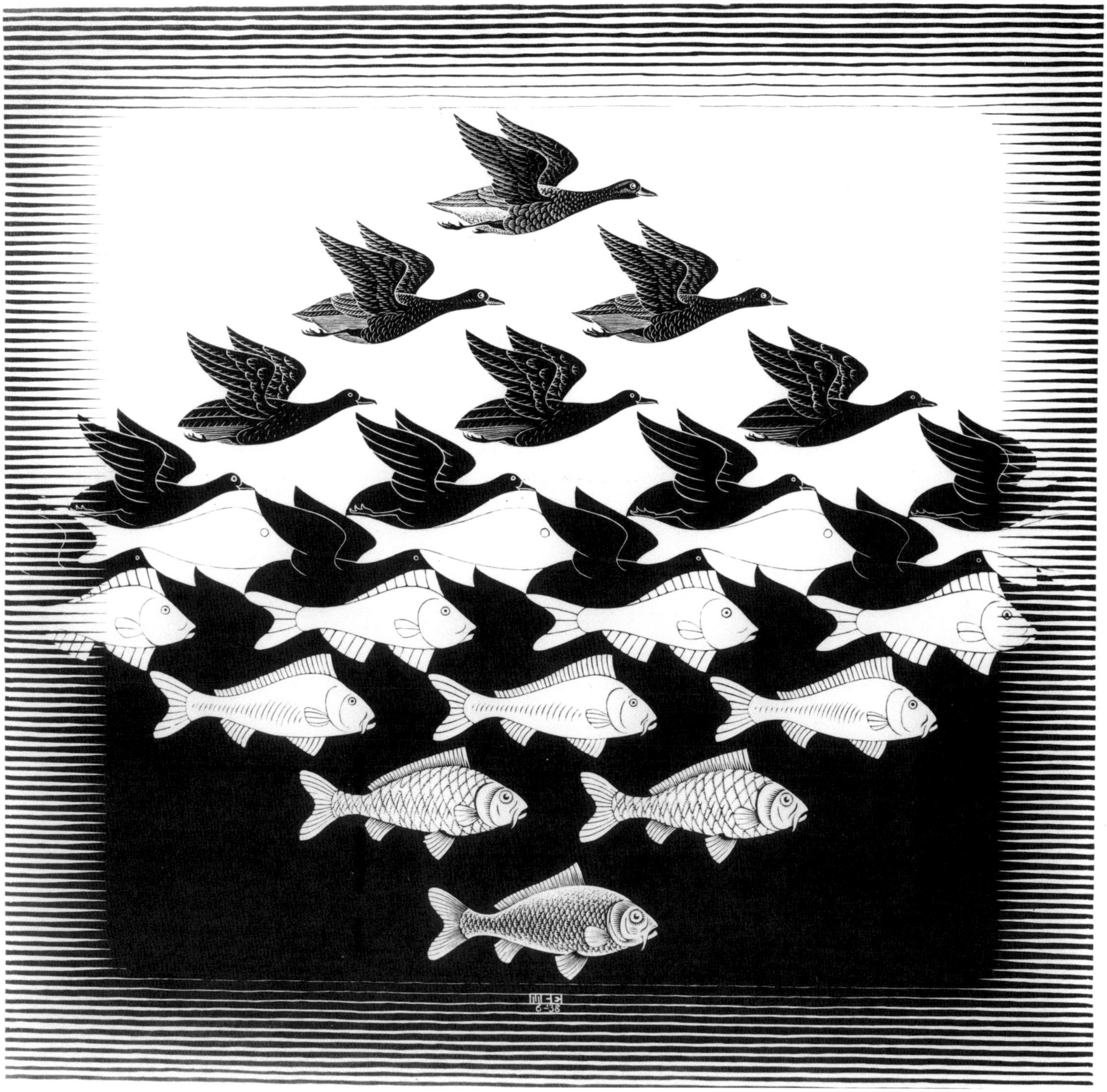

Birds and fish
Birds and fish alternate with each other in the horizontal middle strip. Each figure constantly shifts sidewards. As the birds and fish in each row look slightly different, there is not perfect translation symmetry. The diamond shape they are drawn in stems from the underlying diamond grid.

Sky and Water I, 1938
M.C. Escher
Woodcut
Collection M.C. Escher Foundation

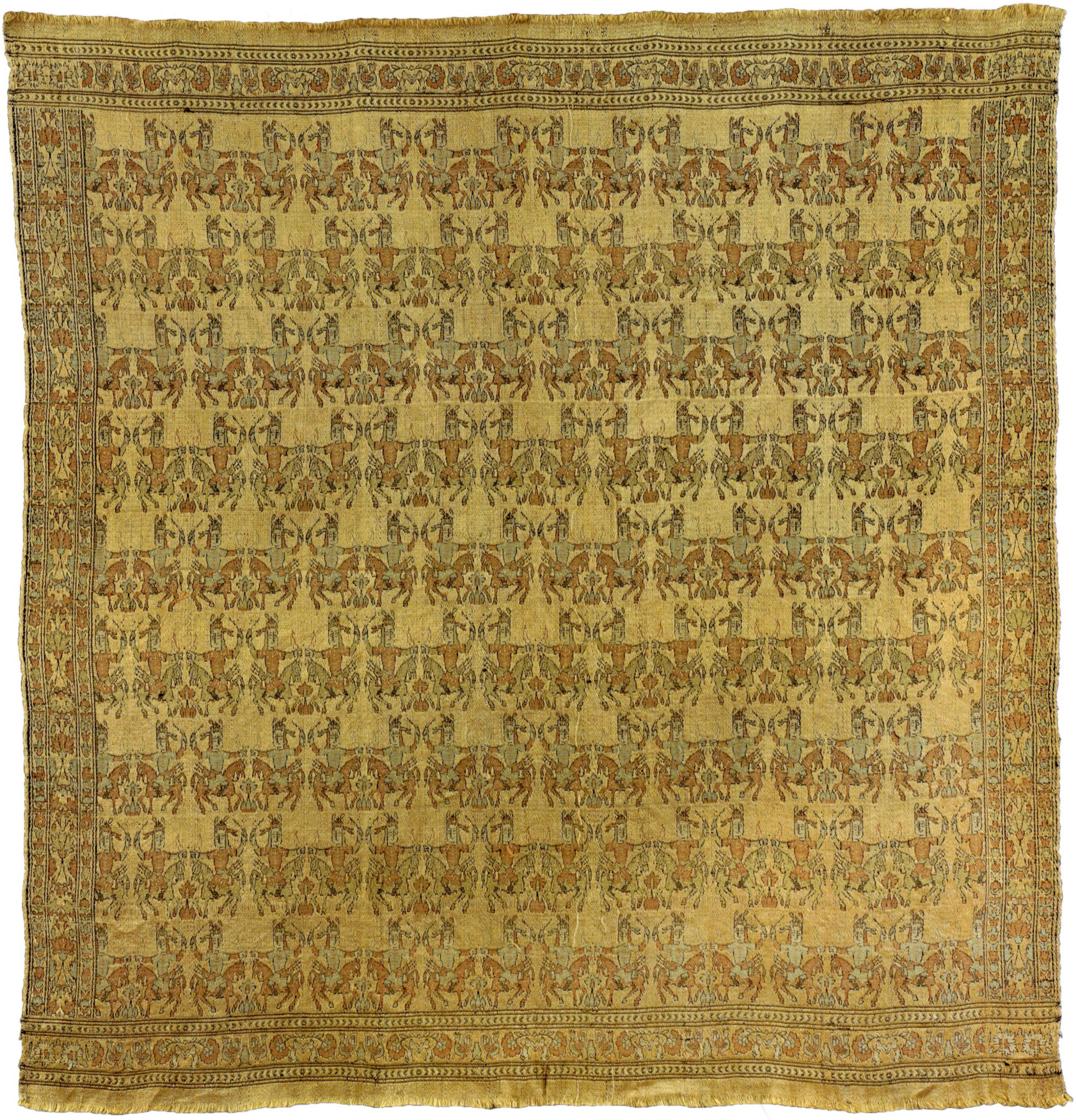

Reflection symmetry
The hunting life of rulers and other eminent people was a popular subject in Persian art. The pattern on this fabric comprises pairs of reflected horse riders that are repeated diagonally upwards and downwards.

Textile, 17th century
Iran, Safavid period
Silk brocade
Collection Wereldmuseum, Rotterdam

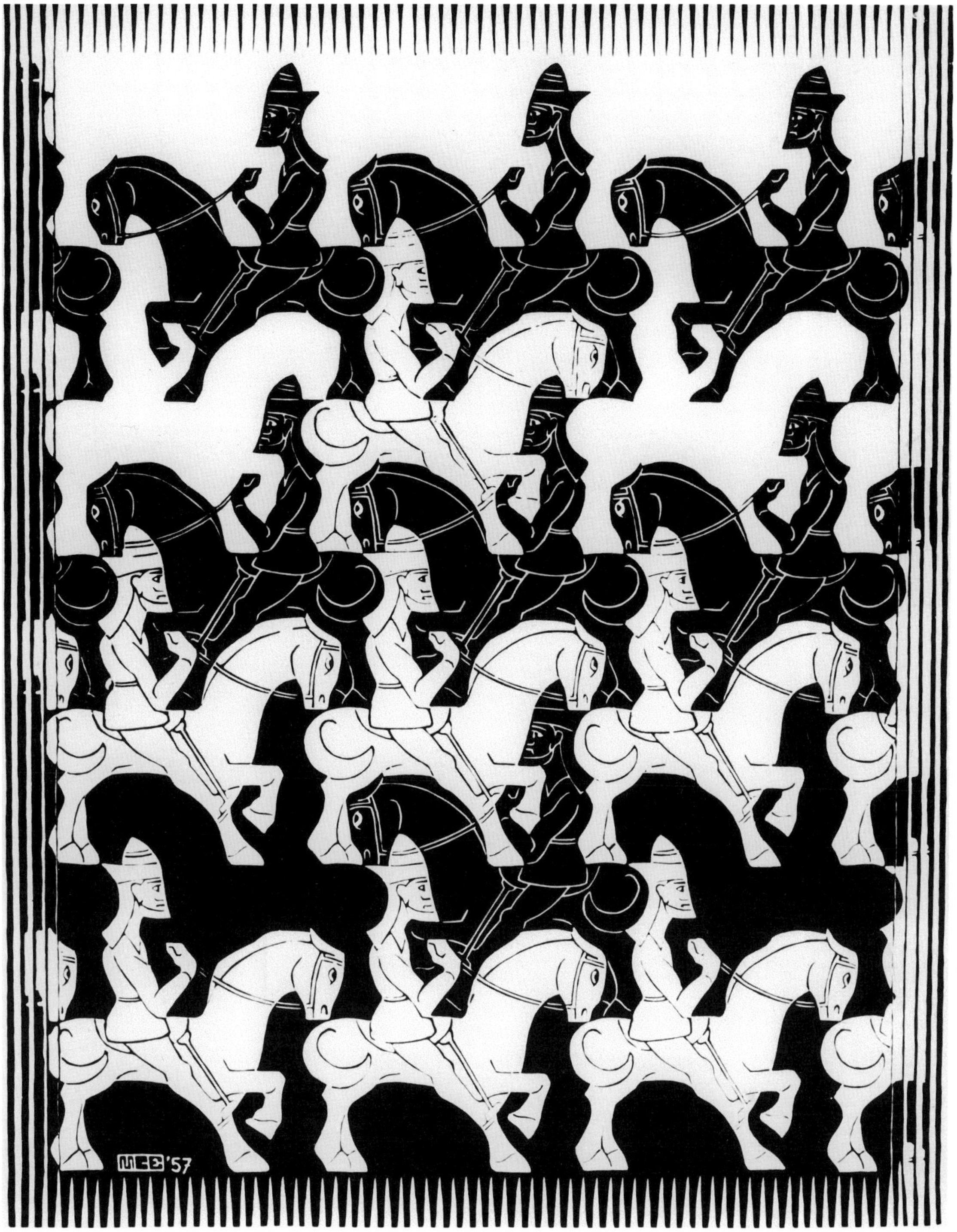

Horsemen
Escher considered shapes that were simply reflected to be boring and static. To put more vivacity into his patterns he often used glide reflection, whereby figures shift after reflection. As Escher used more than one colour, this pattern looks more complicated than it is.

Regular Division of the Plane III, 1957
M.C. Escher
Woodcut
Collection M.C. Escher Foundation

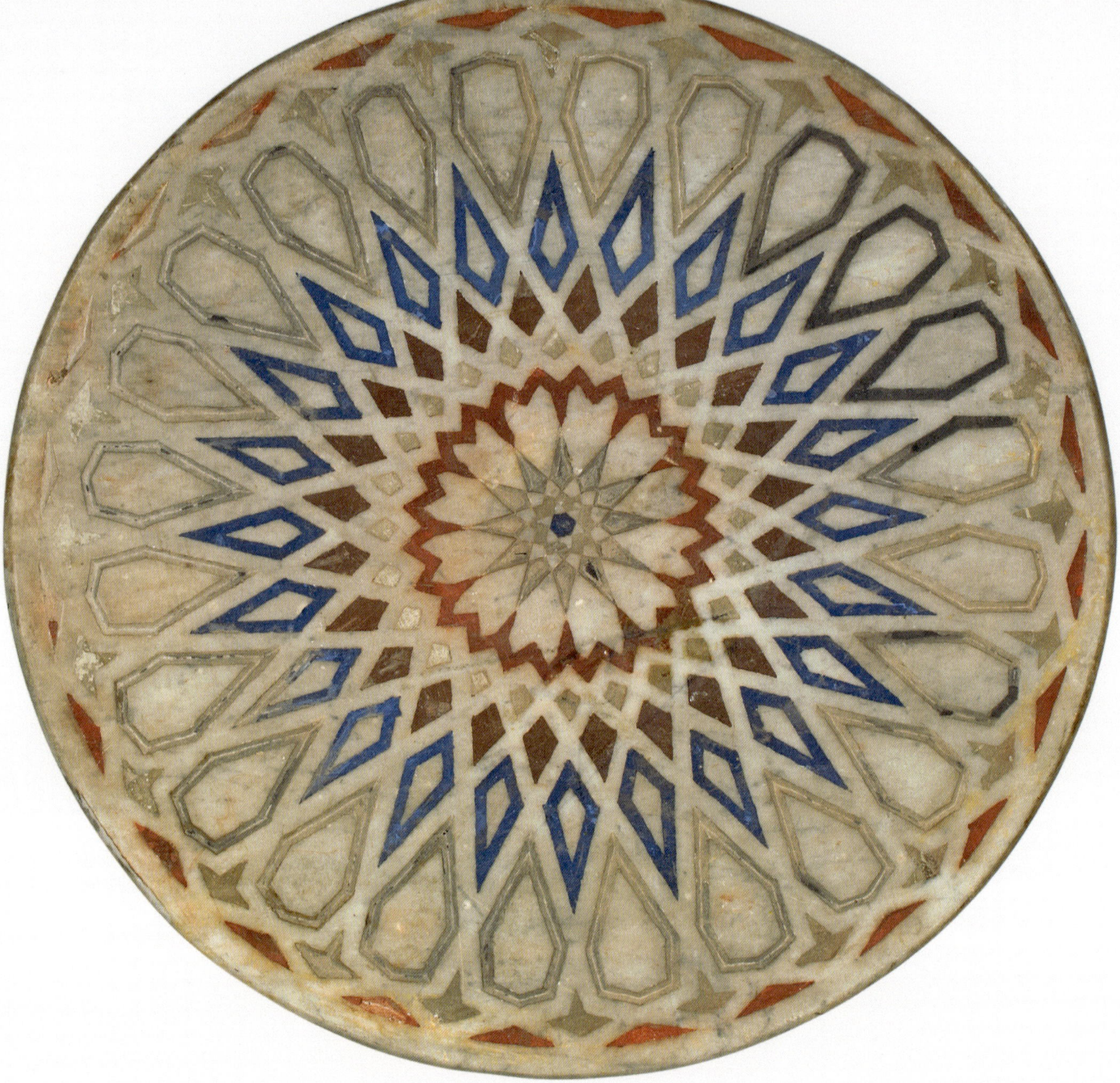

Rotation symmetry
From the small blue hexagon in the middle the pattern is divided into six segments which rotate. Each segment comprises two reflected parts. Multicoloured panels such as these decorated the walls of monumental buildings like mosques and tombs built by the Mamluk sultans.

Panel, 1350–1500
Egypt, Mamluk period
Marble, glass paste
Collection Tropenmuseum, Amsterdam

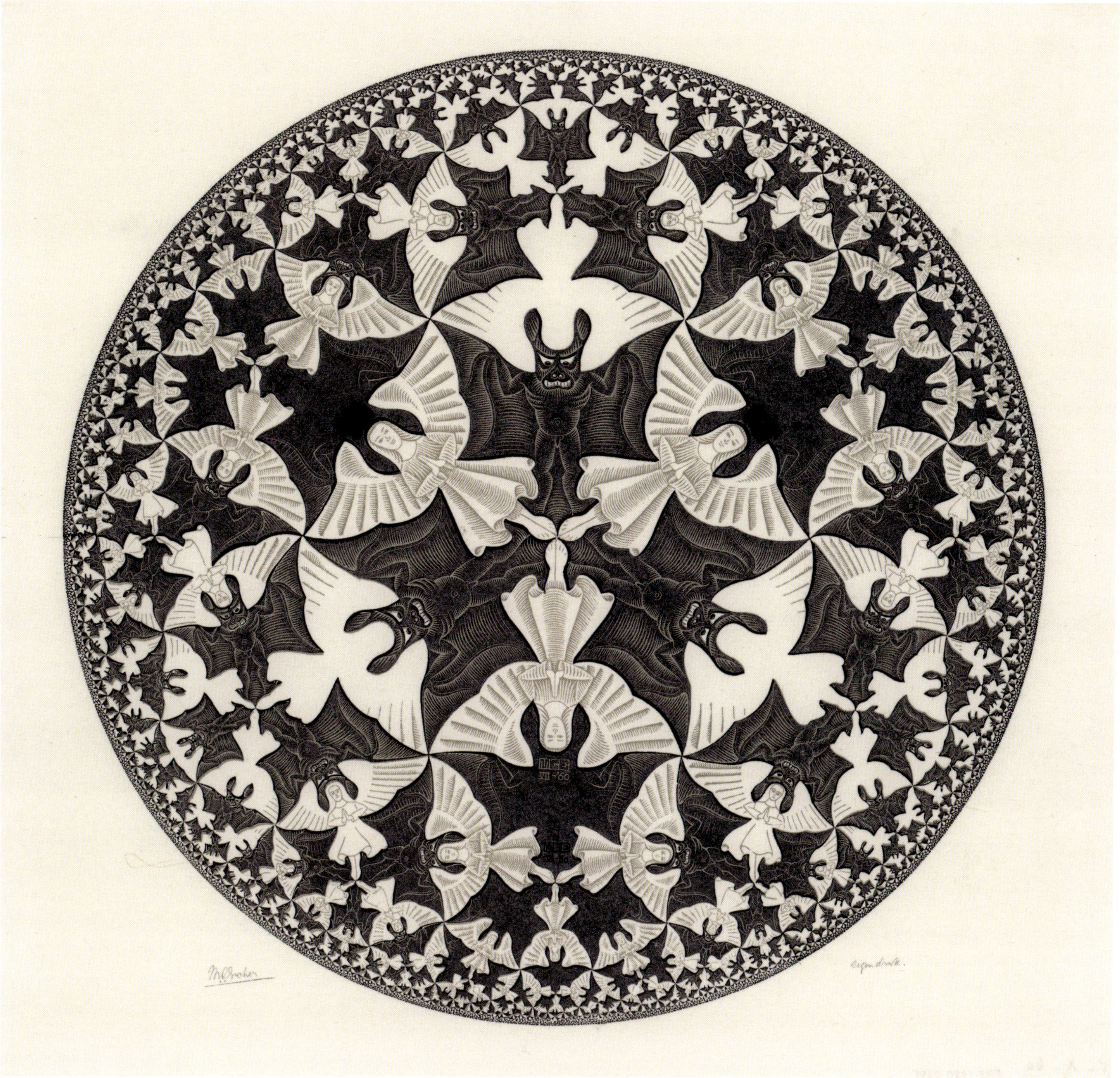

Angels and devils
This print acquired the subtitle 'Heaven and hell'. Angels and devils alternate with each other and rotate around the central points. The six large figures in the middle reveal the grid, a hexagon. Towards the edge the figures become smaller and smaller. With the circle limit series Escher attempted to transform the mathematical figure of the hyperbola into an image.

Circle Limit IV, 1960
M.C. Escher
Woodcut
Collection Gemeentemuseum Den Haag

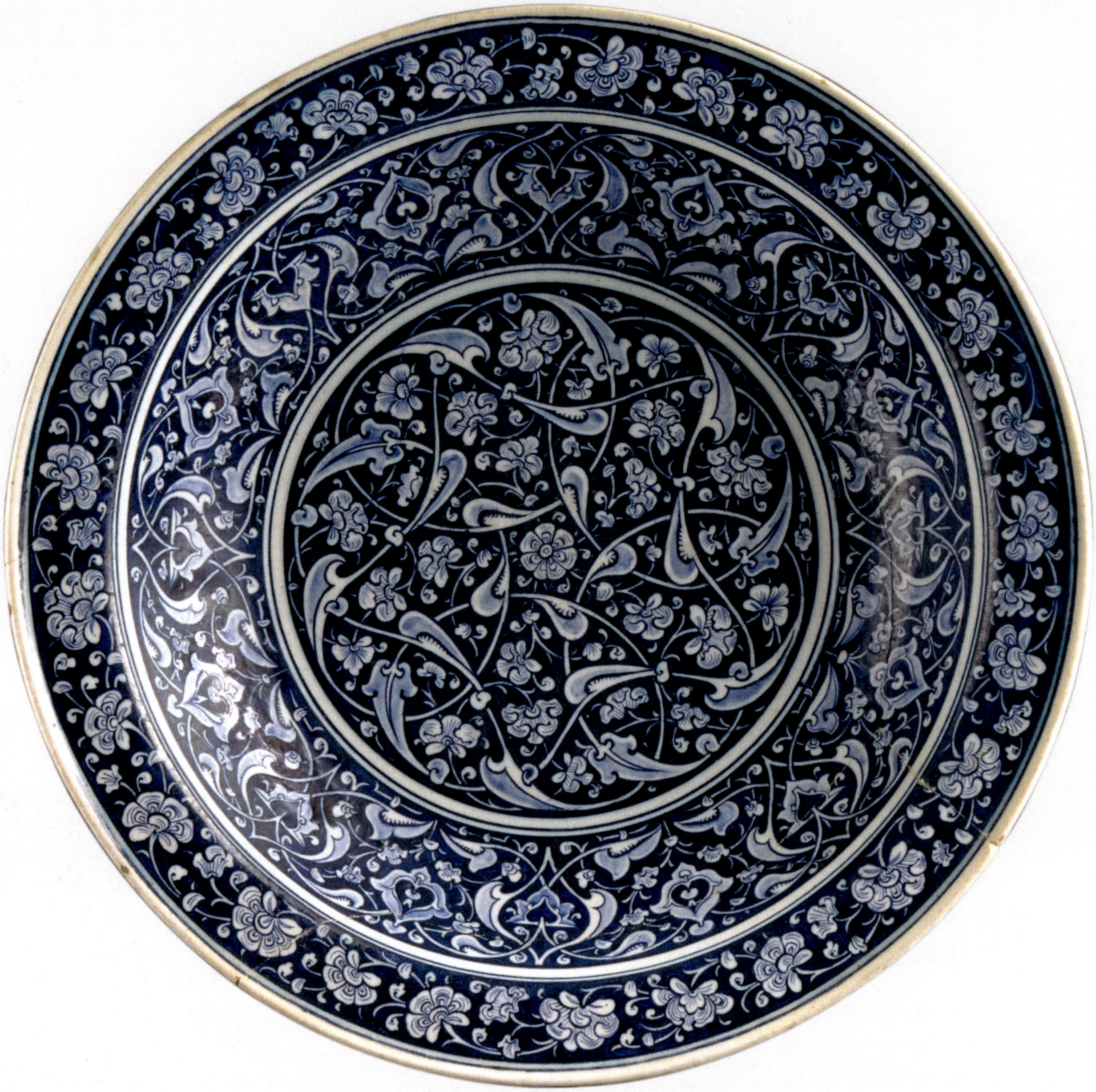

Rotation symmetry
The pentagon in the middle of this dish is created by rotating arabesque shapes around a flower in five steps. The circles are construction lines which have become part of the decoration. The dish is a rare, early example of Iznik pottery. This famous ceramic tradition originated when Turkish potters began copying blue and white porcelain from China. The flower motif on the rim of the dish is therefore of Chinese origin.

Dish, c. 1480
Iznik, Turkey, Ottoman period
Fritware, glaze
Collection Gemeentemuseum Den Haag

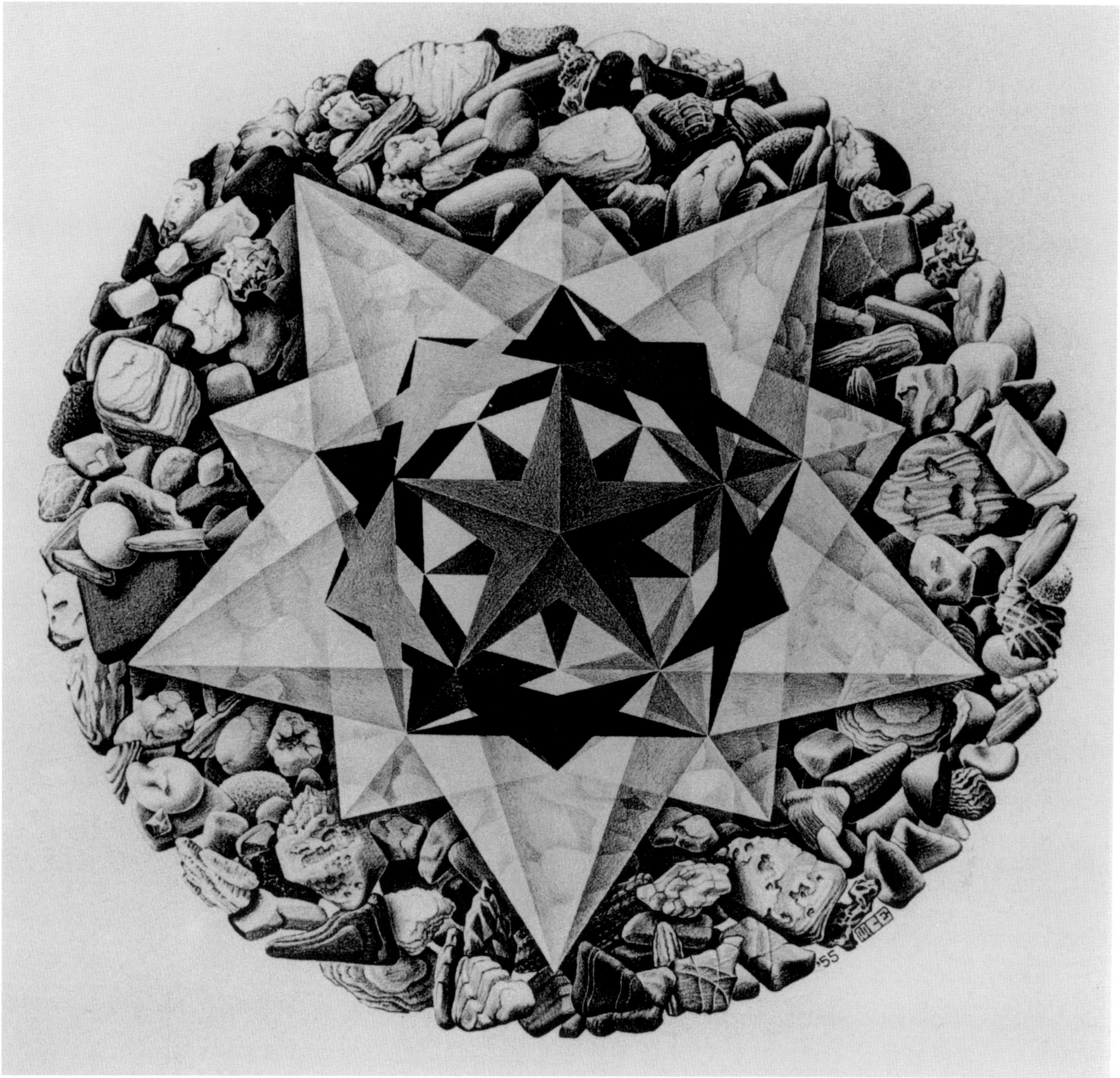

Pentagram
If this pattern was in only one colour, it would be clear that the star in the middle comprises five identical flat parts. By applying light and dark planes Escher gives the impression that the figure is spatial. For Escher the regular star figure was a symbol of order and beauty. The contrast with the chaos of the background filled with irregularly shaped stones emphasizes this.

Order and Chaos II, 1955
M.C. Escher
Lithography
Collection M.C. Escher Foundation

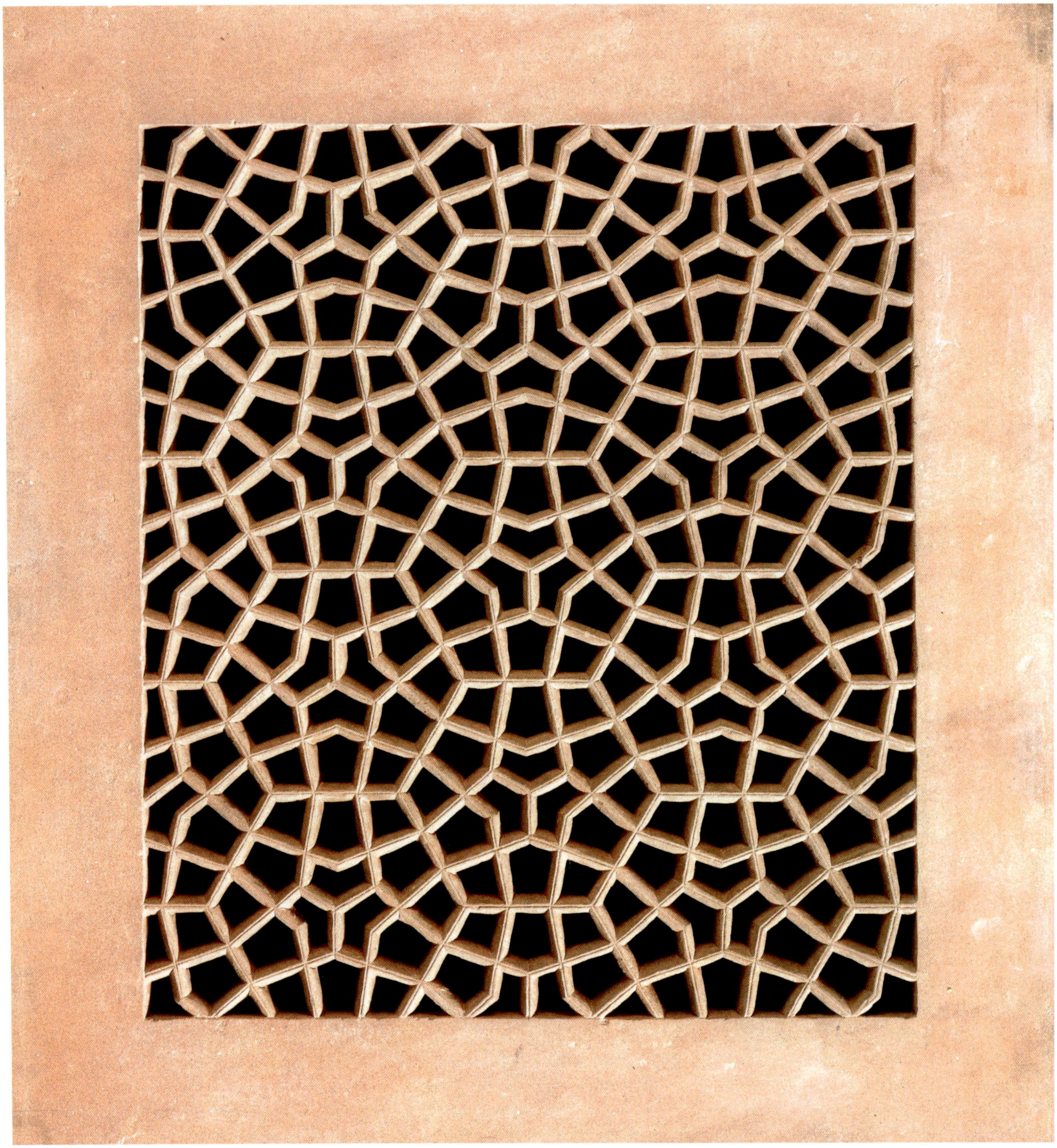

Hexagonal grid
This open screen, called *jali*, was intended to put in a window to circulate air and act as a sunblind. Women could look outside through the screen without being seen themselves. The abstract pattern follows a hexagonal grid.

Jali screen, 19th century
Agra, India, Mughal style
Sandstone
Collection Victoria and Albert Museum, London

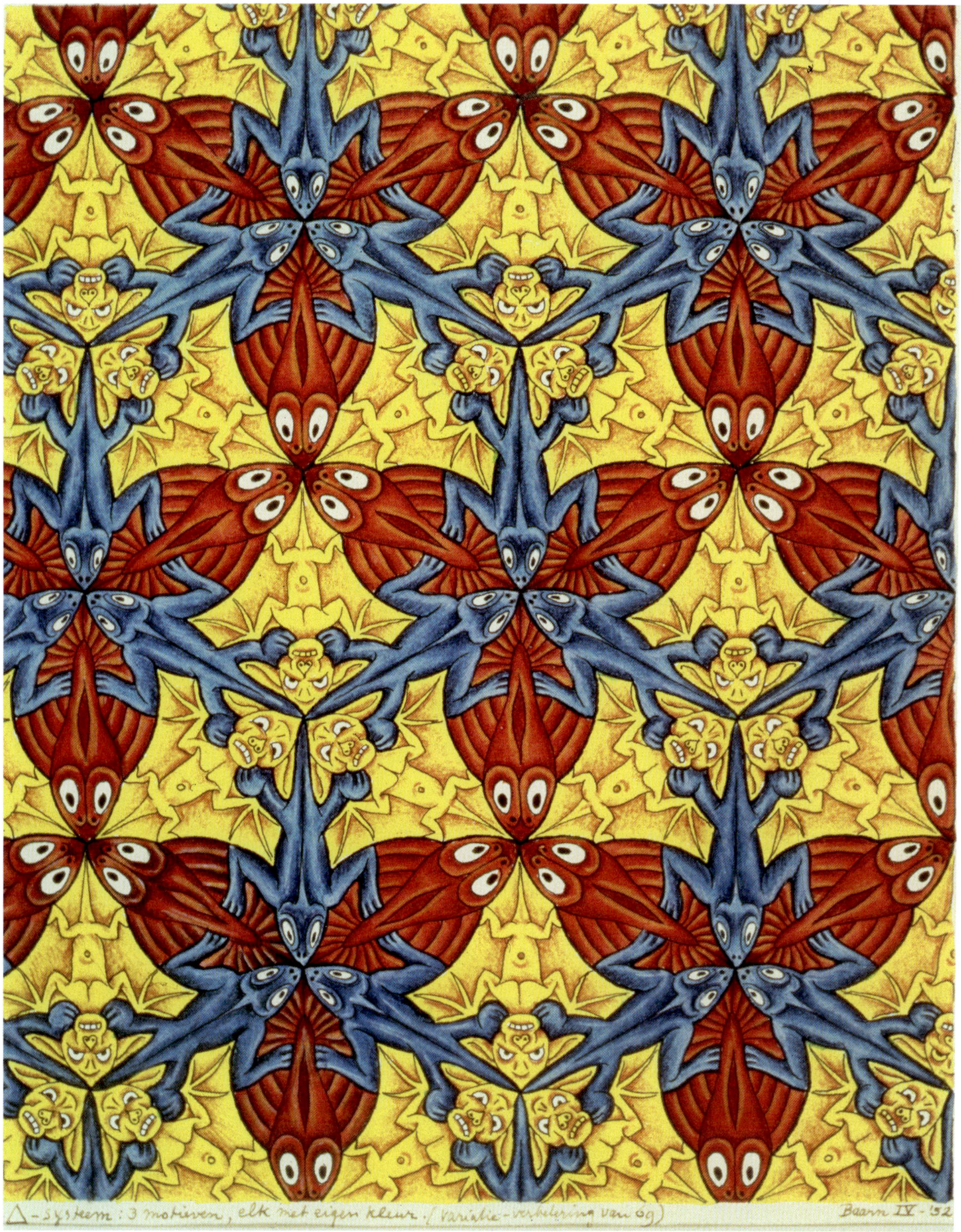

Triangular grid

This drawing of lizards, birds and bats is based on a grid of triangles but exact repetition is only possible by dividing the pattern into hexagons. Four different hexagonal grids are then possible; each follows another animal.

Triangular system, 1952
M.C. Escher
Ink, pencil, watercolour
Collection M.C. Escher Foundation

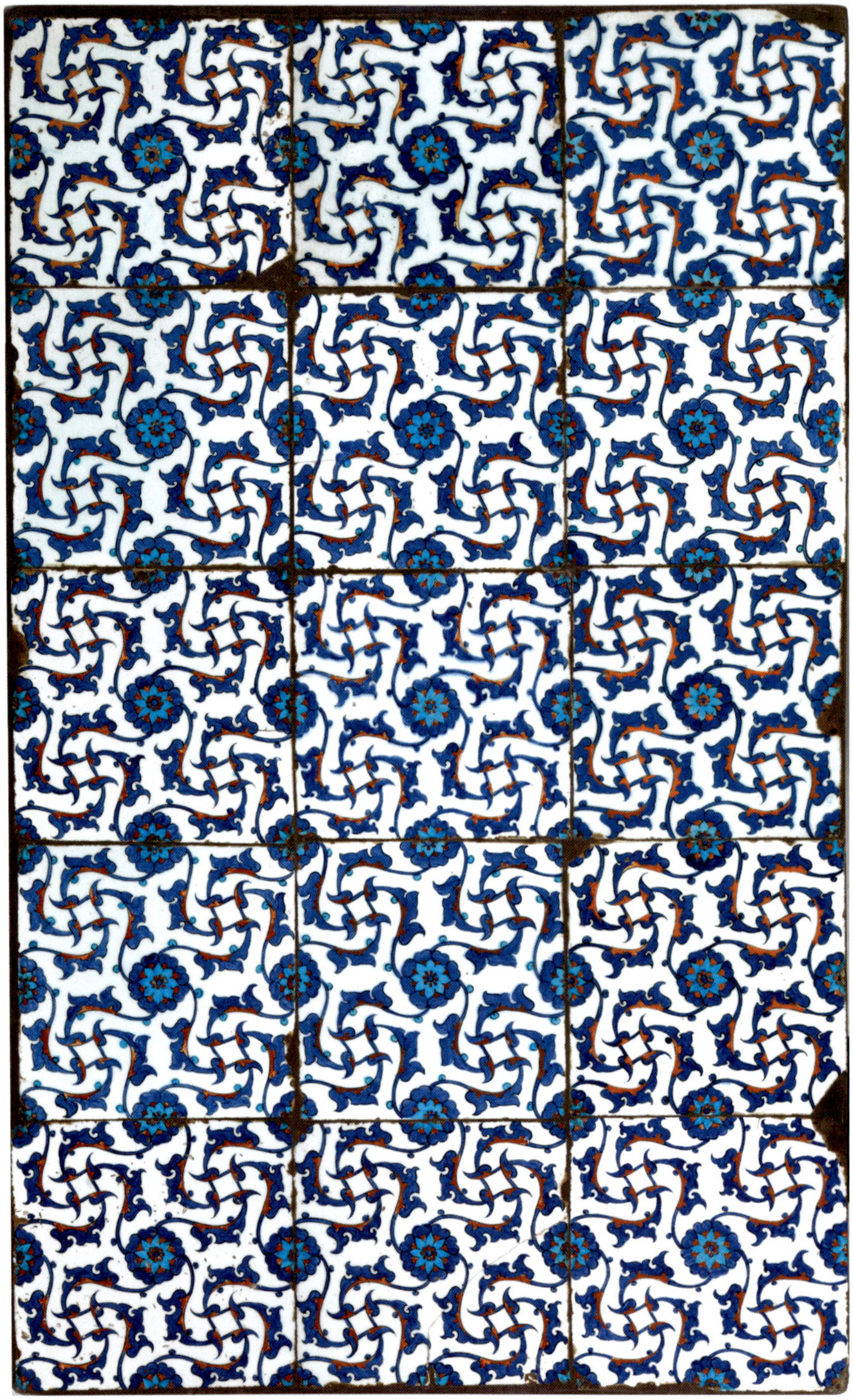

Square grid
The pattern is formed by constantly shifting the figure (translation symmetry) in this square grid. The figure itself is a plant motif that rotates four times (rotation symmetry). The Rüstem Pasha mosque in Istanbul, built c. 1561 by the famous architect Sinan, has identical tiles.

Tile panel, 1550–1600
Iznik, Turkey, Ottoman period
Fritware, glaze
Collection Museum Boijmans Van Beuningen, Rotterdam

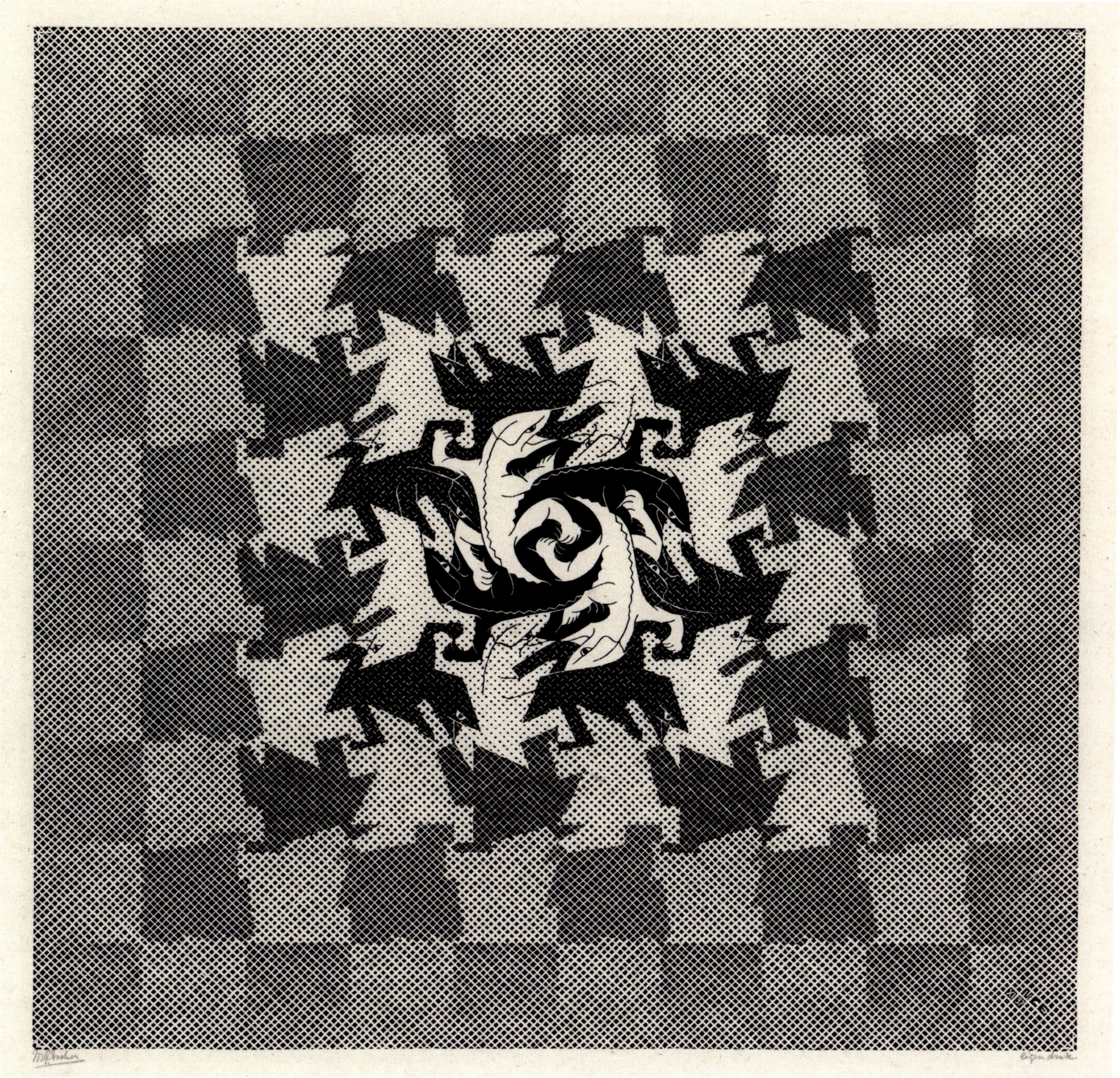

Reptiles
The square gird is clearly visible on the edges of this print. Towards the middle the abstract shapes are transformed into black and white reptiles that are reaching out to each other. The print is an example of how Escher made metamorphoses by playing with shape and colour.

Development I, 1937
M.C. Escher
Woodcut
Collection Gemeentemuseum Den Haag

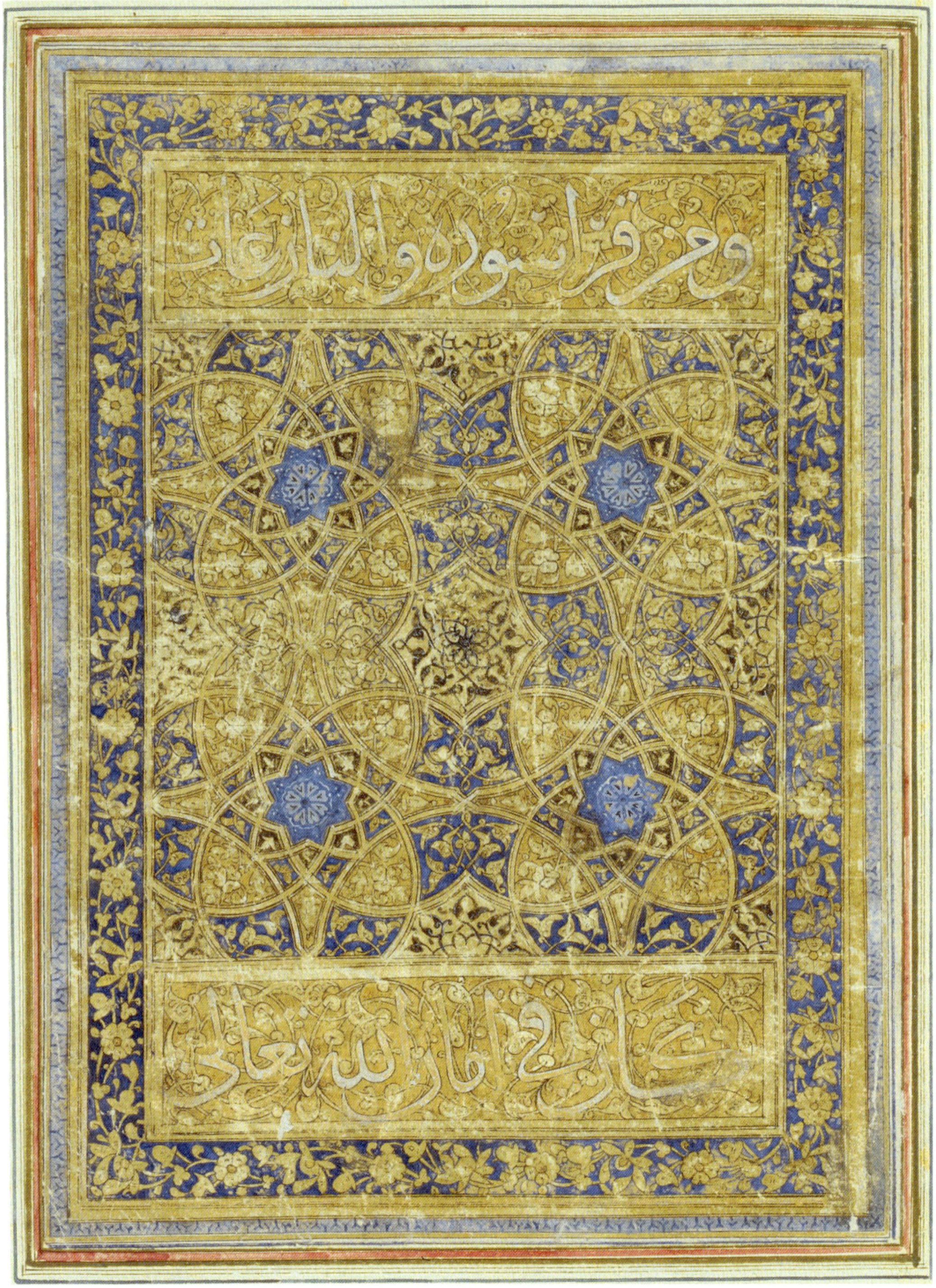

Square grid
The opening pages of this manuscript, part of the Qur'an, are decorated with a pattern that appears complicated but really is very simple. The basis is a square grid with flower motifs which are formed by rotation symmetry. The circles, in fact lines to construct the figure, have been coloured in and become part of the decoration.

Qur'anic manuscript, 1330–1340
Iran, Ilkhanid period
Gold, ink and gouache
Collection Victoria and Albert Museum, London

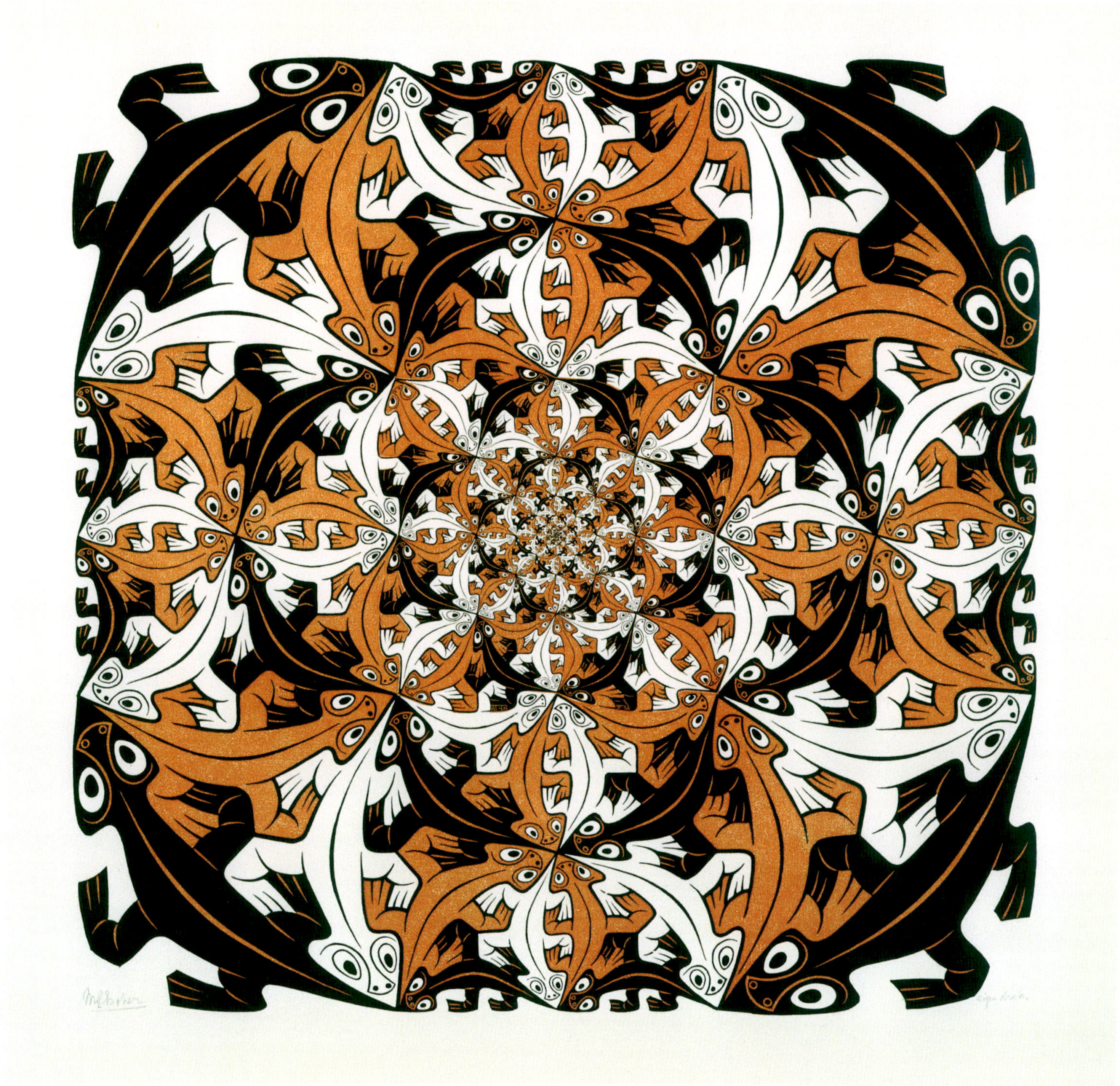

Square grid
This print belongs to a series in which Escher made the figures smaller and smaller towards the centre or towards the edges. The grid is based on squares with a red, a white and a black reptile in each separate square. If you look carefully, you can see that Escher cheated to make the pattern fit – the black reptile is missing from some of the squares in the middle.

Smaller and Smaller, 1956
M.C. Escher
Wood engraving
Collection M.C. Escher Foundation

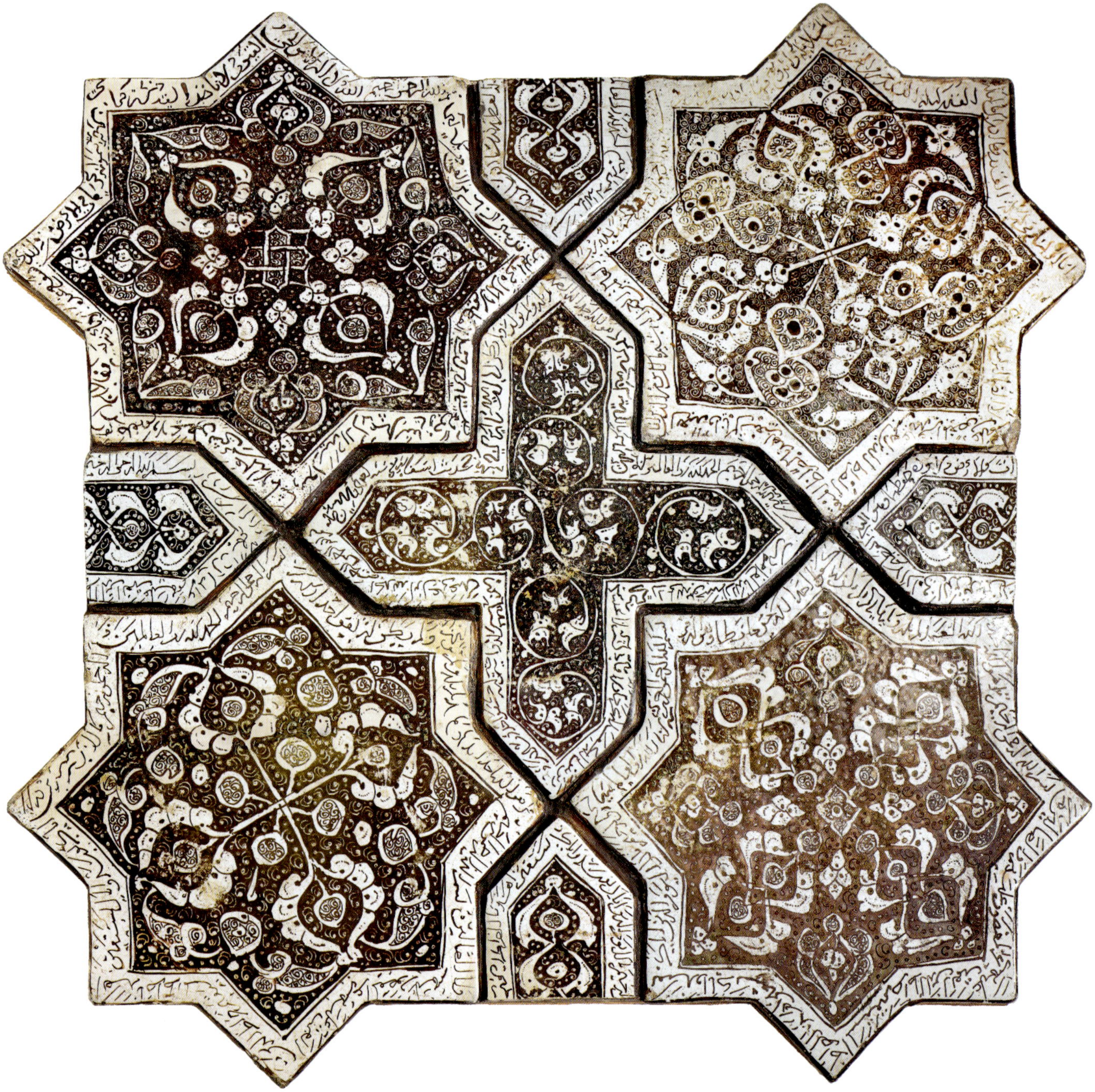

Diamond grid
The pattern of stars and crosses follows a simple diamond grid. Tiles shaped like this were frequently found in both religious and non-religious buildings in Iran. This panel is decorated in lustre, a complicated technique that tried to imitate the colour and shine of precious metal on ceramics.

Tile panel, 1220–1300
Kashan, Iran, Seljuk period
Fritware, glaze
Collection Gemeentemuseum Den Haag

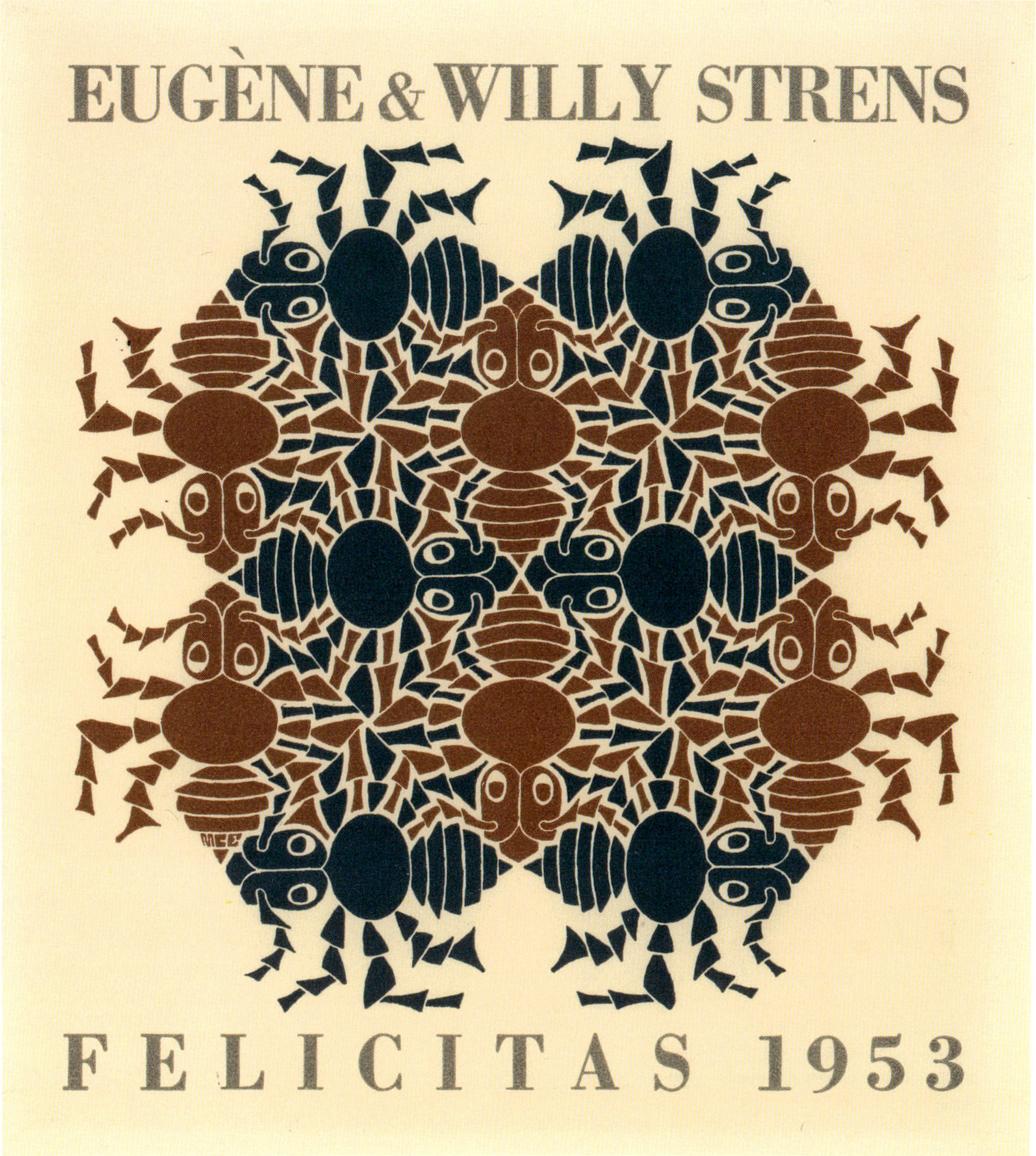

New Year's greeting
Between 1952 and 1956 Escher made a series of New Year's cards each featuring one of the four elements. This is 'earth'. At first sight it seems the depiction on this card has a square grid as basis, but the insects rotate in a diamond grid. The axes through the middle show reflection symmetry.

Earth, New Year's greeting card 1953, 1952
M.C. Escher
Cliché print
Collection M.C. Escher Foundation

DESIGN

Escher and the makers of Islamic art used the same basic instruments to design their patterns: a pair of compasses and a ruler. Before Escher started work on a print, he first drew the grid and the symmetry. He then designed the figures for the tessellation and worked out the entire design. Designers of abstract Islamic patterns approached their work differently. They created figures by drawing circles and lines and linking intersections.

Craftsmen themselves used a pair of compasses and a ruler for simple patterns in Islamic art. They directly executed the designs in buildings or on objects. They also used

ESCHER AND THE MAKERS OF ISLAMIC ART USED THE SAME BASIC INSTRUMENTS TO DESIGN THEIR PATTERNS: A PAIR OF COMPASSES AND A RULER

templates of part of the design. A bigger pattern was created by continually repeating the template. Specialist mathematical knowledge was necessary for the more complex patterns; design and execution were sometimes separated.

Escher virtually always executed his designs himself, working with various graphic techniques, such as lithography and woodcutting. He himself didn't think he was good at drawing. What he meant was, he couldn't depict a figure directly from memory. He always copied human and animal figures. Every print required months of thought and many preliminary studies.

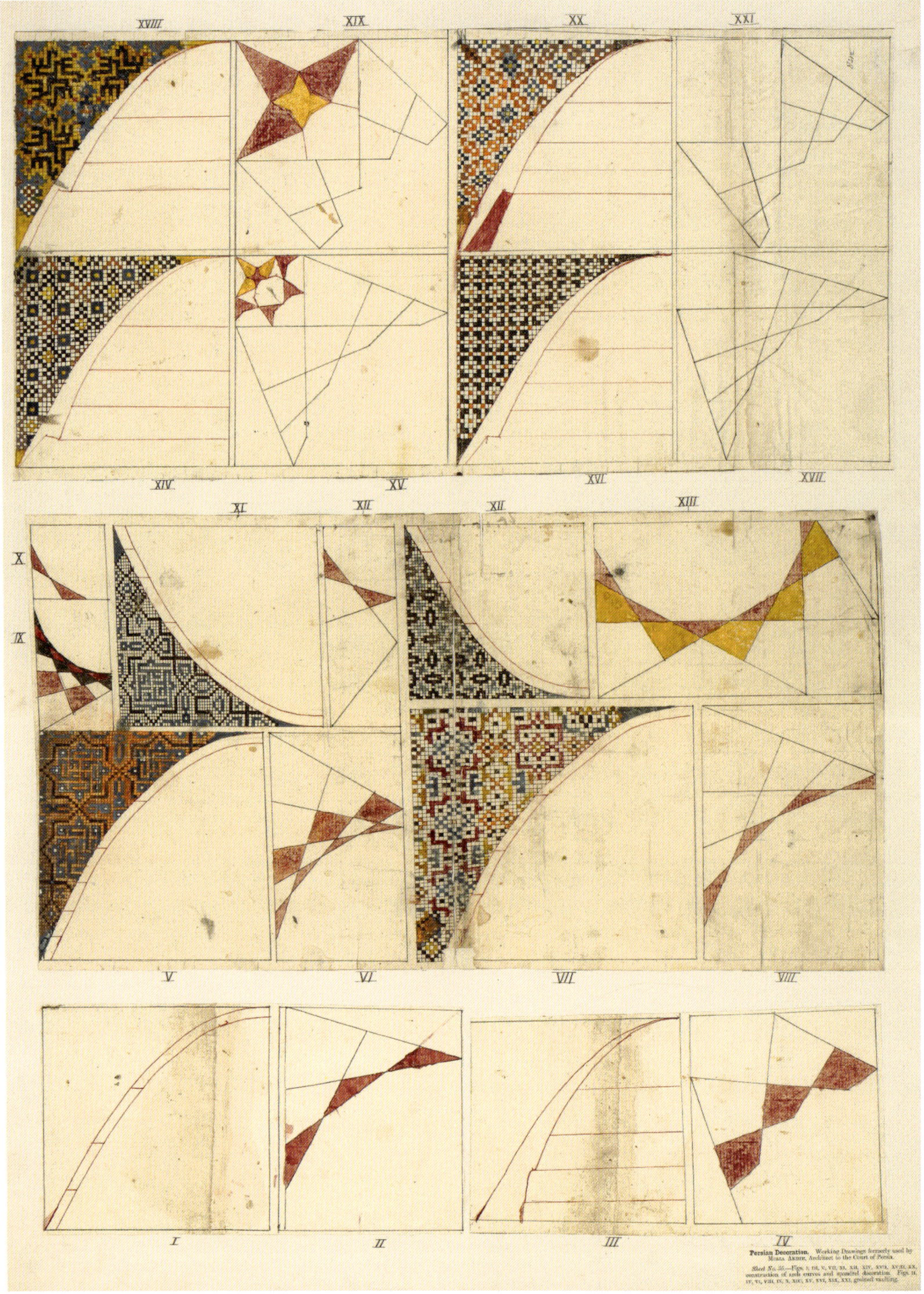

Pattern drawings
These pattern drawings were originally in scrolls in the possesion of court architects who worked for the Persian shahs. It's unclear whether they were working plans or sketches of designs already implemented. The coloured sketches are patterns for arches and cross vaults; the complex line drawings are designs for *muqarnas*, three dimensional abstract ornaments.

Designs from the 'Mirza Akbar' scrolls, 1840–1870
Tehran, Iran, Qajar period
Graphite, ink, paint
Collection Victoria and Albert Museum, London

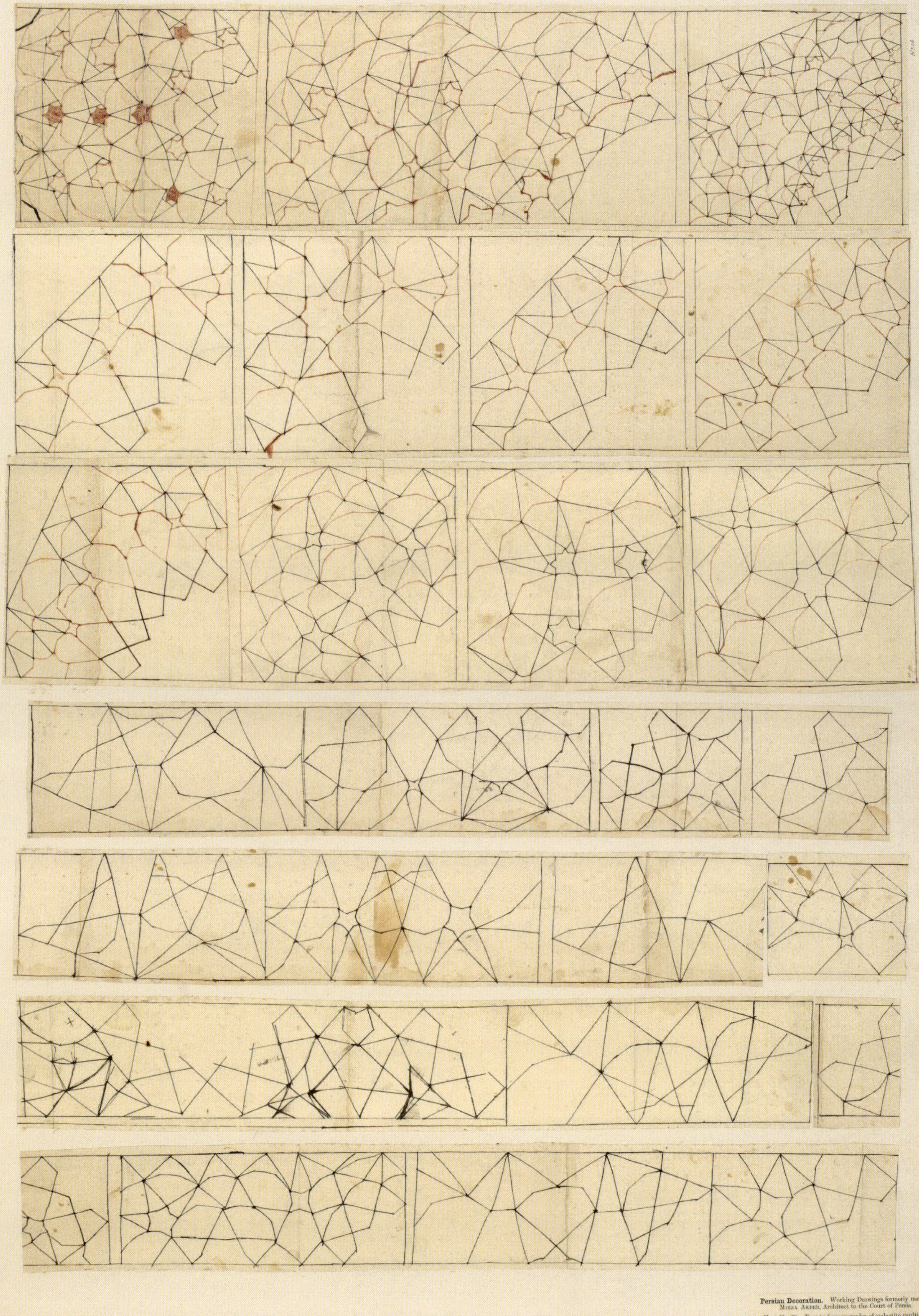

Persian Decoration. Working Drawings formerly used by Mirza Akber, Architect to the Court of Persia.

Sheet No. 39.—Twenty-four examples of stalactite vaulting.

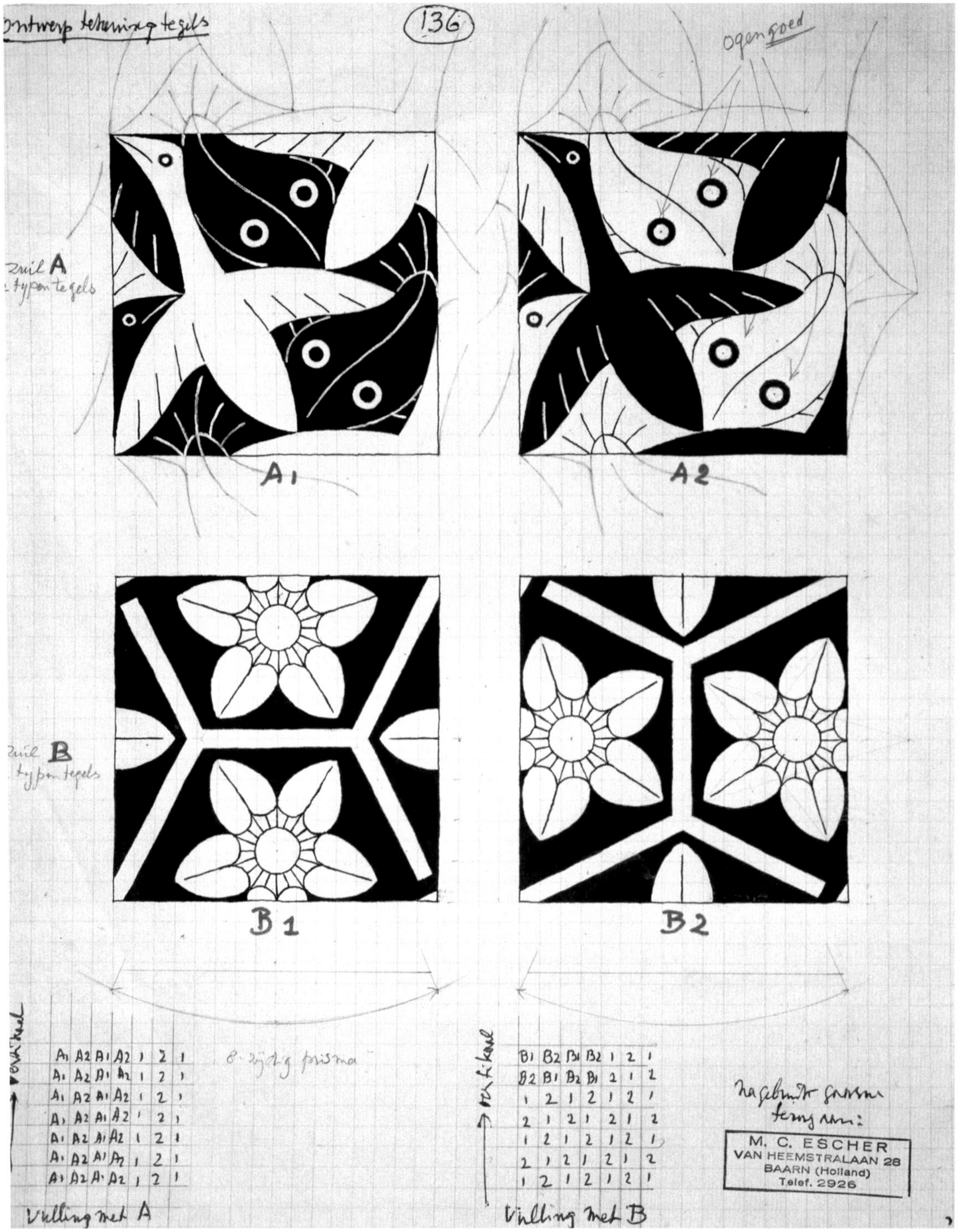

Sketches for tessellation
Escher designed two tiled columns in a school in Baarn. Two sorts of tiles were needed for each column for a continuous tessellation. To make the pattern of birds and fish for one column, the tiles had to be glazed in positive and negative (A1 and A2). For the flower motif on the other column, two tile versions were also necessary because the lines were sometimes interrupted and sometimes not.

Architectural drawings, 1967
M.C. Escher
Pencil, ink
Collection Gemeentemuseum Den Haag

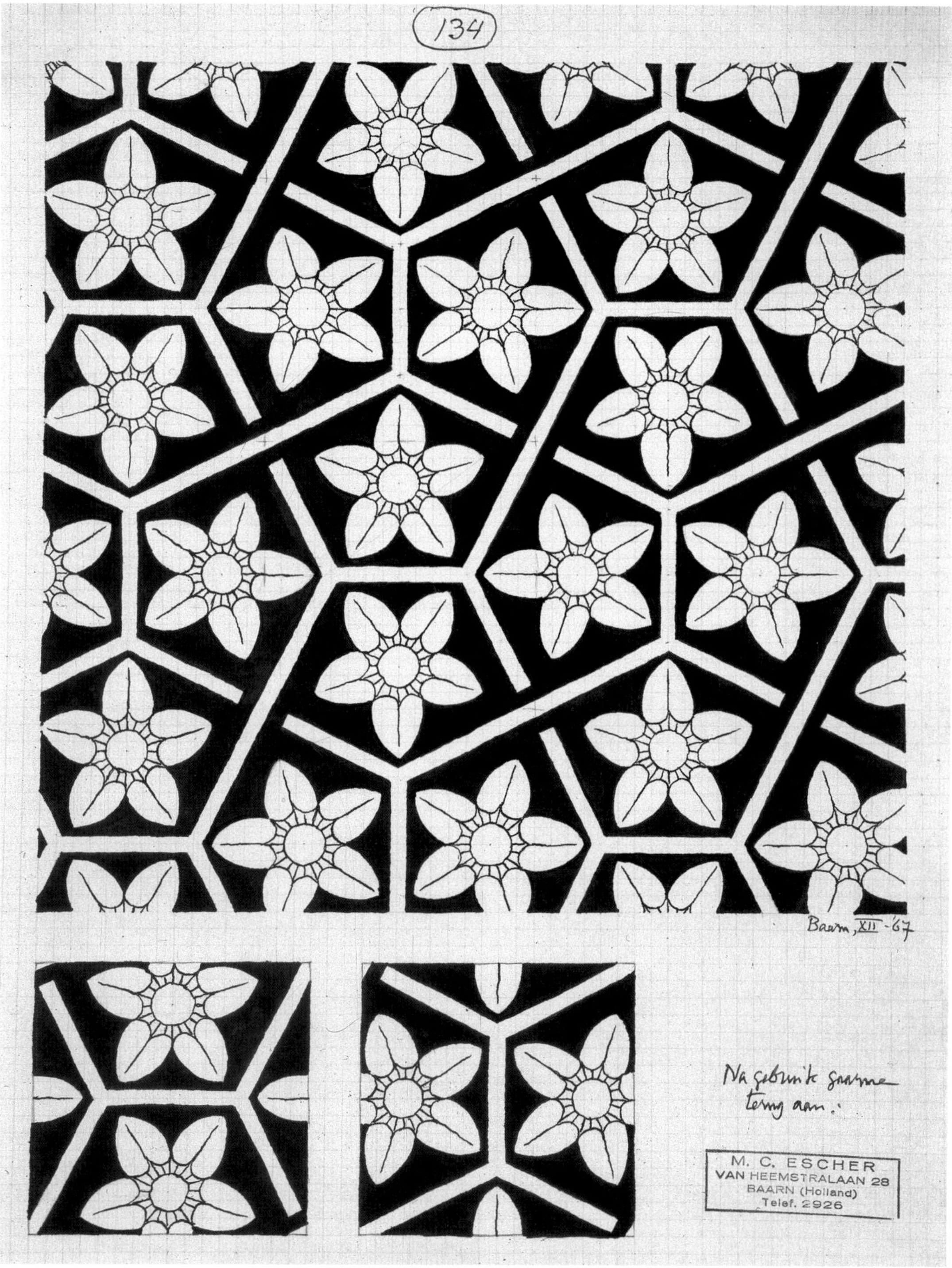
134
Baarn, XII-'67
Na gebruik gaarne terug aan:
M. C. ESCHER
VAN HEEMSTRALAAN 28
BAARN (Holland)
Telef. 2926

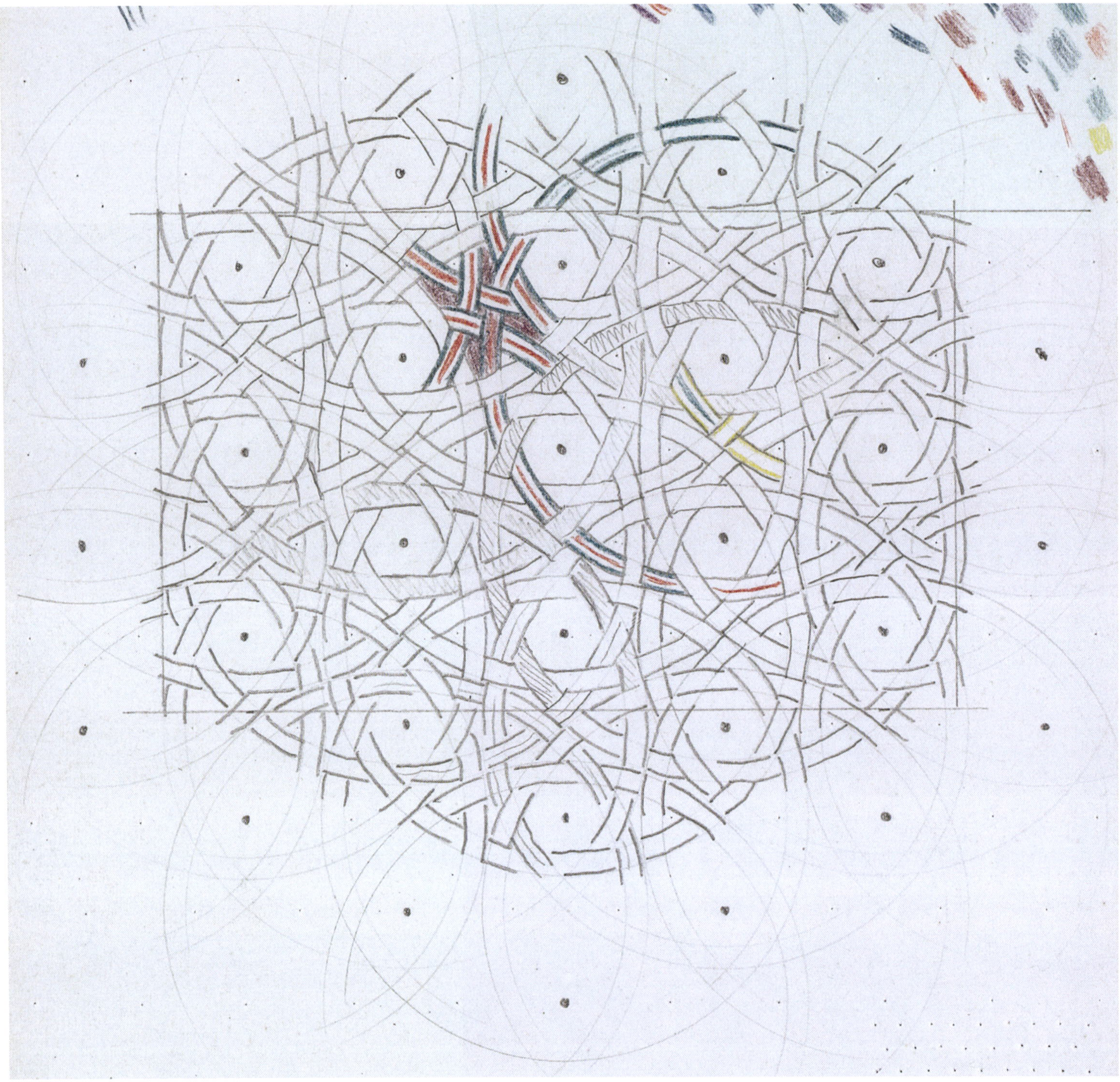

Abstract sketches
These sketches by Escher are from his notebook of abstract motifs in which he precisely researched how a plane could be divided regularly. The geometric patterns are based on overlapping circles, a motif that often occurs in Islamic art too. Escher used a pair of compasses and ruler to draw them.

Regular division of the plane, abstract motifs, 1941–1942
M.C. Escher
Pencil, colour pencil
Collection Gemeentemuseum Den Haag

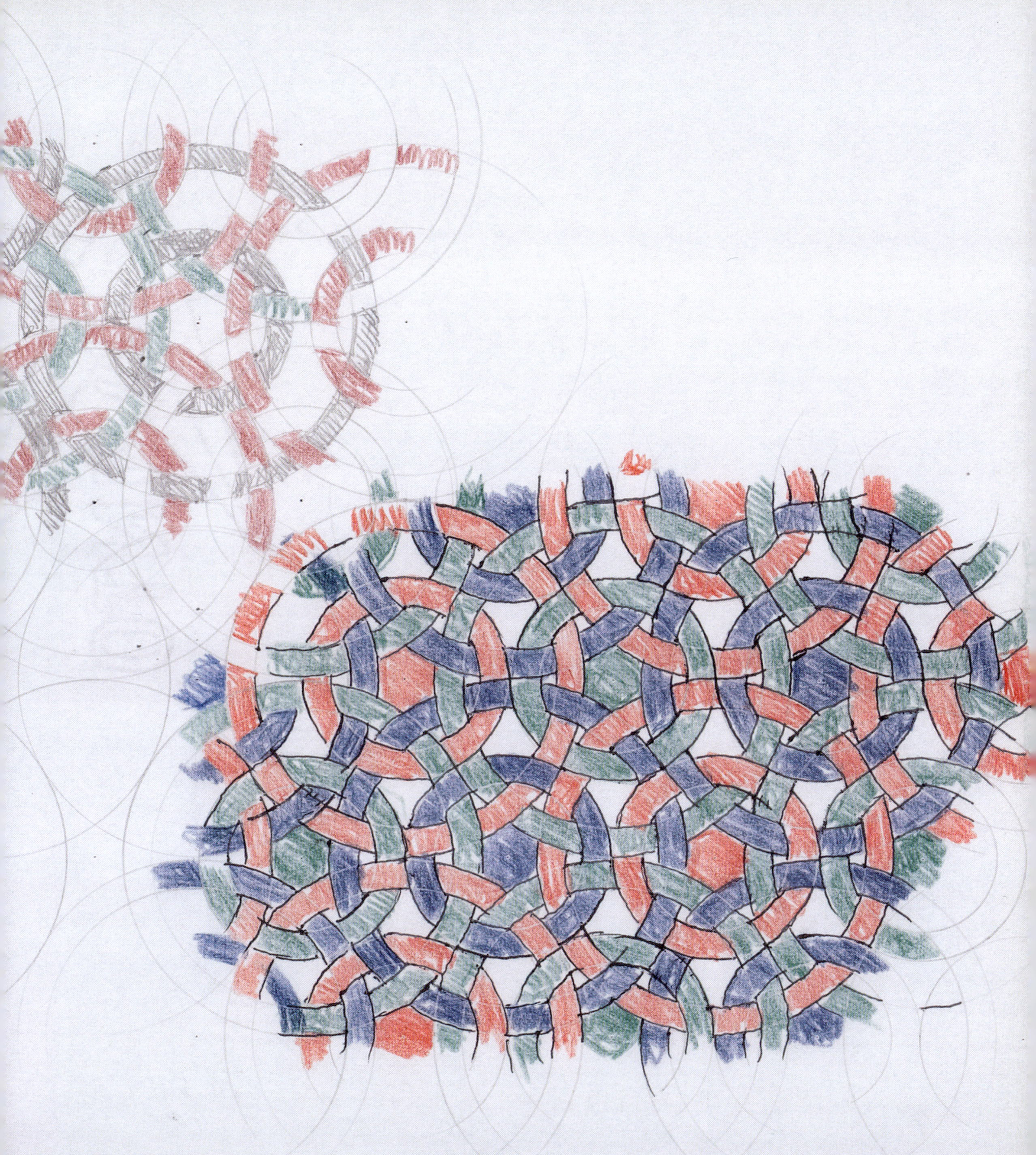

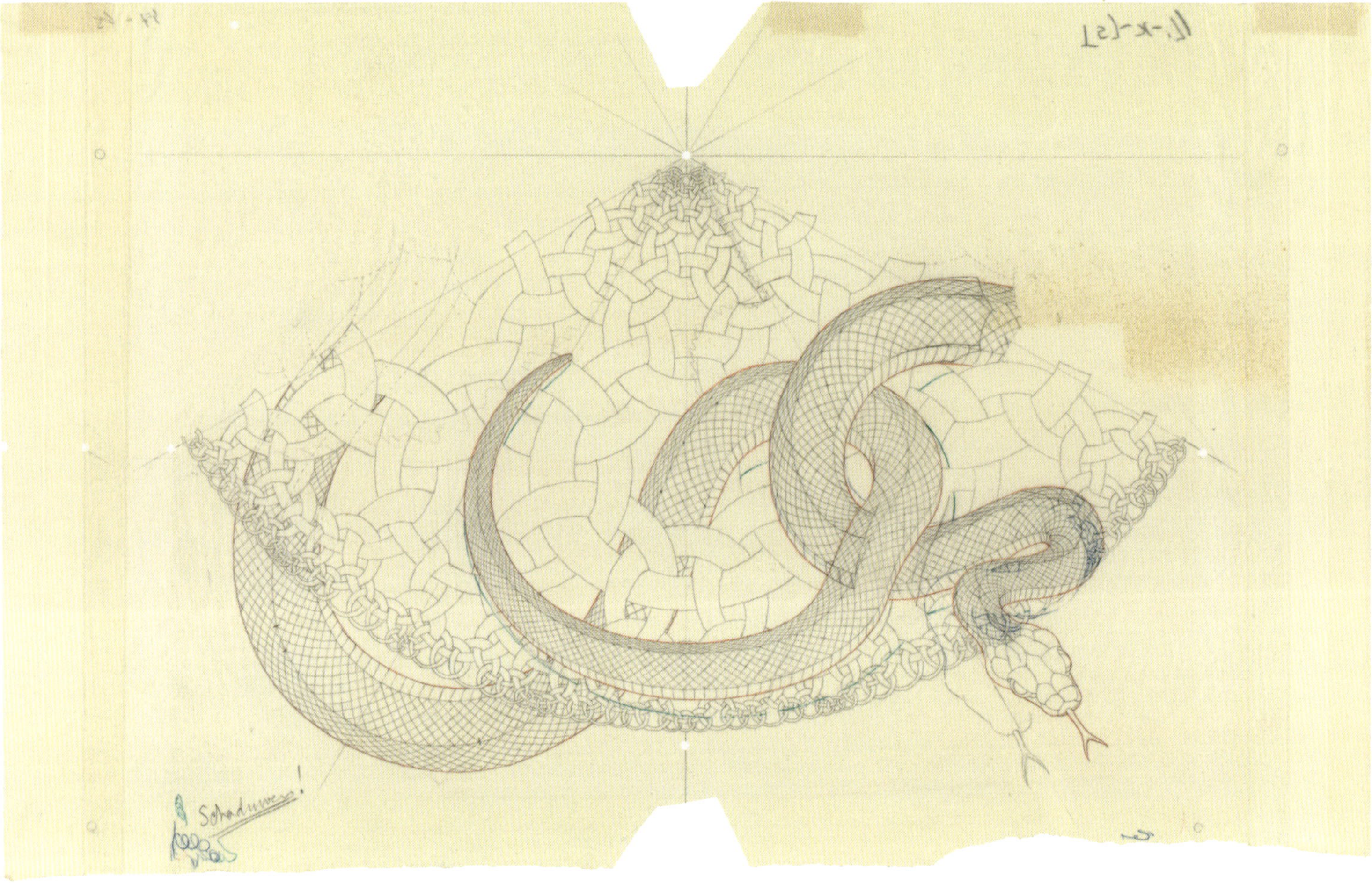

Sketches
'Snakes' was the last print Escher made. The fine draughtsmanship in these preliminary sketches shows how he meticulously drew every detail before he started the definitive woodcut. The snakes are not drawn from nature but from photos that Escher had acquired especially for this work.

Sketches for Snakes, 1969
M.C. Escher
Pencil, chalk
Collection Gemeentemuseum Den Haag

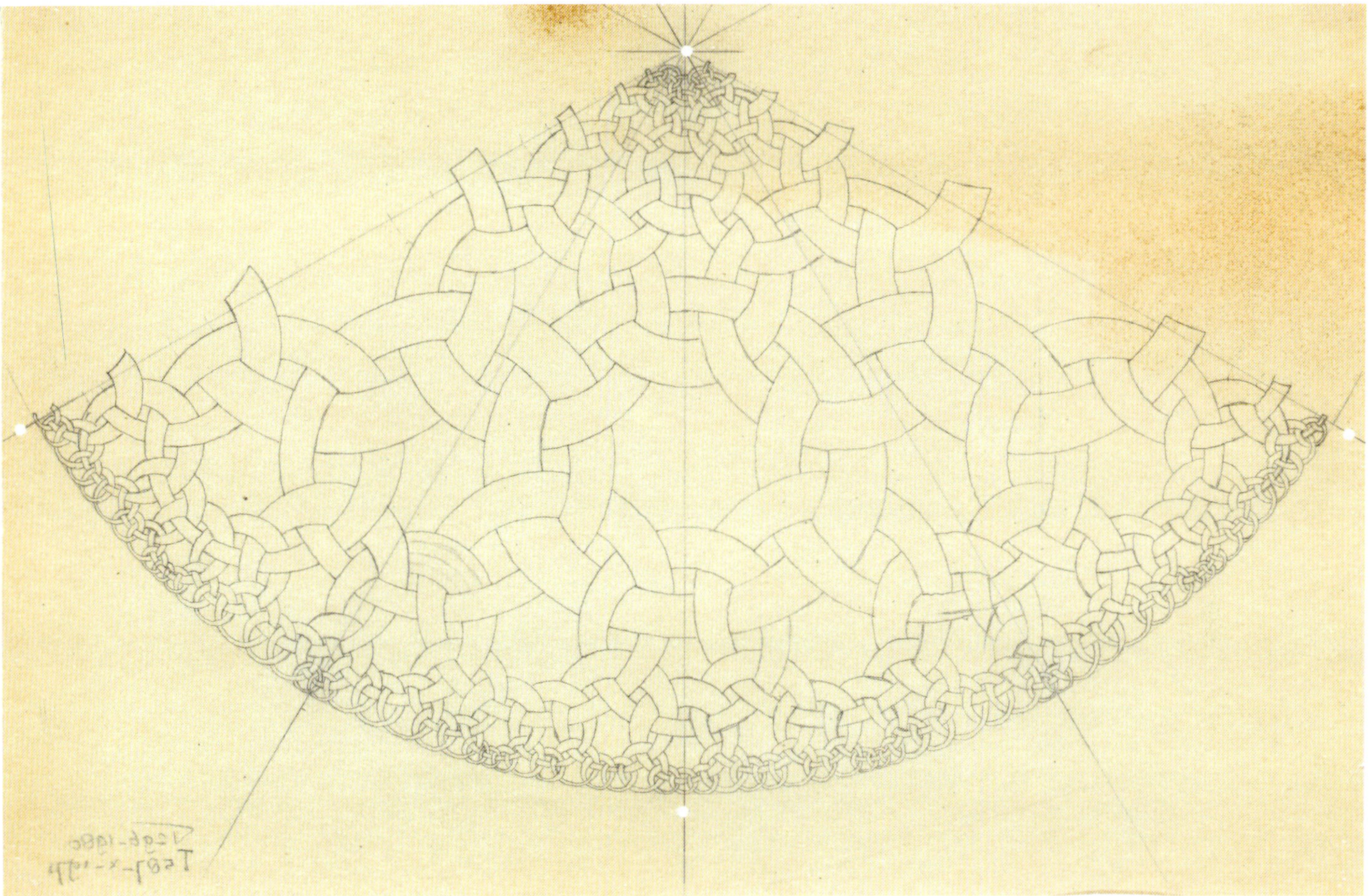

VARIATIONS

For M.C. Escher the tessellation was the ideal means of expressing eternity and infinity. He often used a tessellation in his prints in an unexpected and playfully refined way. Escher was impressed by the sophisticated, sometimes complicated tessellations he copied in Andalusia. He could, however, only give his fantasy free rein after his older brother Berend Escher had told him more about the scientific background, including the seventeen systems of symmetry. (See also the essay *Escher in Andalusia* in this catalogue.)
M.C. Escher worked on these systems for years in exercise books, on loose sheets of squared paper and in coloured studies.
This arsenal formed the nigh-on inexhaustible source of inspiration for his art: the prints.

The tessellations from Islamic art were based on these same systems. Hence there are visual similarities between Escher's prints which partly comprise tessellations or where the whole print is a tessellation, and objects from Islamic art with tessellations, or large wall tile panels that in their entirety are a tessellation. Escher and the Islamic artists used the same simple geometrical instruments to design their basic patterns – a pair of compasses and a ruler.

The following selection comprises prints and objects, such as a carved wooden ball and a confectionary tin by M.C. Escher, as well as tiles, dishes, bowls and a single jug from the internationally renowned collection of Islamic art of the Gemeentemuseum Den Haag.

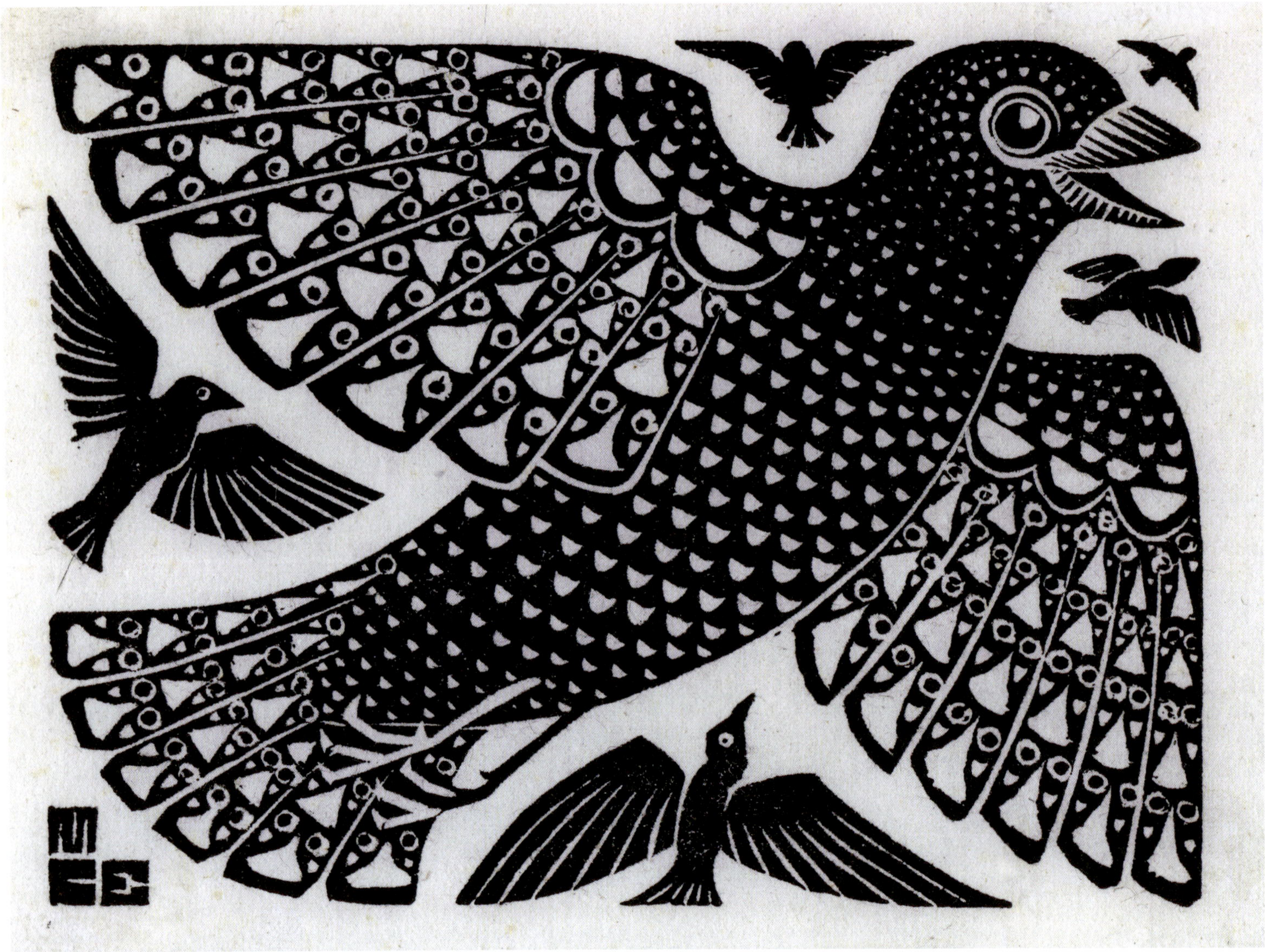

Birds, 1926
M.C. Escher
Woodcut
Collection Gemeentemuseum Den Haag

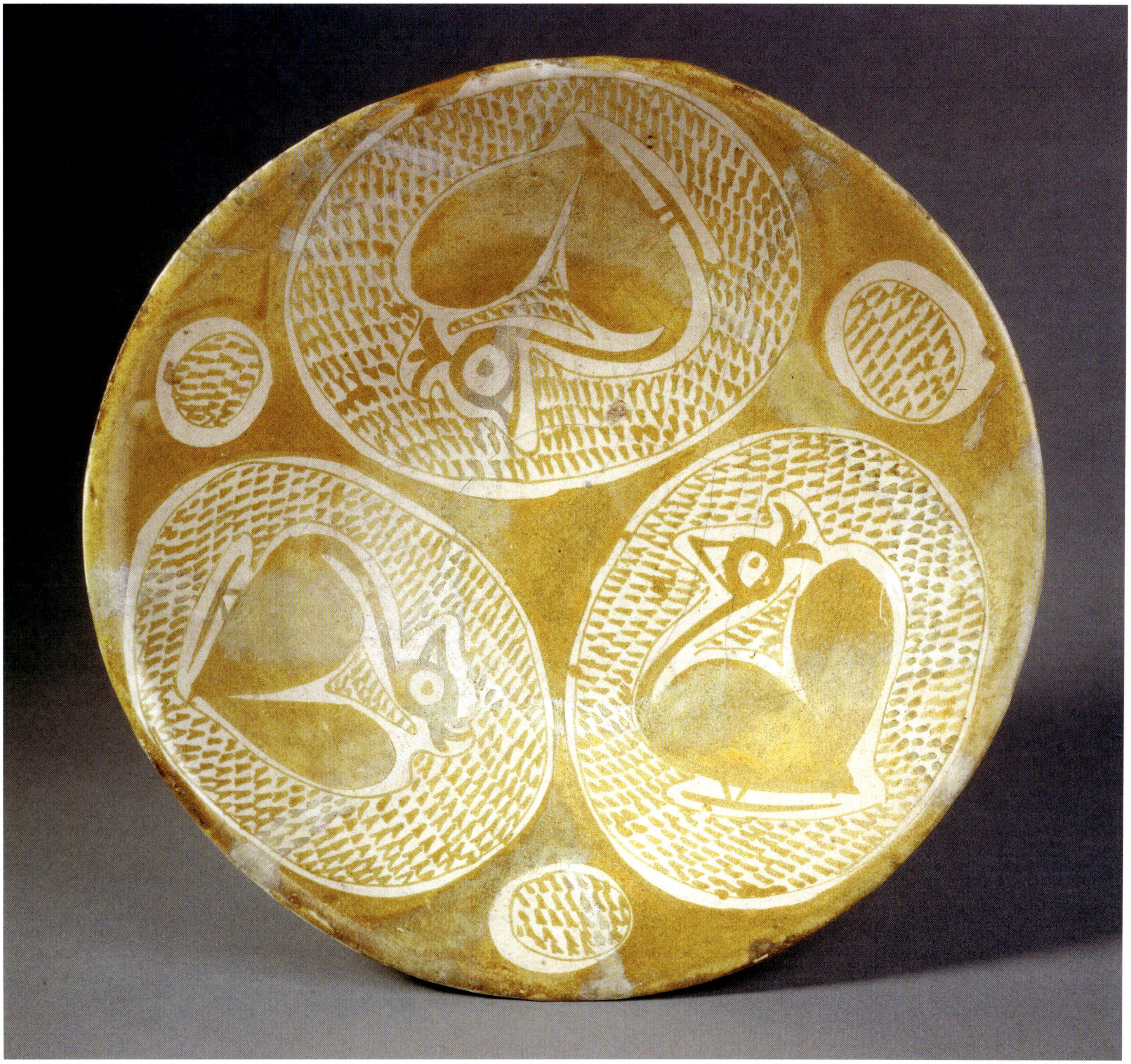

Bowl, 850–950
Iraq
Fritware, glaze
Collection Gemeentemuseum Den Haag

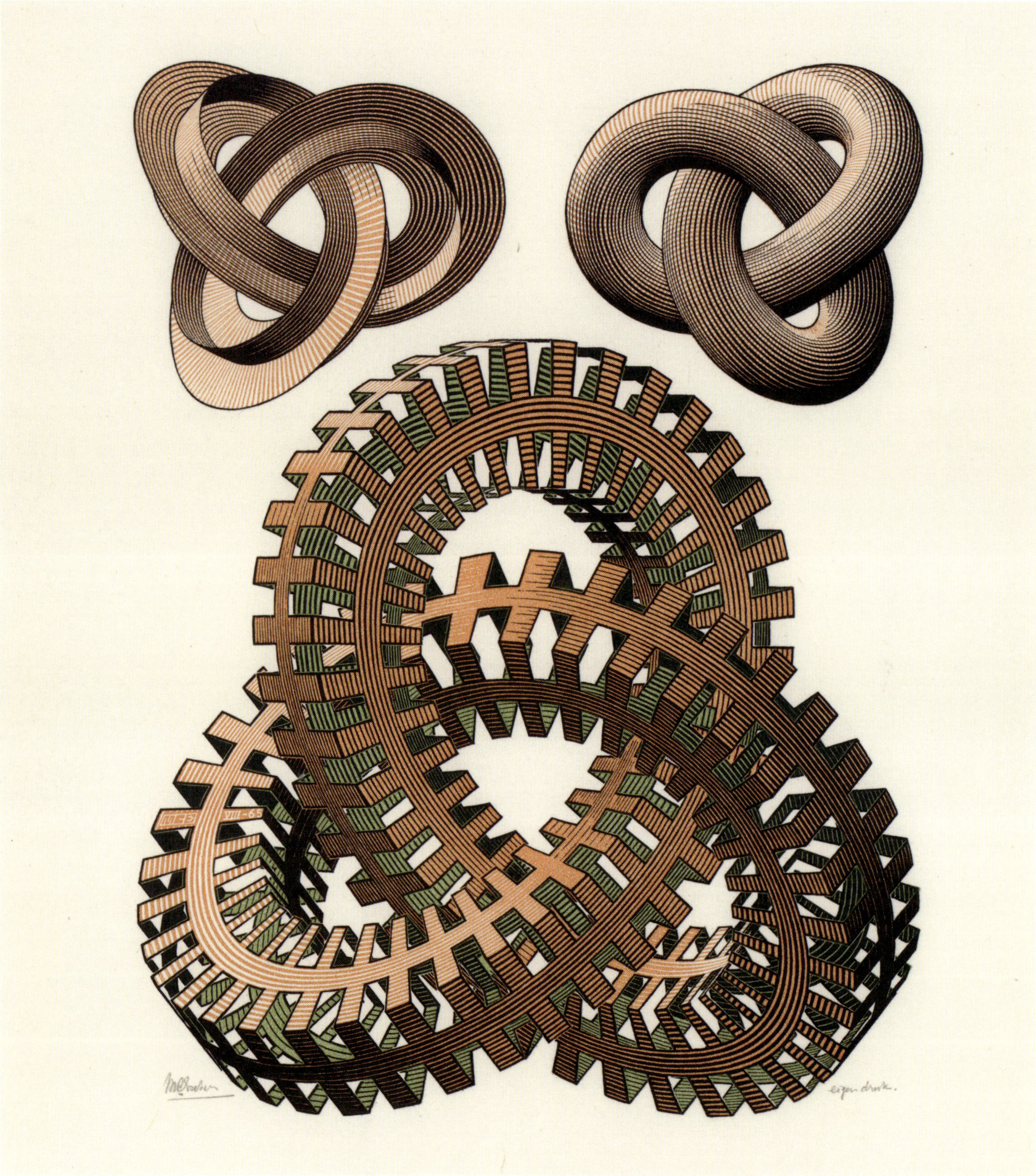

Knots, 1965
M.C. Escher
Woodcut in black, green and brown printed from three blocks
Collection Gemeentemuseum Den Haag

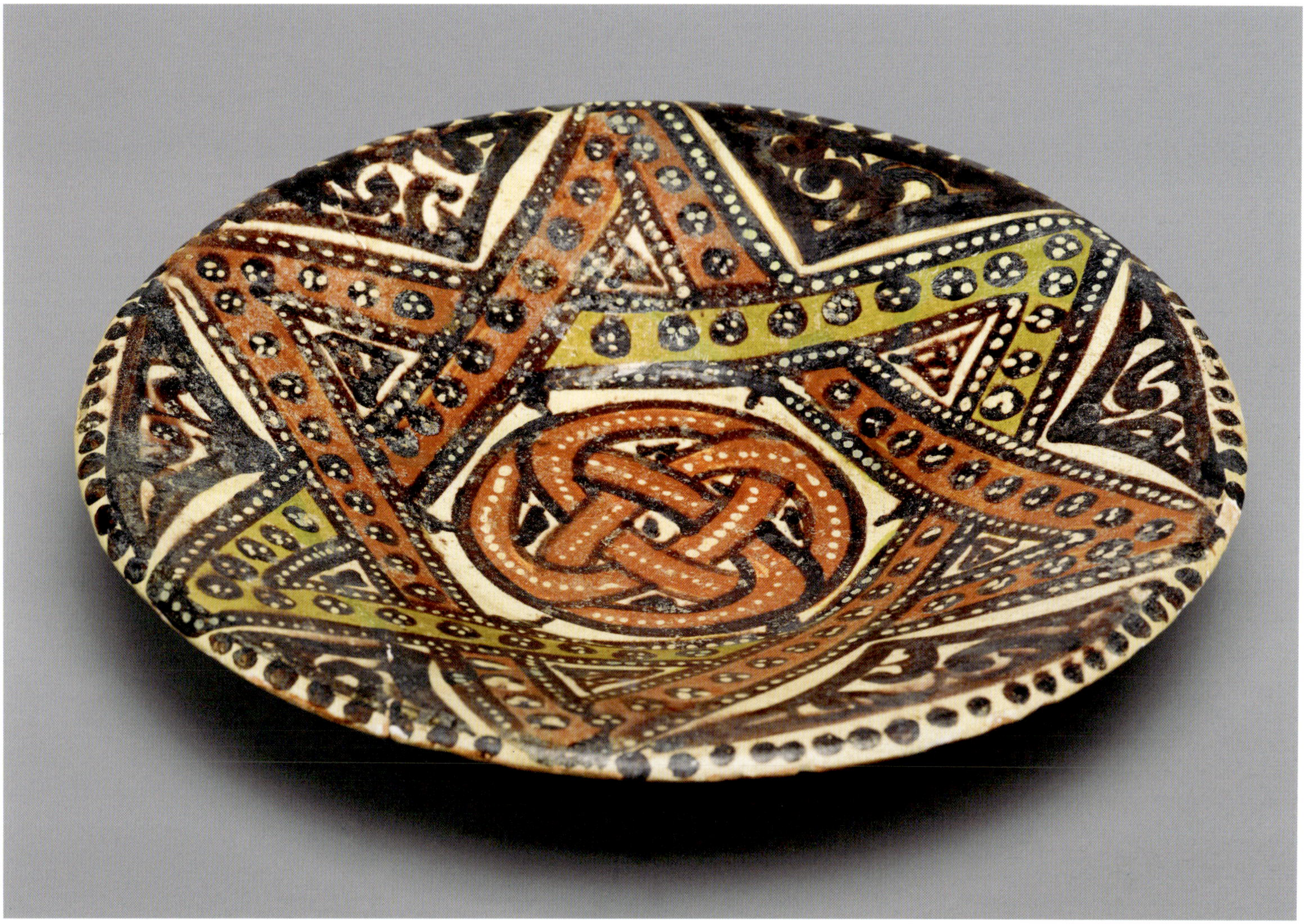

Dish, 14th century
Iran
Fritware
Collection Gemeentemuseum Den Haag

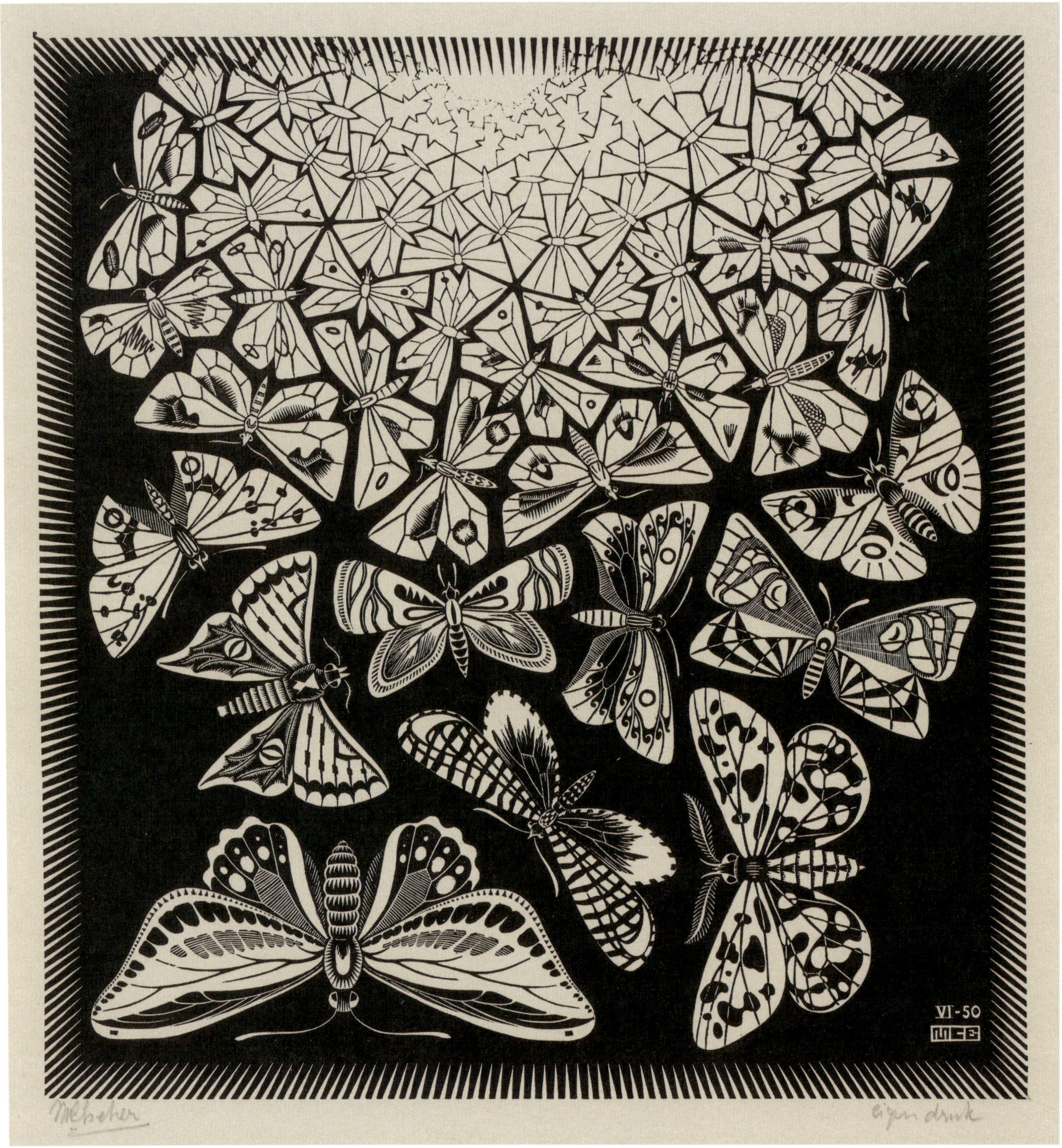

Butterflies, 1950
M.C. Escher
Wood engraving
Collection Gemeentemuseum Den Haag

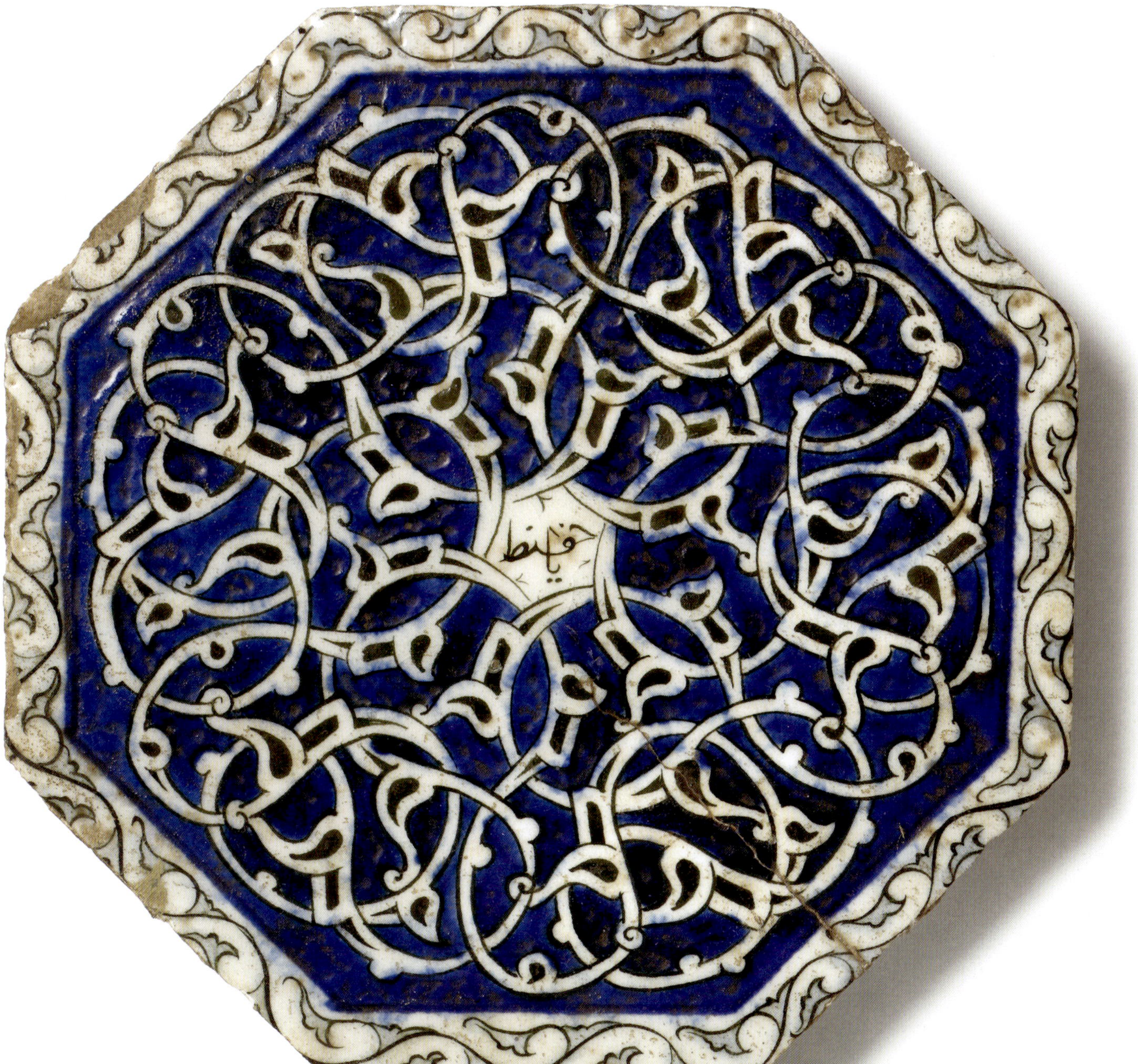

Tile, 15th century
Iran
Fritware, glaze
Collection Gemeentemuseum Den Haag

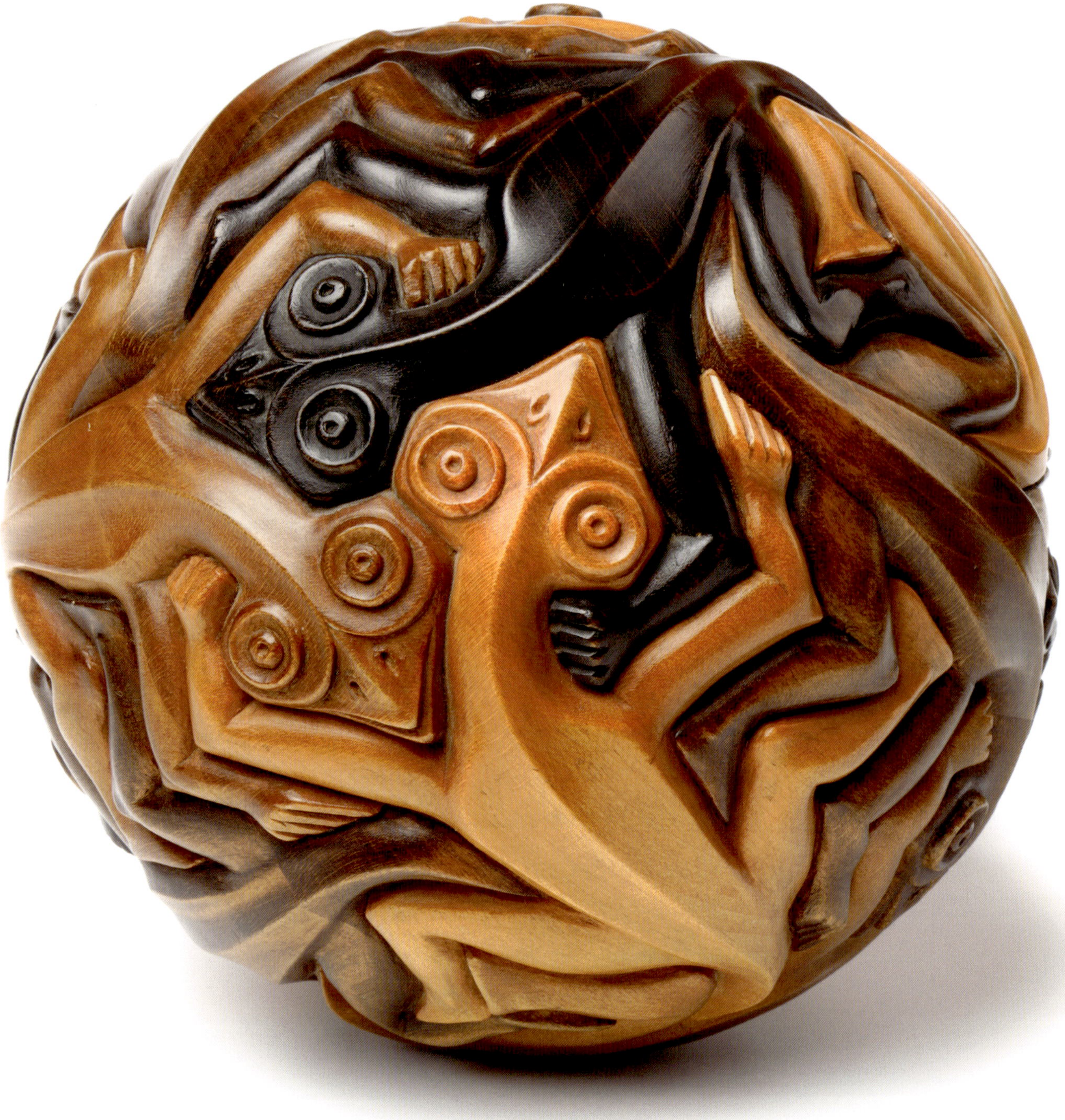

Wooden ball with reptiles, 1949
M.C. Escher
Ahorn wood
Collection Gemeentemuseum Den Haag

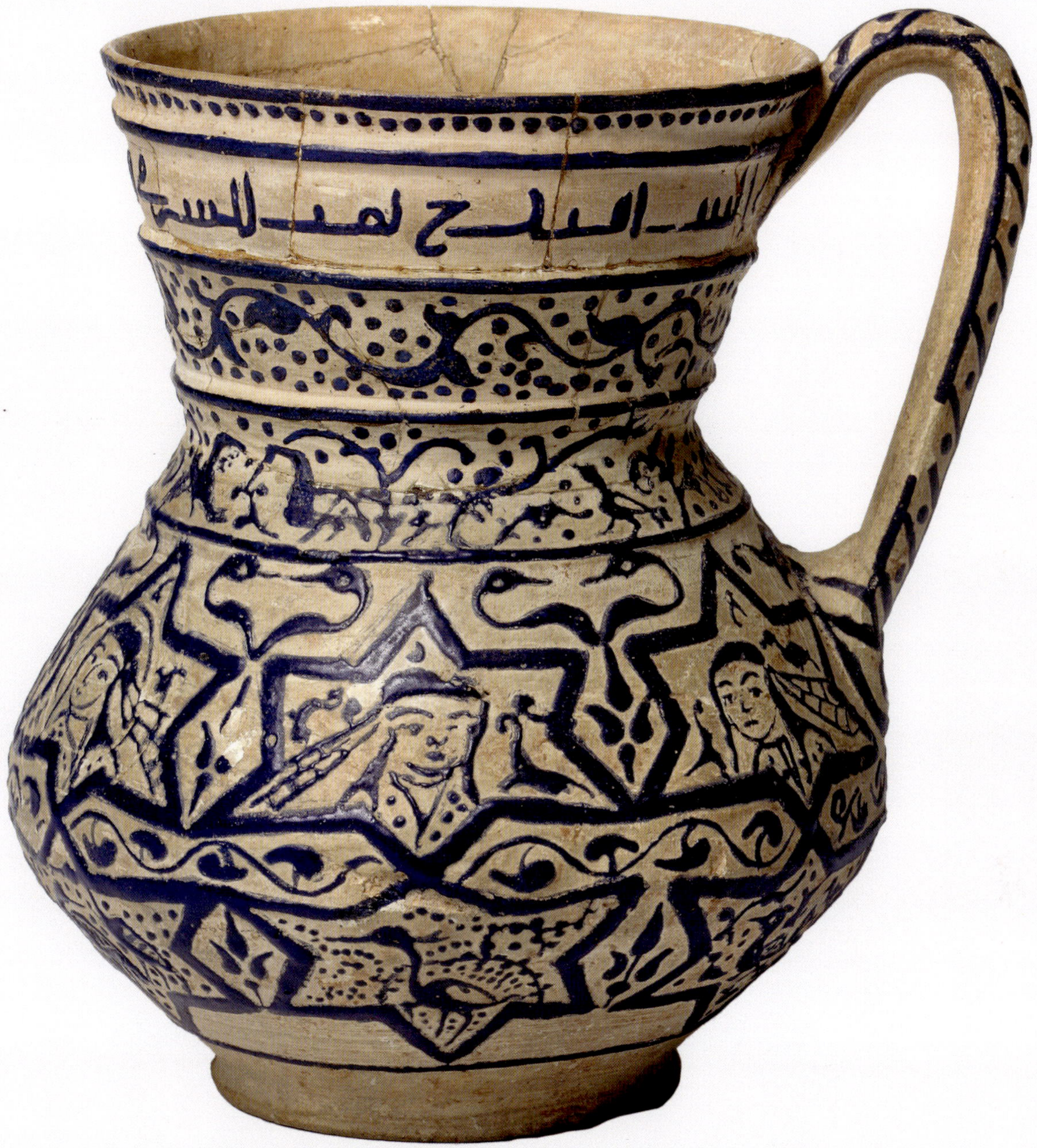

Jug, 19th/early 20th century
Iran
Earthenware
Collection Gemeentemuseum Den Haag

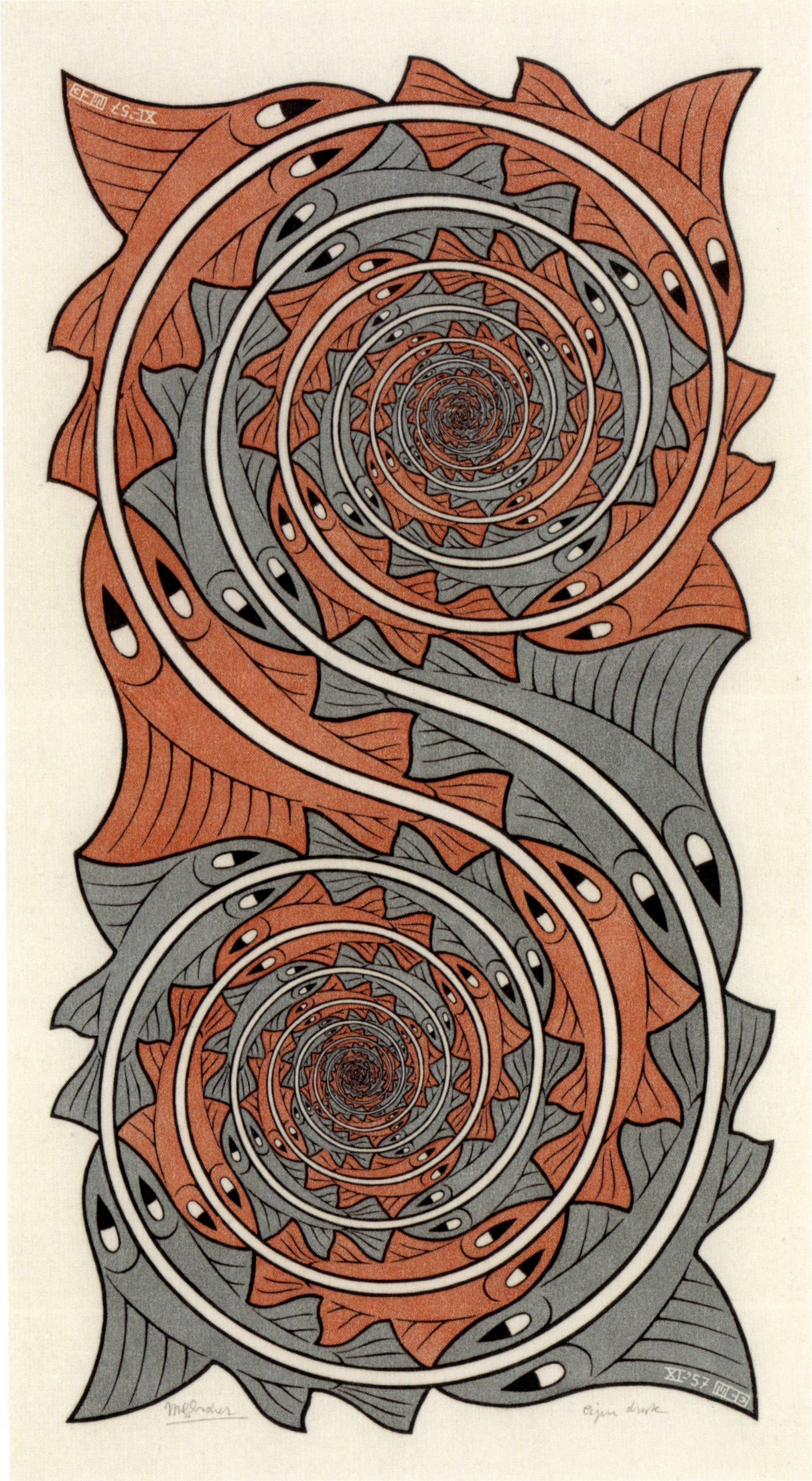

Whirlpools, 1957
M.C. Escher
Wood engraving and woodcut, second state, in red, grey and black, printed from two blocks
Collection Gemeentemuseum Den Haag

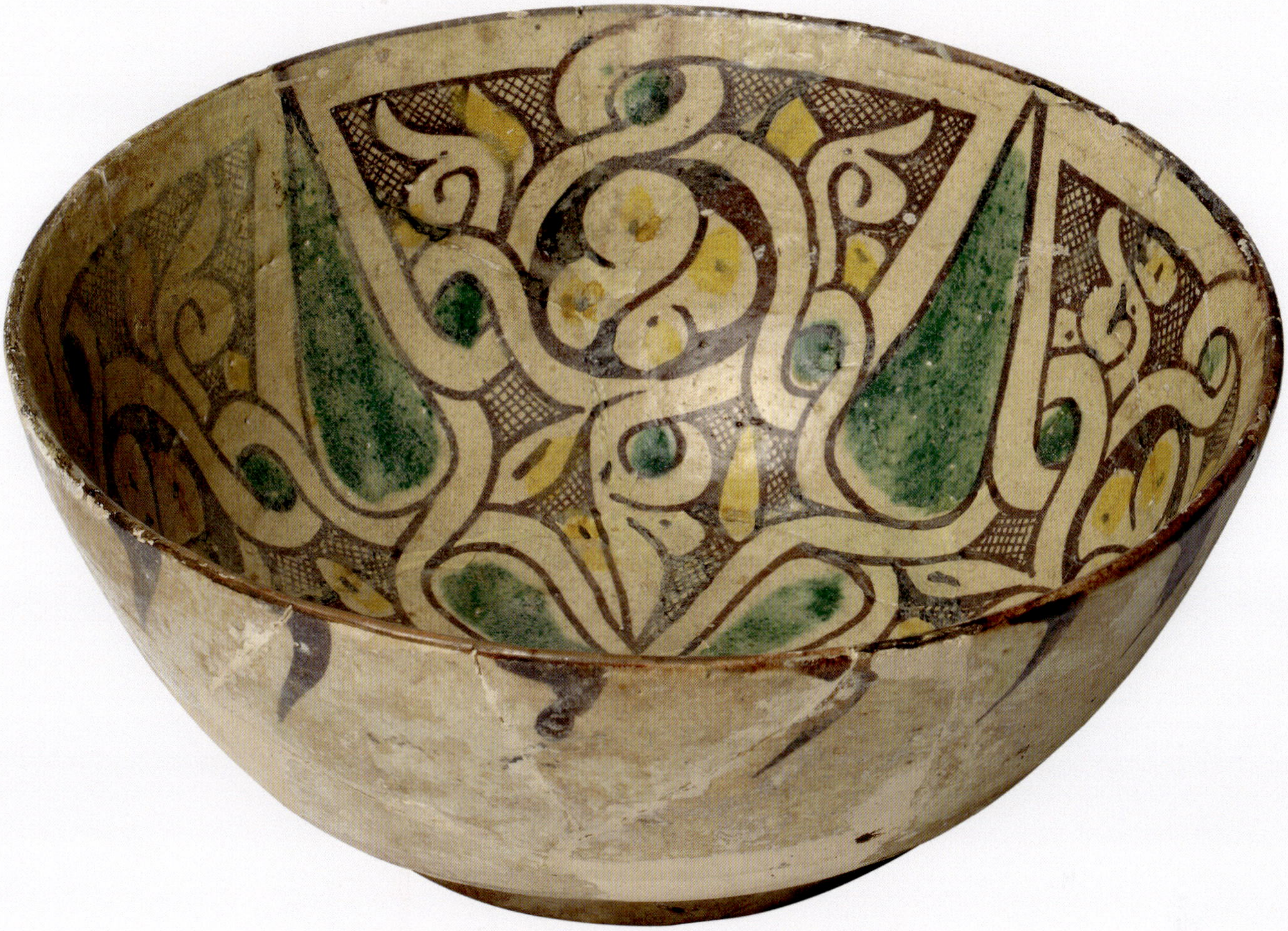

Bowl, 10th century
Khorasan, Iran
Fritware, glaze
Collection Gemeentemuseum Den Haag

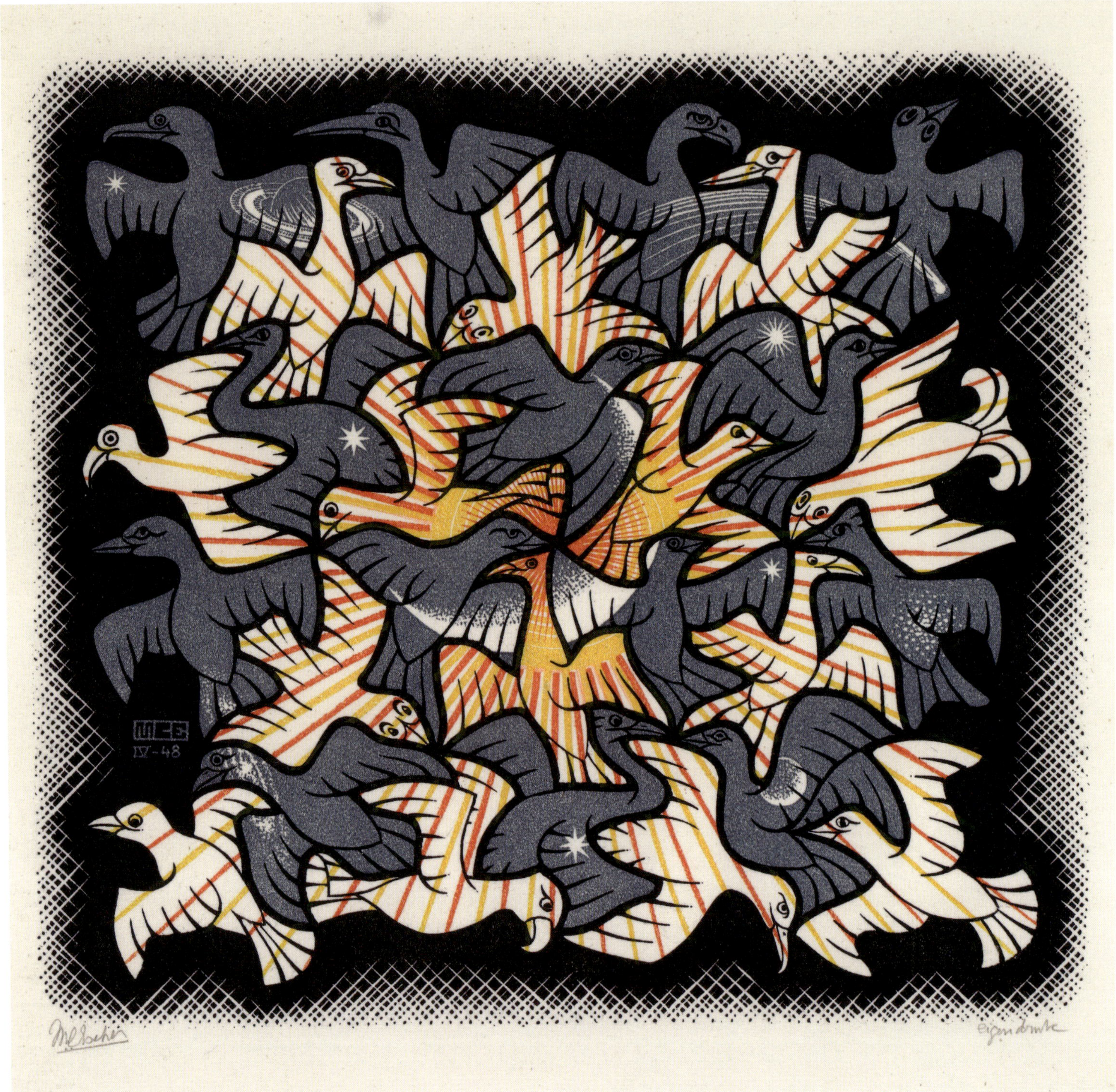

Sun and Moon, 1948
M.C. Escher
Woodcut, in blue, red, yellow and black,
printed from four blocks
Collection Gemeentemuseum Den Haag

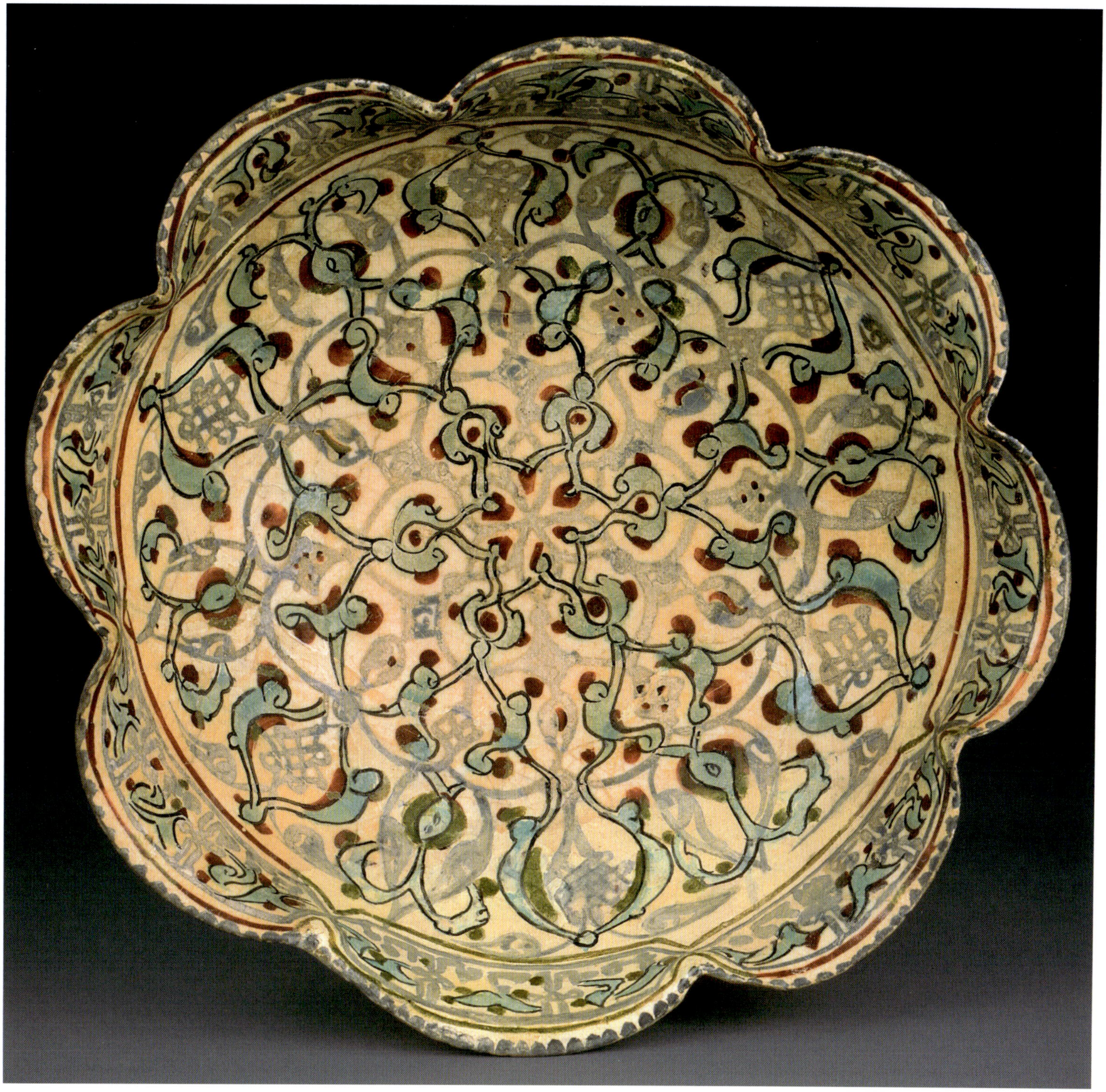

Bowl, c. 1200
Iran
Fritware, glaze
Collection Gemeentemuseum Den Haag

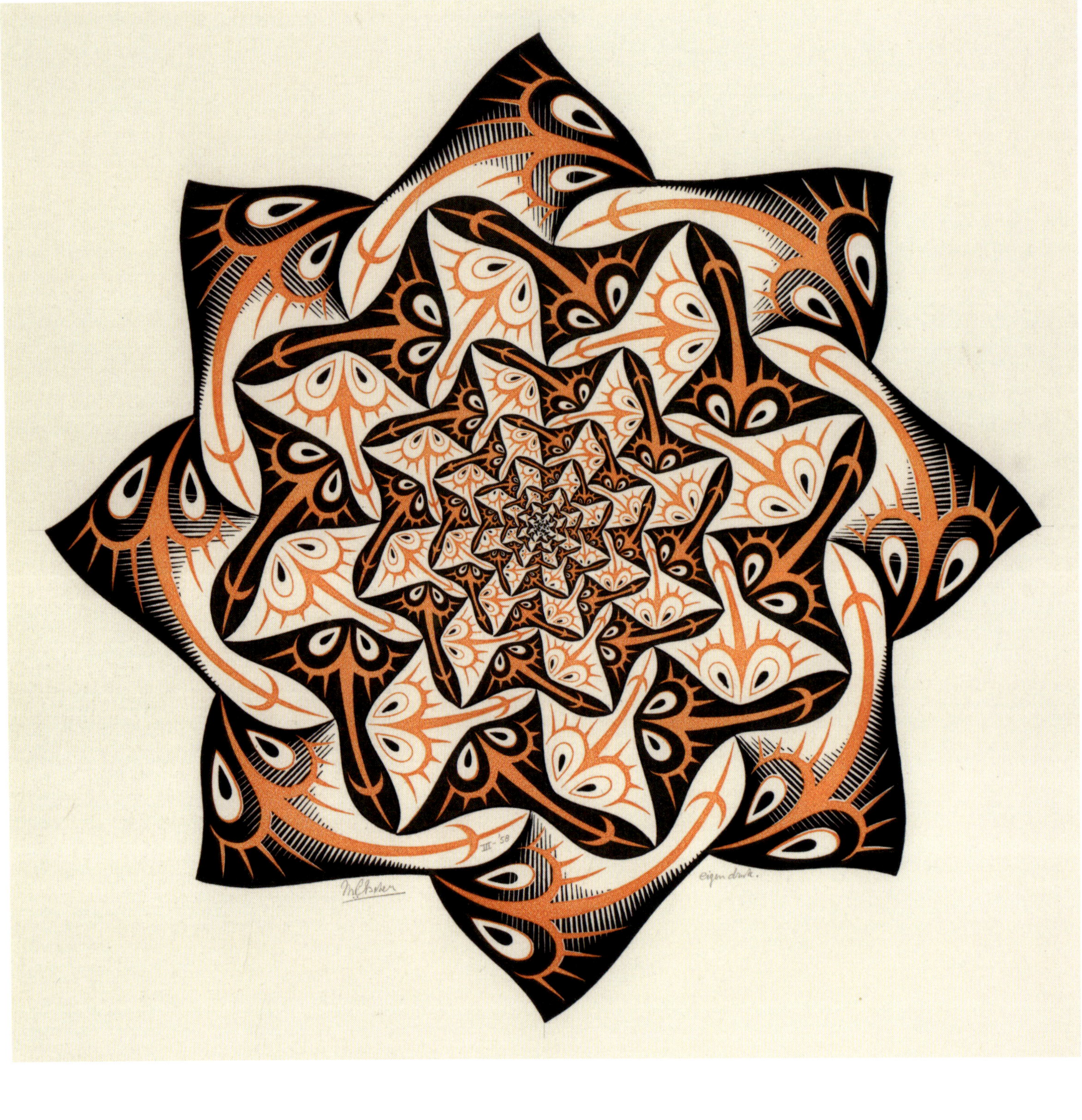

Path of Life I, 1958
M.C. Escher
Woodcut, in red and black, printed from two blocks
Collection Gemeentemuseum Den Haag

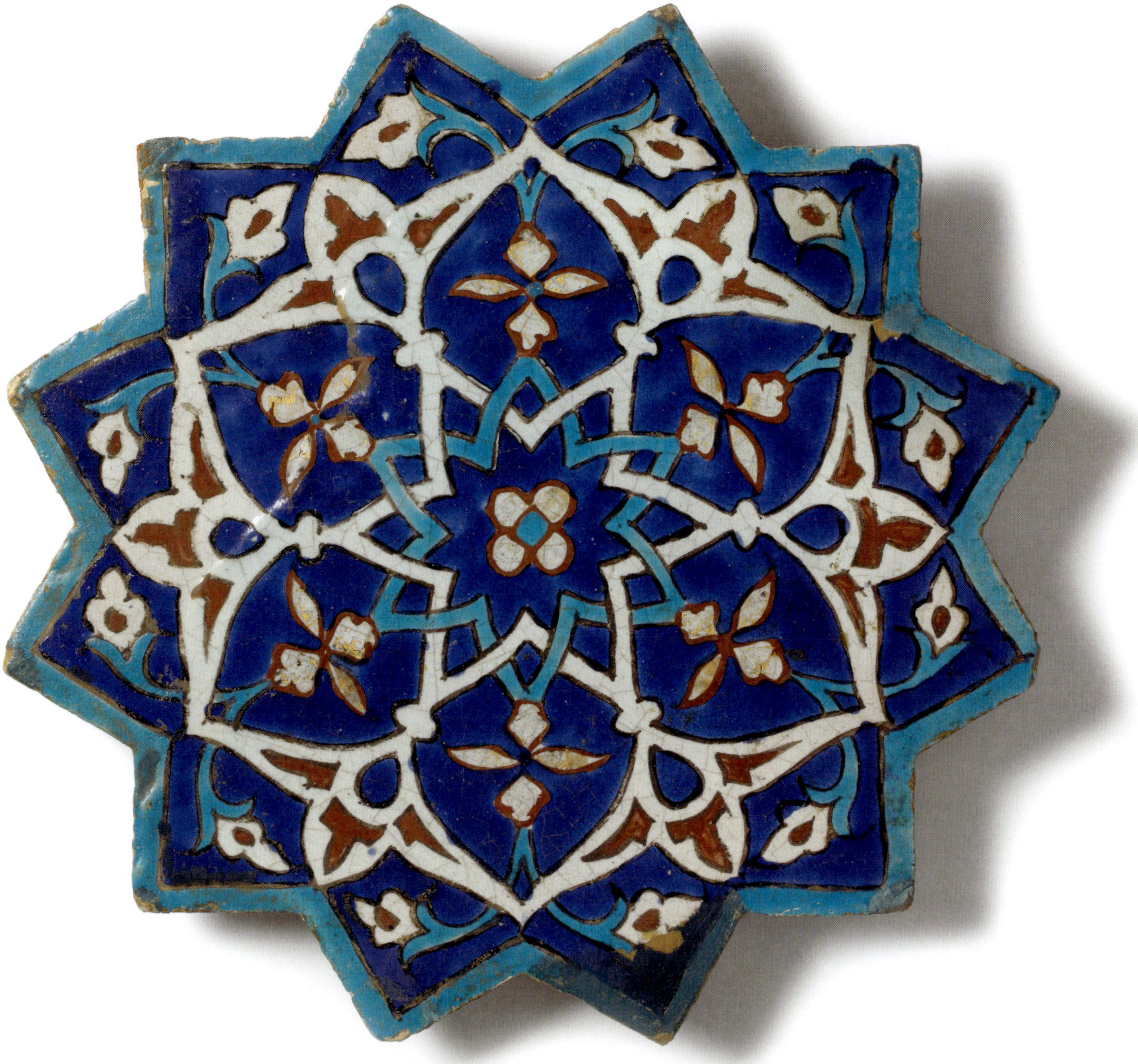

Tile, early 15th century
Iran
Fritware, glaze
Collection Gemeentemuseum Den Haag

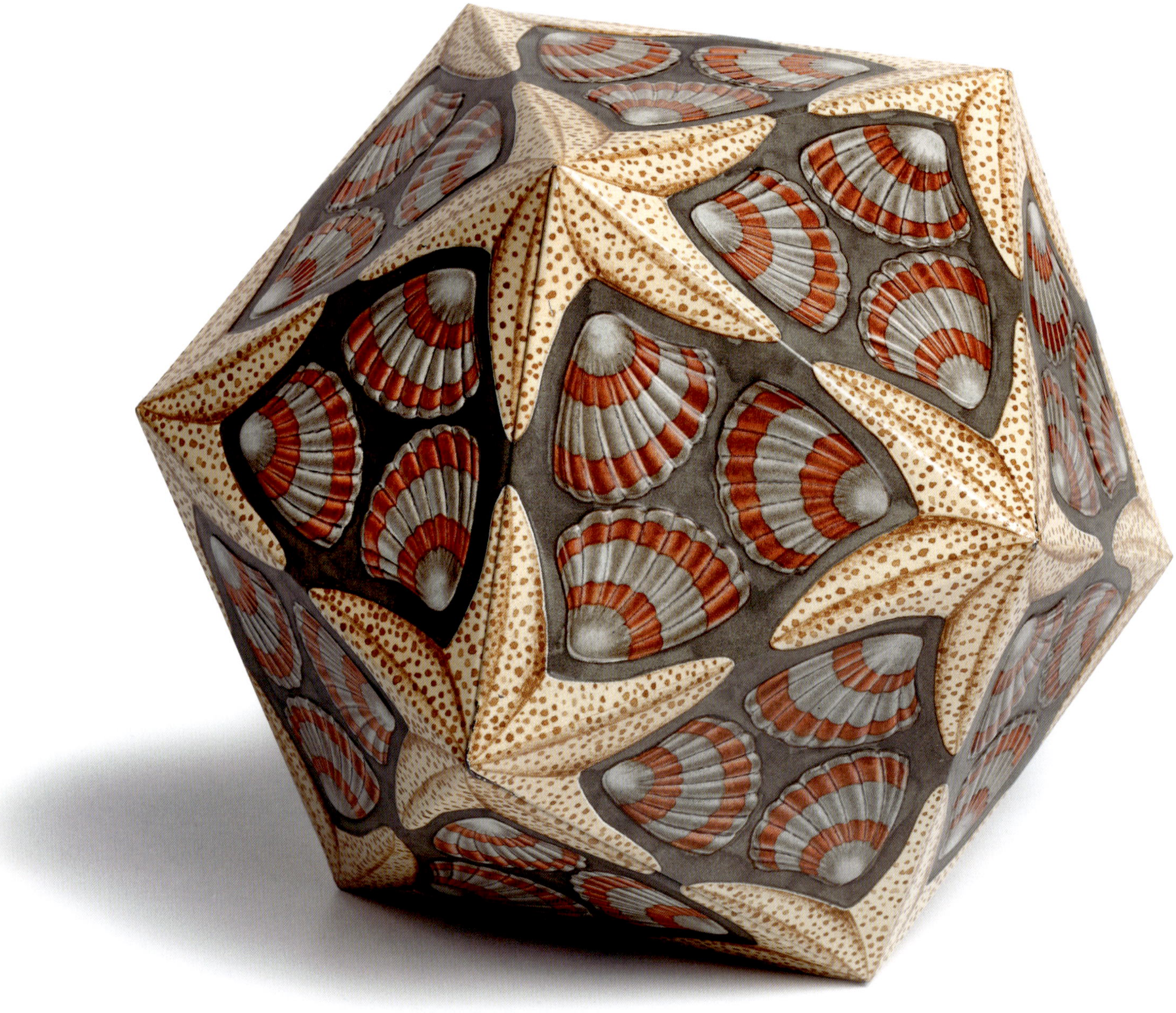

Confectionery tin, 1963
M.C. Escher
Tin designed by Escher, commissioned by Verblifa (Vereenigde Blikfabrieken) a firm that manufactured tins. This tin was a business gift to commemorate its 75th anniversary
Collection Gemeentemuseum Den Haag

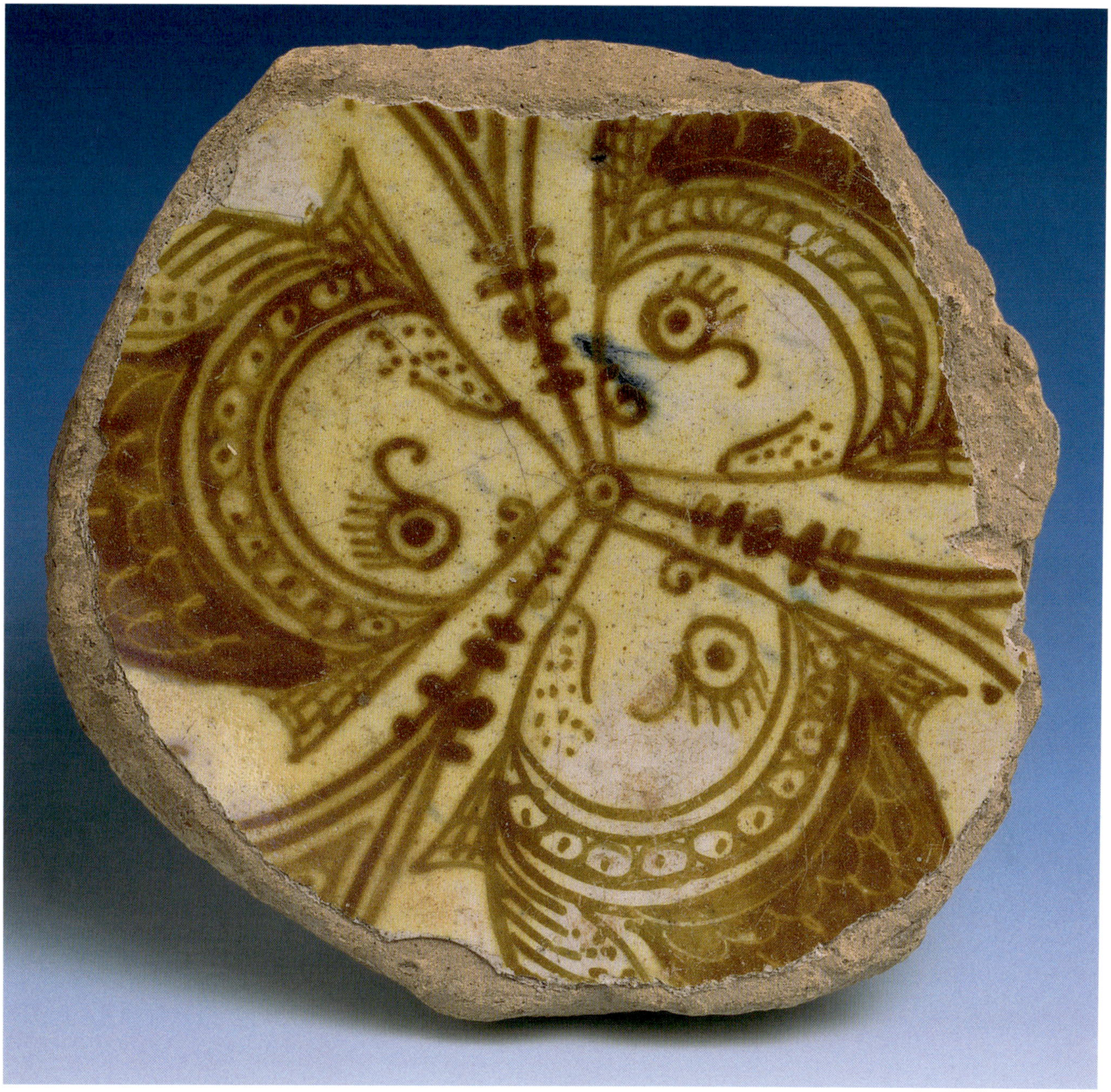

Fragment, c. 11th century
Fustat, Egypt
Earthenware, glaze, lustre
Collection Gemeentemuseum Den Haag

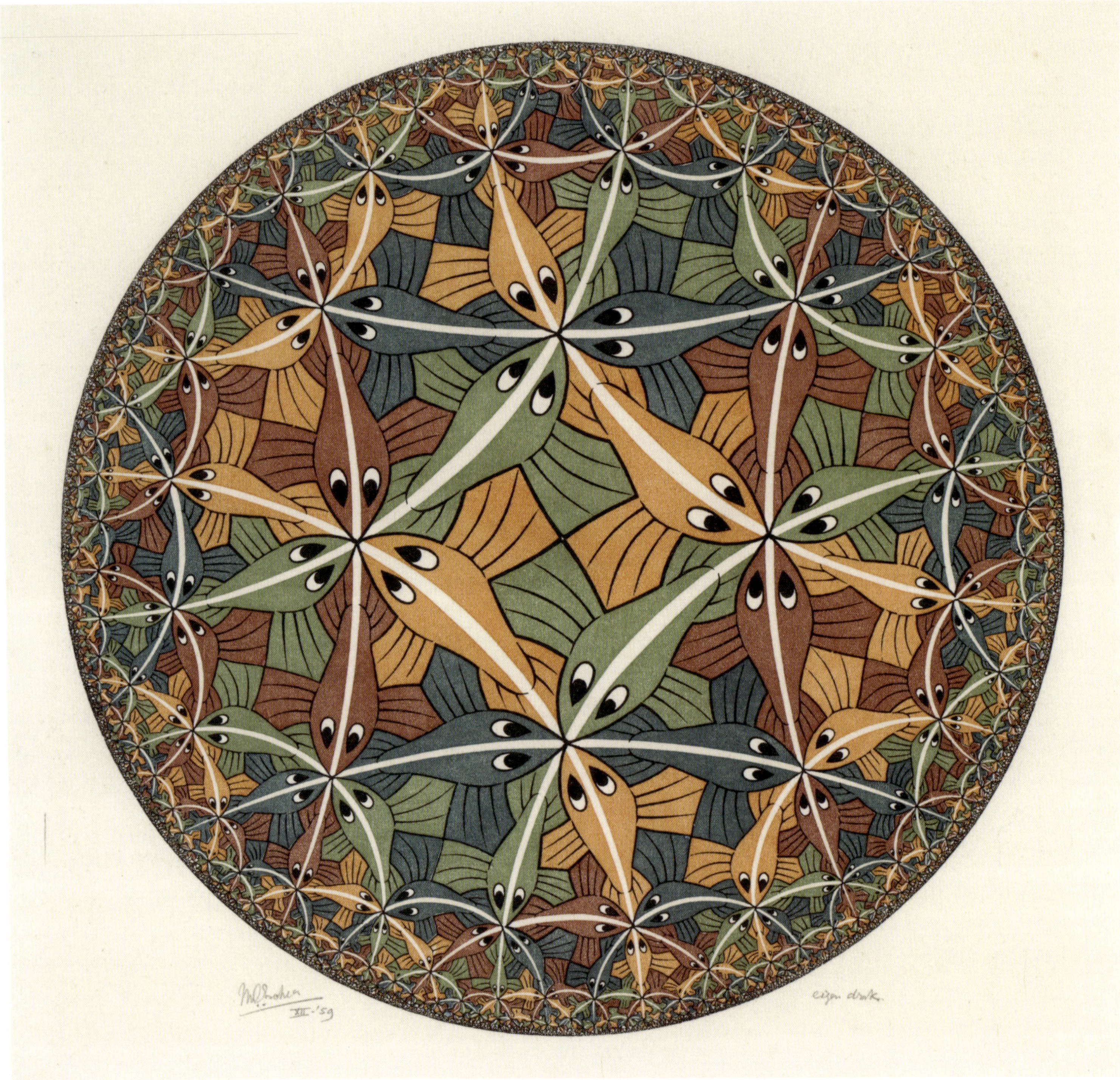

Circle Limit III, 1959
M.C. Escher
Woodcut, second state, in yellow, green, blue, brown and black, printed from five blocks
Collection Gemeentemuseum Den Haag

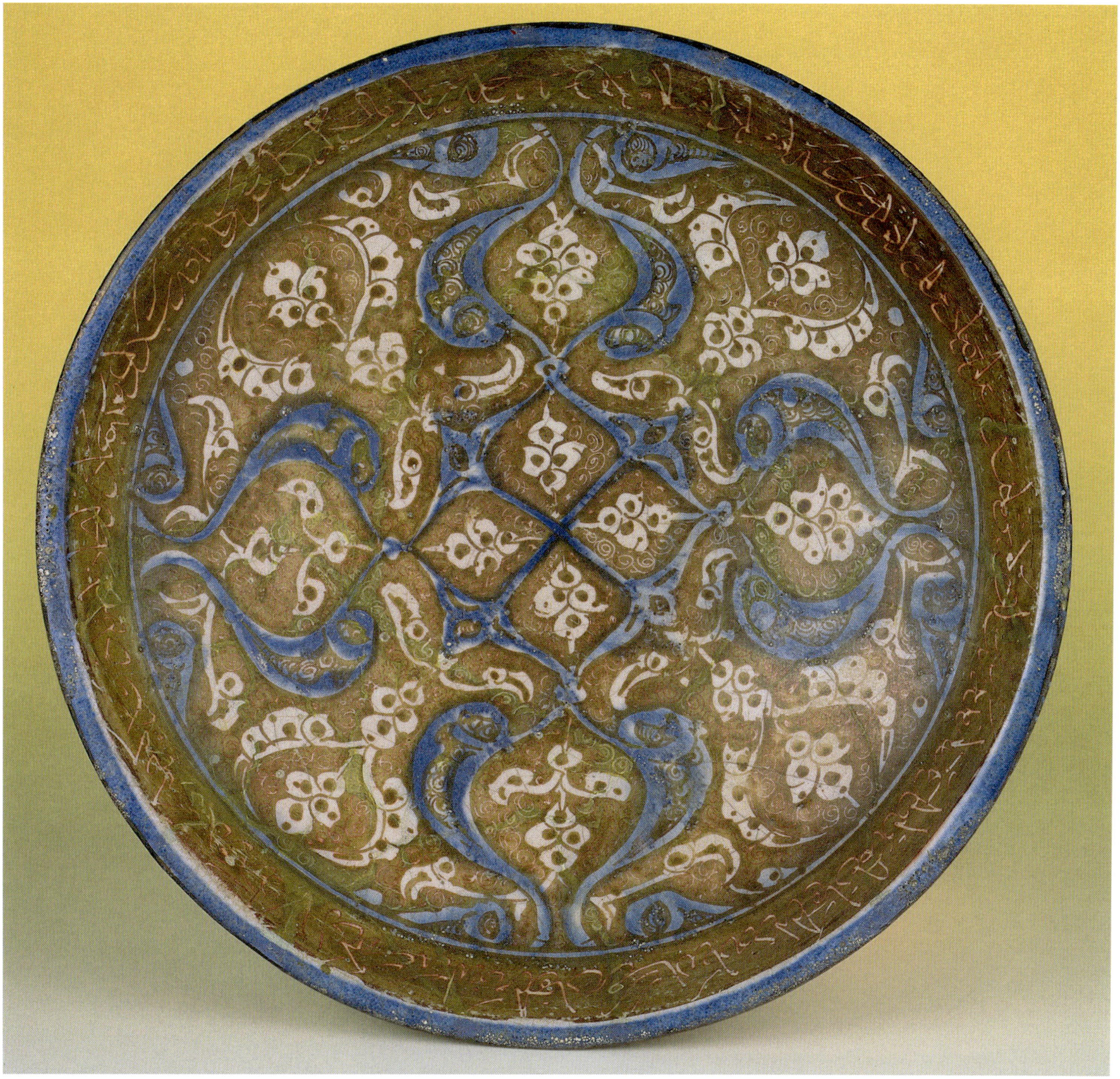

Dish, early 13th century
Iran
Fritware, glaze, lustre
Collection Gemeentemuseum Den Haag

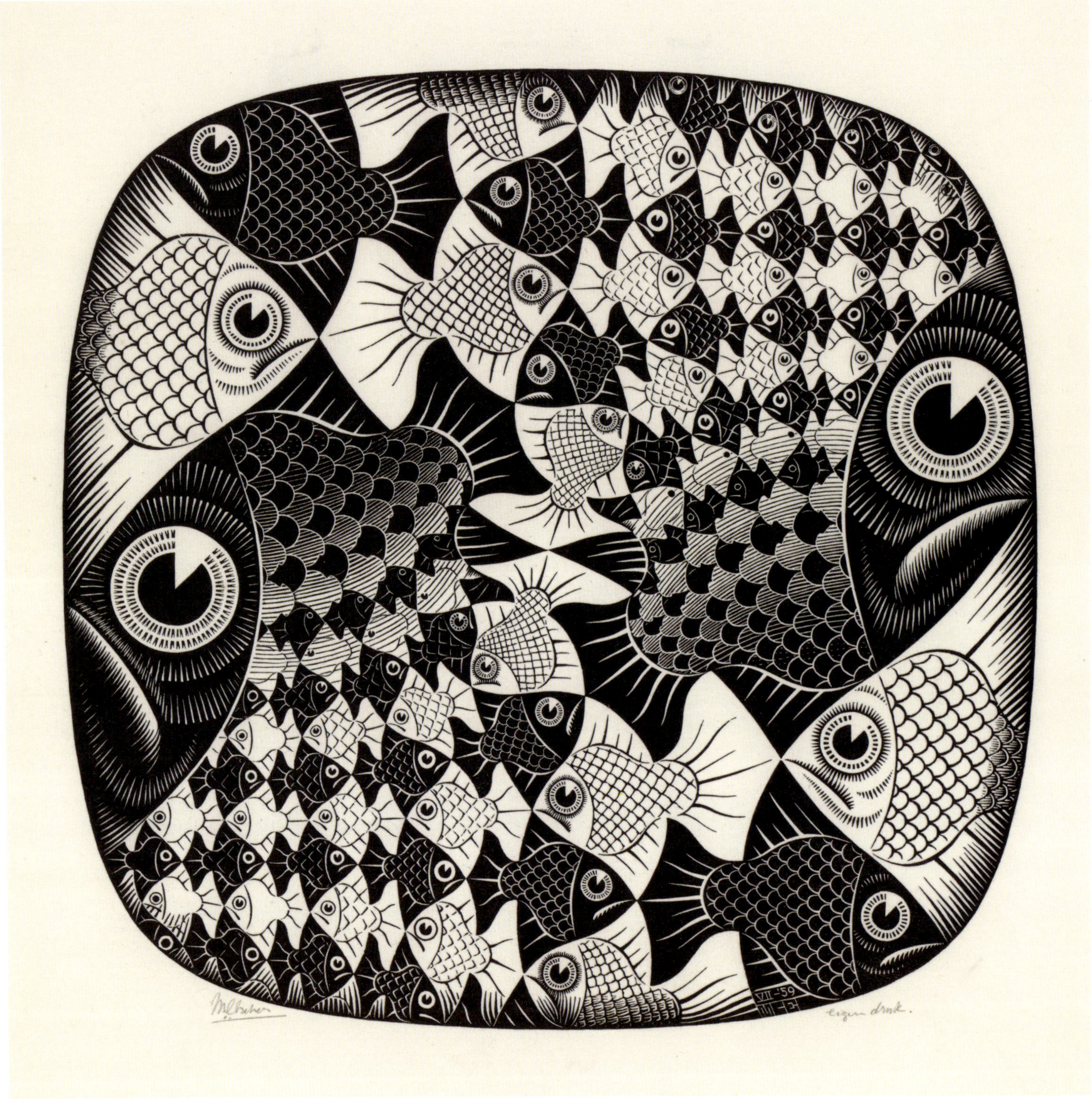

Fish and Scales, 1959
M.C. Escher
Woodcut
Collection Gemeentemuseum Den Haag

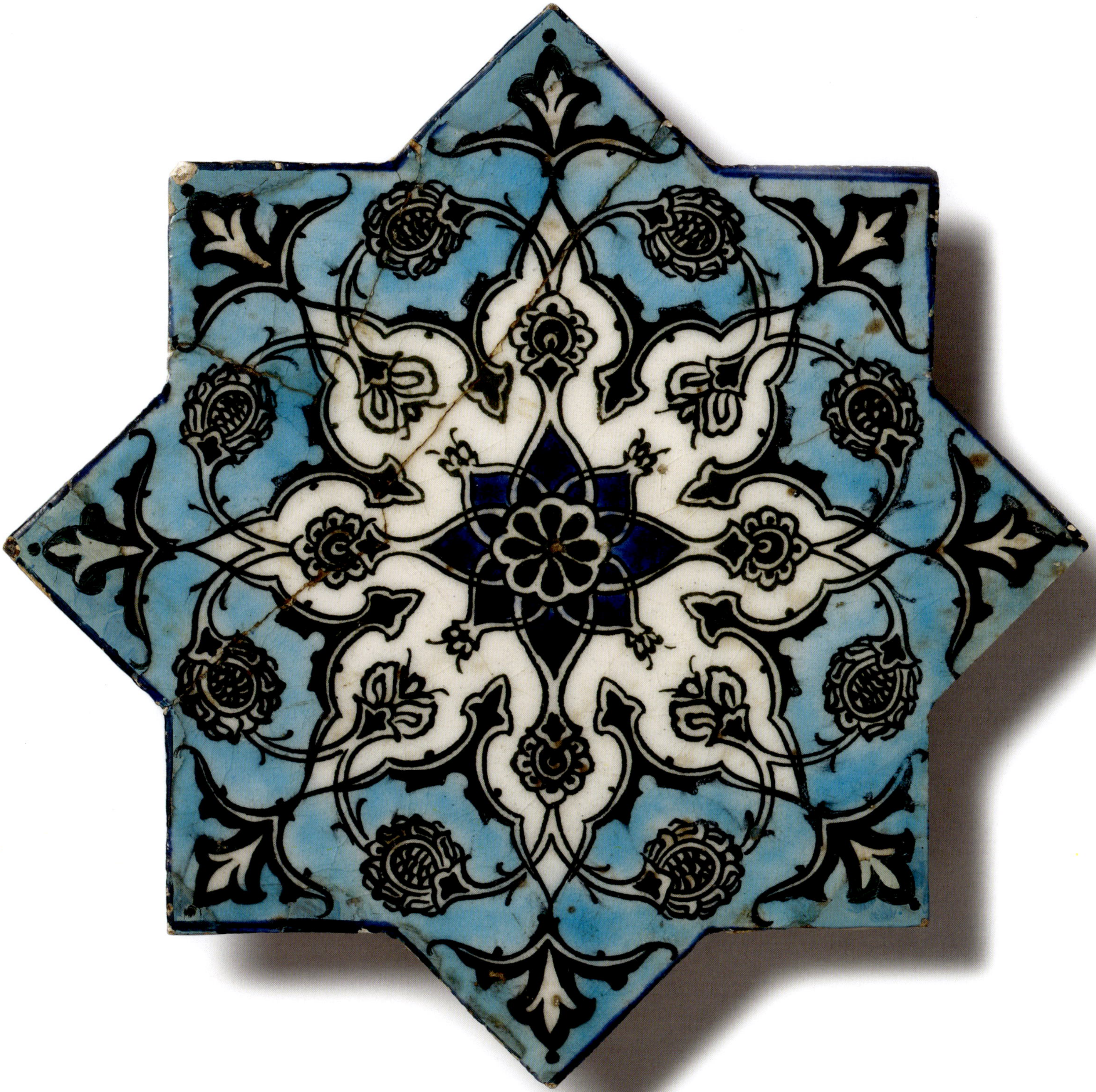

Tile, 19th/early 20th century
Iran (possibly)
Fritware, glaze
Collection Gemeentemuseum Den Haag

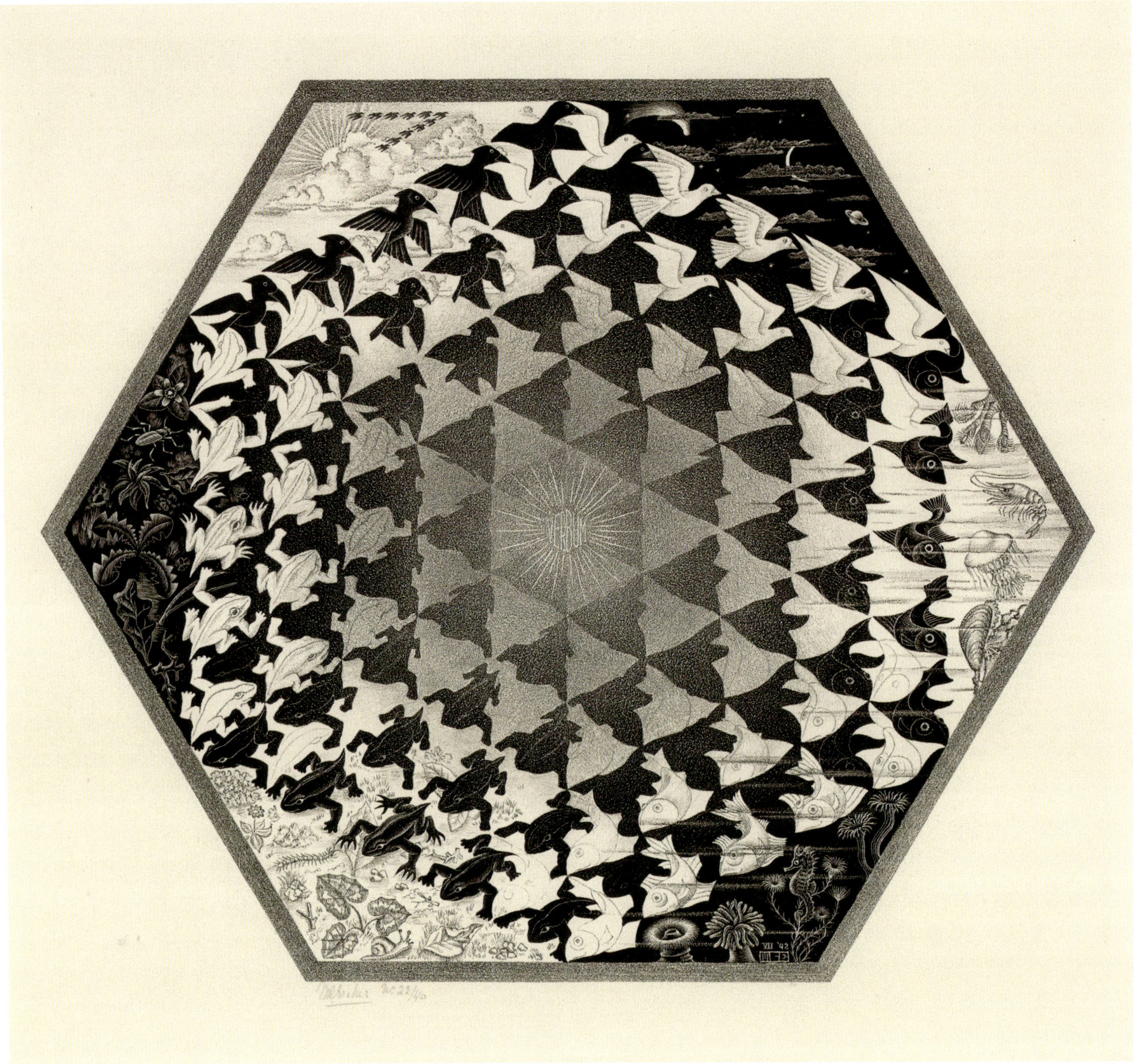

Verbum (Earth, Sky and Water), 1942
M.C. Escher
Lithograph, second state
Collection Gemeentemuseum Den Haag

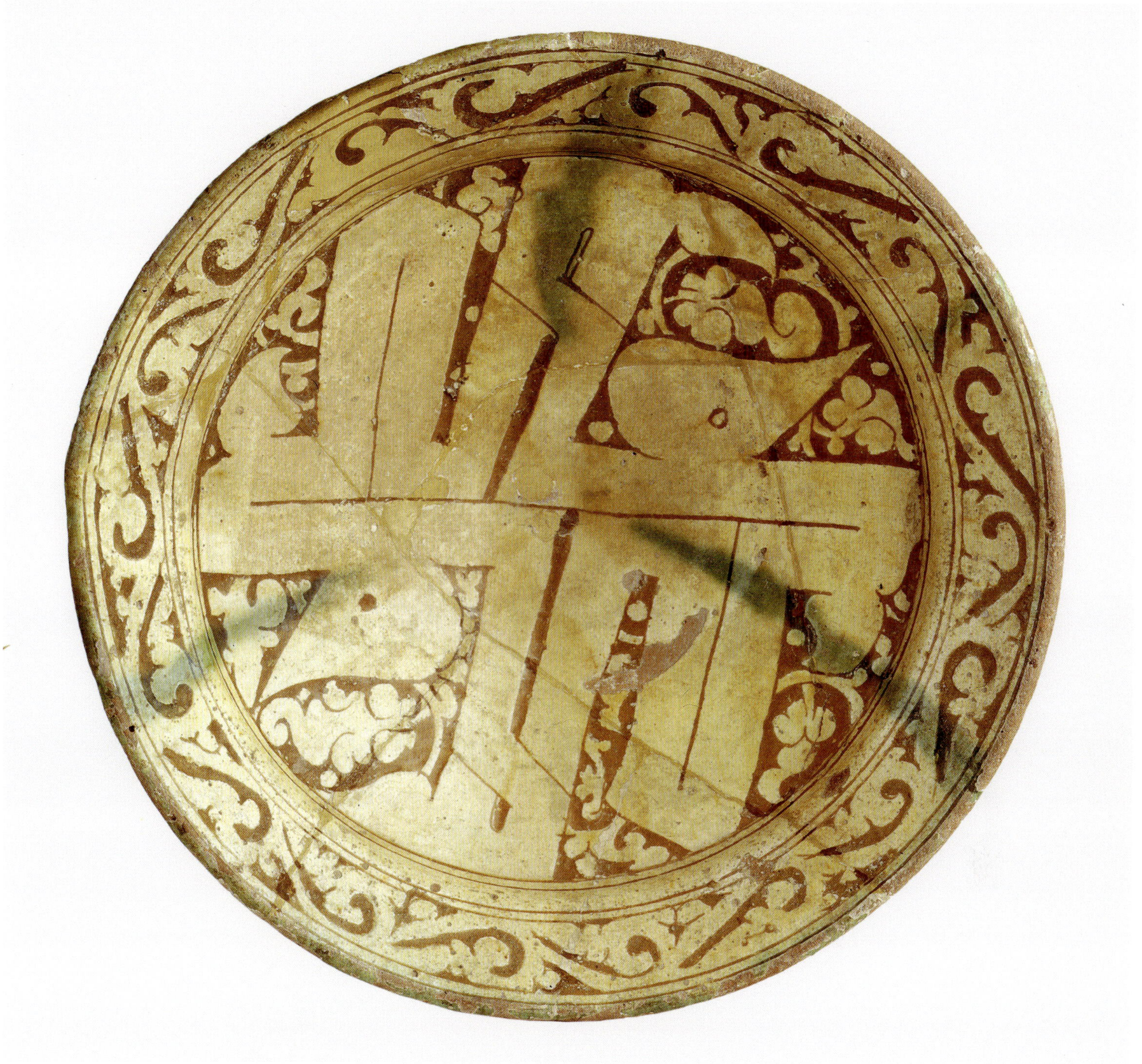

Bowl, 13th century
Iran
Fritware, glaze
Collection Gemeentemuseum Den Haag

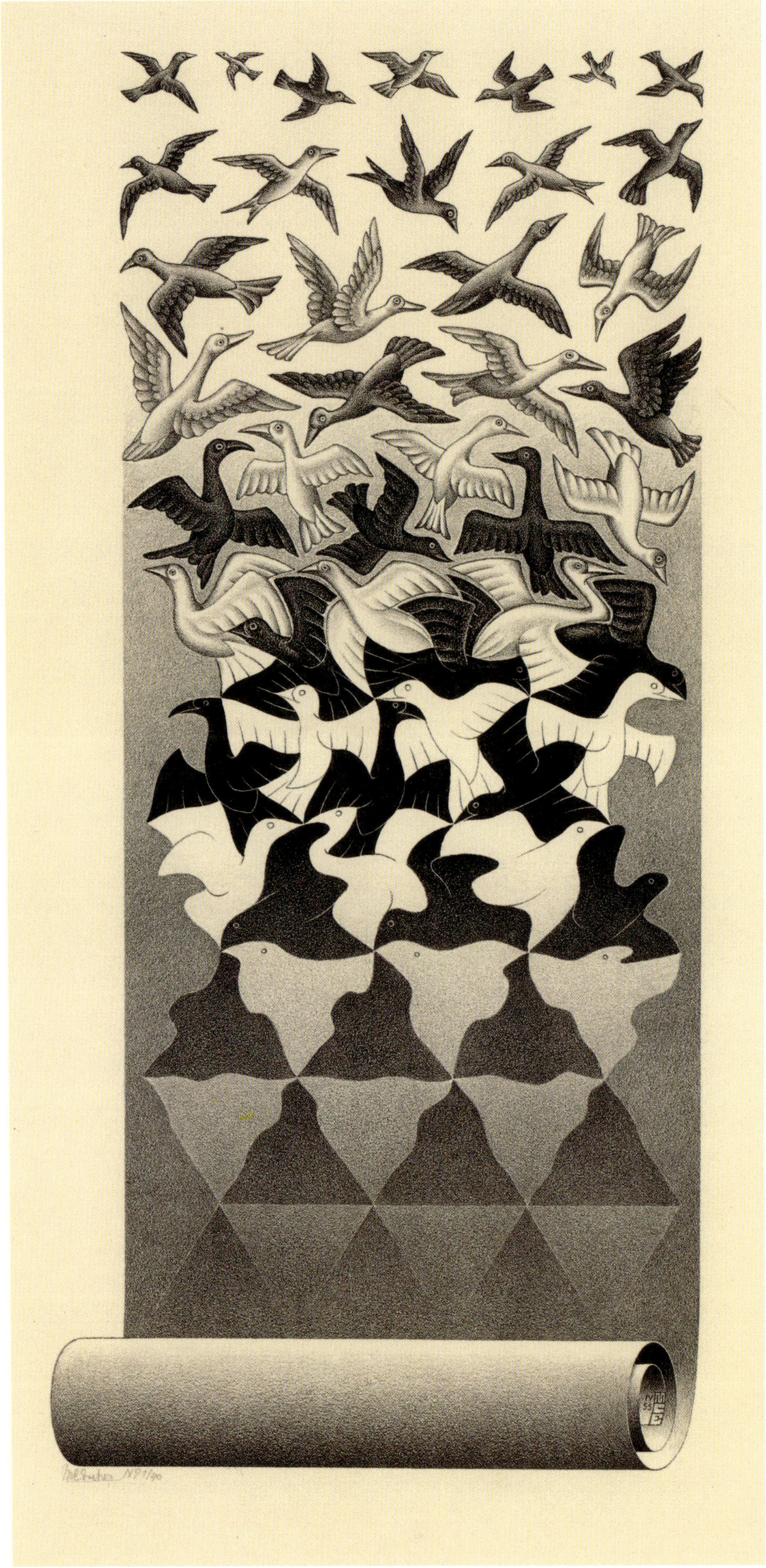

Liberation, 1955
M.C. Escher
Lithograph
Collection Gemeentemuseum Den Haag

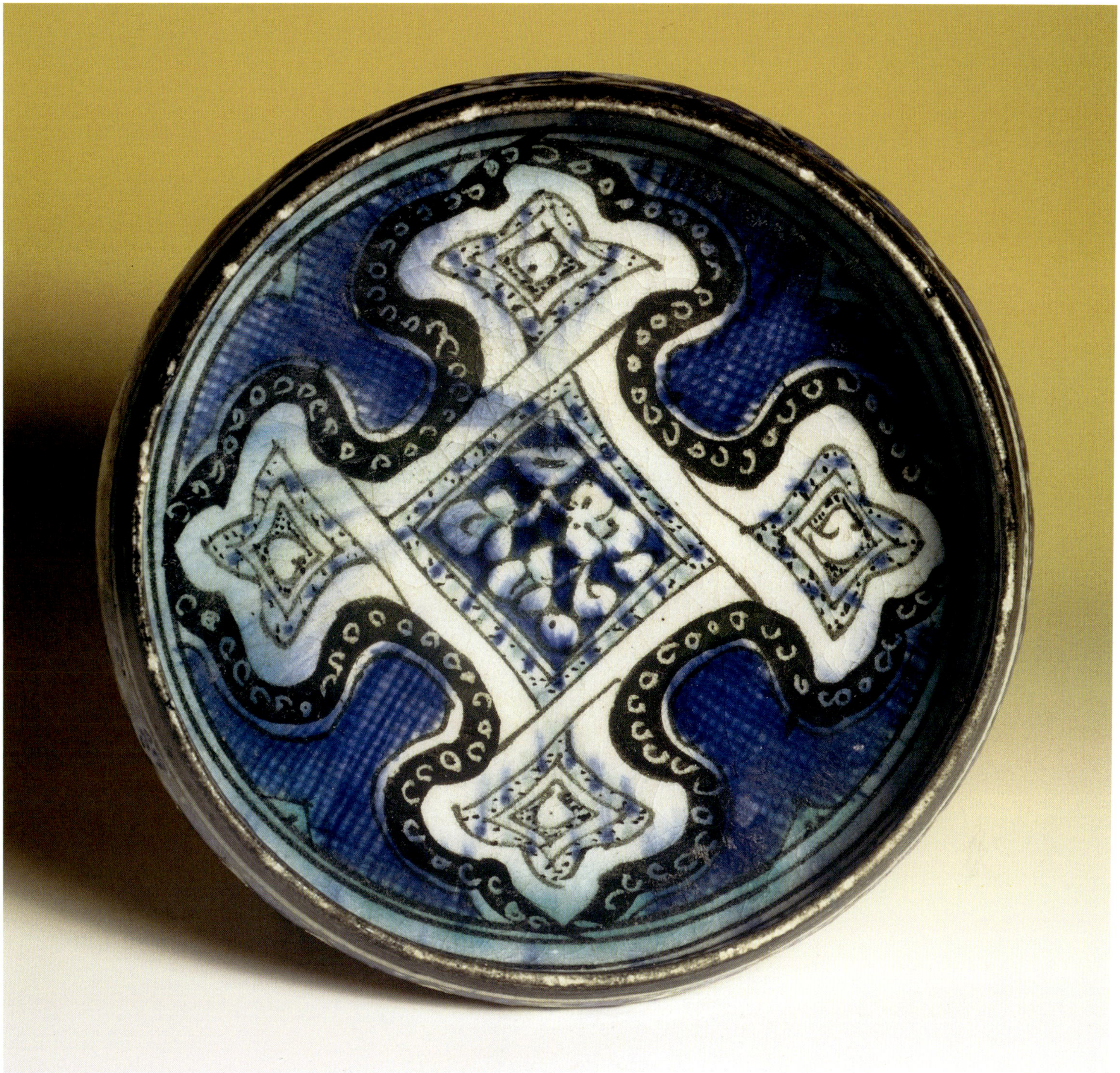

Bowl, 14th century
Iran
Fritware, slip, glaze
Collection Gemeentemuseum Den Haag

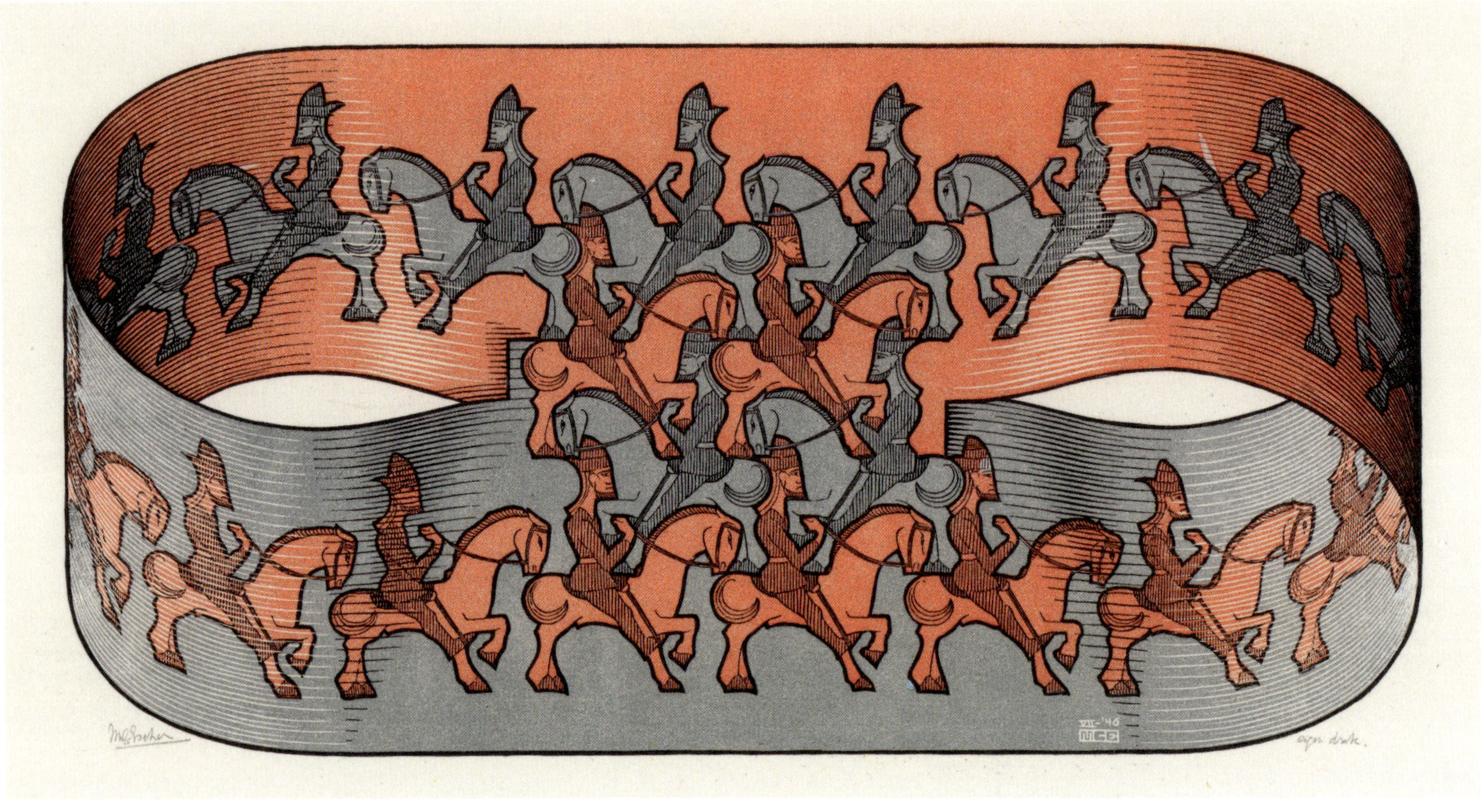

Horseman, 1946
M.C. Escher
Woodcut in red, black and grey printed from three blocks
Collection Gemeentemuseum Den Haag

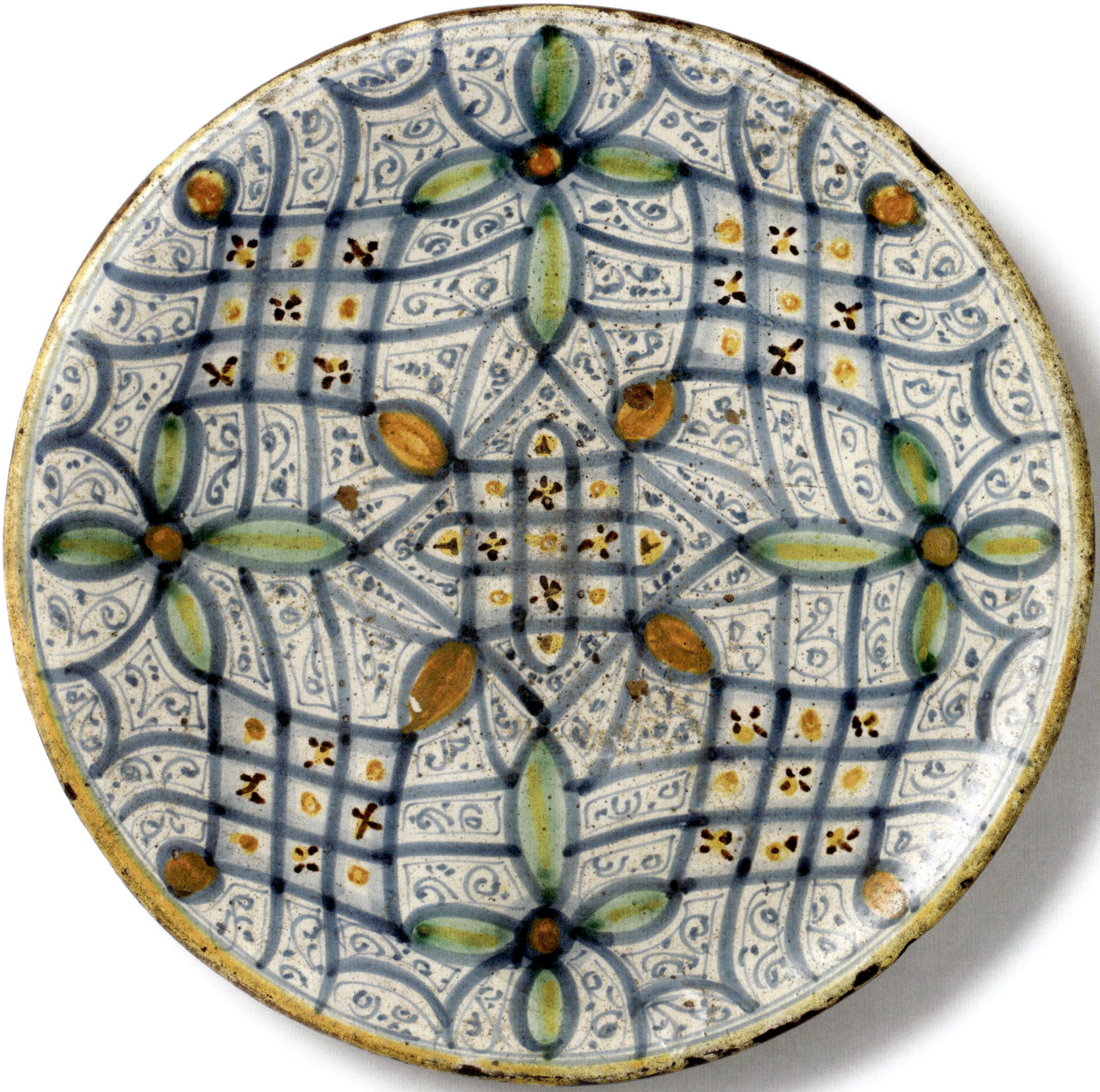

Dish, 16th century
Italy
Earthenware
Collection Gemeentemuseum Den Haag

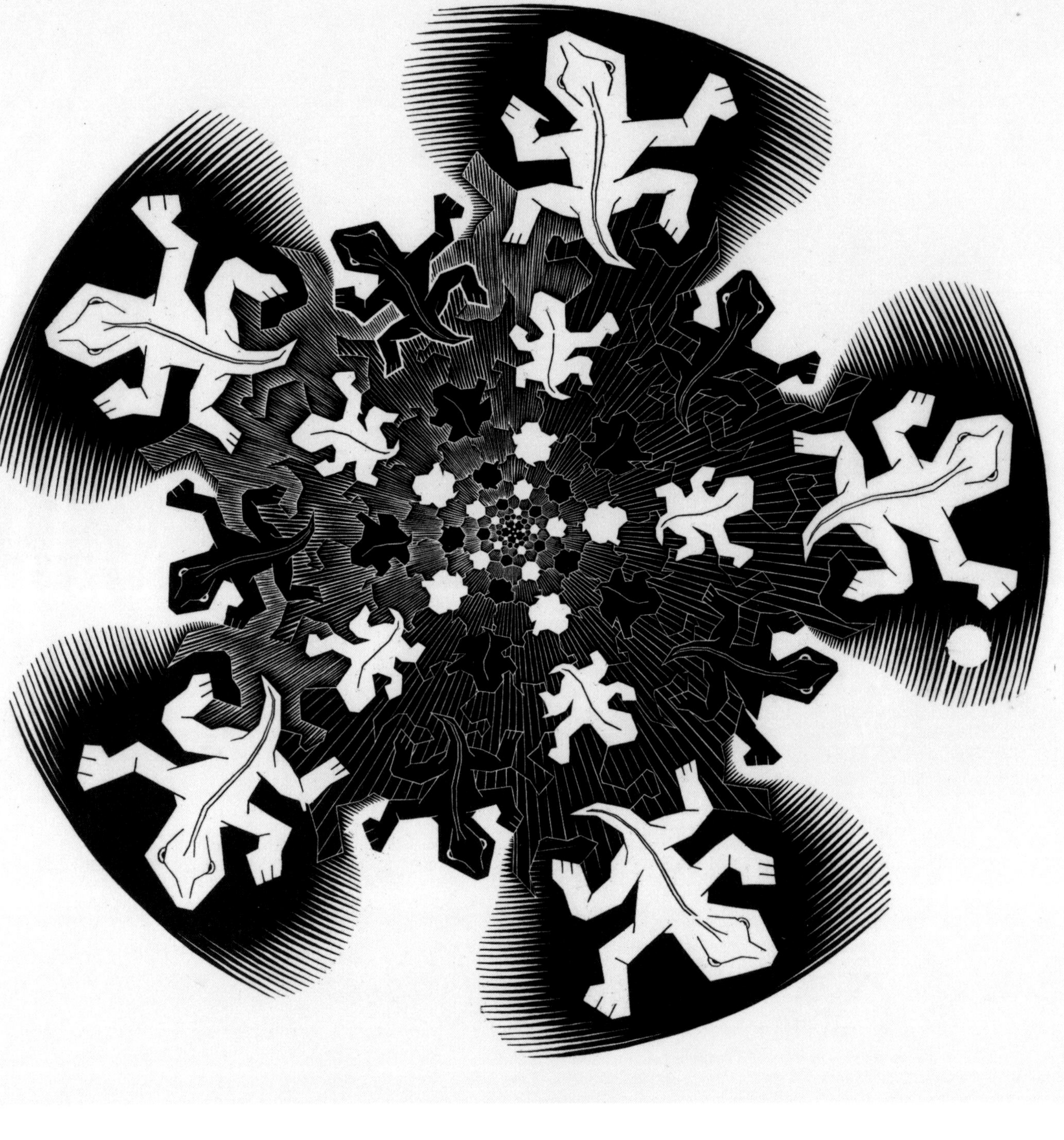

Development II, 1939
M.C. Escher
Woodcut, first version
Collection Gemeentemuseum Den Haag

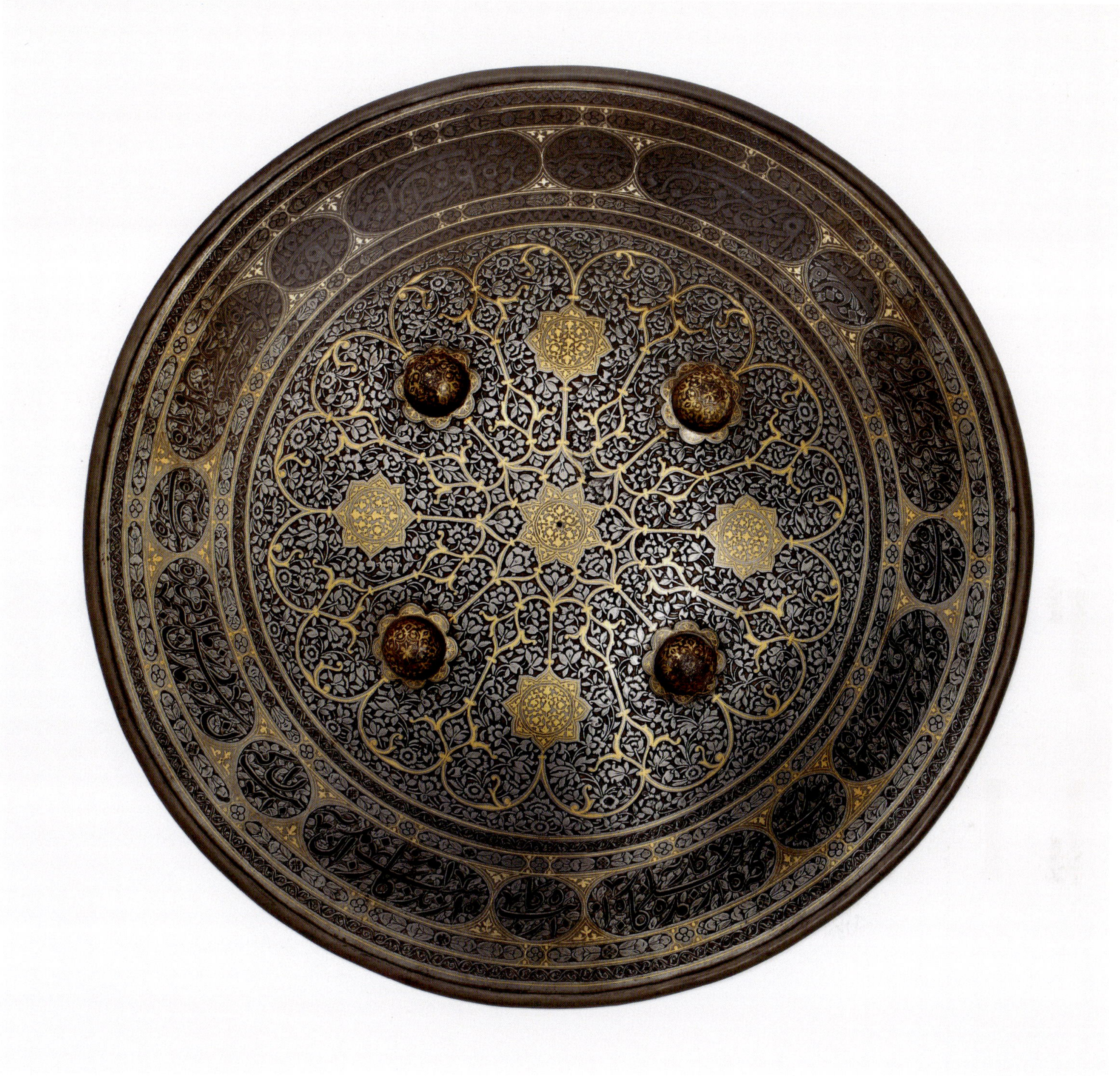

Shield, 19th/20th century
Iran
Incrustated metal
Collection Gemeentemuseum Den Haag